SOME OF C-124 GLOBEMASTER II ACCIDENTS LISTED
P-49   BELOW -- 44?

C-124A, 22 MAR, 51 - SAC, 13 Crew 40 pass TOTAL (53)
ATLANTIC
P-55
55 C-124A, 20 DEC, 52 - TROOP CARRIER, { 5 of the 10 CREW MEMBERS
MOSES LAKE   { 87 of the 115 PASSENGERS
-56 5 124A, 18 JUN, 53, USAF CREW 7, TOTAL 129 TACHI
54- 124 A-(51-107A) MATS-ALASKA, OUT OF McCHORD AFB (crew 11, pass 41   TOTAL 52

THIS BOOK LEAVES OUT A LOT OF
SIGNIFICANT ACCIDENS, I THINK, IN
MY OPINION.

Page 116 - C-141A 8th Sqd (my squadron)

Page 164- Bird Strike, 22 Sept, 95, Elmendorf AFB, AK.

Page 62
Insert by Bob Corene, Oct 15, 2000
        This book does not list any C-133
accidents, some of which I would say were
significant. There were 50 C-133's built
with the loss of 13, which is considered a
high ratio loss to number built and
opperated. I lost a former aircraft commander
on a C-133 which disapeared over ocean flight
without a trace of it being found. He was
Maj Cerithie whom I served with in the 50th ATS
at Hickam AFB, in 1954 to 1957. He was
with M.A.T.S. flying out of Dover AFB at the time
of the accident which I believe was in the
early 60's. This was to be his last flight
before retereing from the A.F. He was going OVER

into the lumber business his brother had
established.

Military Aviation
Disasters

Military Aviation
Disasters

Significant losses since 1908

David Gero

PSL

Patrick Stephens Limited

AN IMPRINT OF HAYNES PUBLISHING

First published in 1999

A catalogue record for this book is
available from the British Library

ISBN 1 85260 574 X

Library of Congress catalog card no. 98-73715

Note: Metric conversions shown in
parenthesis are approximate only.

Patrick Stephens Limited is an imprint of
Haynes Publishing, Sparkford, Nr Yeovil,
Somerset BA22 7JJ, UK.

Tel. 01963 440635 Fax 01963 440001
Int. tel. +44 1963 440635 Fax +44 1963 440001
E-mail: sales@haynes-manuals.co.uk
Web site: http://www.haynes.com

Haynes North America Inc.,
861 Lawrence Drive, Newbury Park,
California 91320, USA

Designed and typeset by G&M,
Raunds, Northamptonshire
Printed and bound in England by
J. H. Haynes & Co. Ltd

Contents

Introduction

Those familiar with my previous books, *Aviation Disasters* and *Flights of Terror*, which dealt with the subjects of airline disasters and aerial terrorism, will be well aware of the wealth of information that has been amassed on these subjects. Over the years, however, I have also collected a sizeable amount of material on air catastrophes involving the armed forces of the World. The compilation of this information now results in this, my third book, *Military Aviation Disasters*. Due to the nature of the subject matter in this volume, it should be read with a certain amount of caution. Military censorship has played a major role in what is presented here. Whereas some fighting forces are notably forthright in sharing information, such as the Royal Air Force and the US Navy, this is not usually the rule. Although basic details are invariably available, causative factors are often deleted from official reports. Even less material is made available on disasters occurring in Third World and/or non-democratic nations. This problem is complicated during wartime, when censorship frequently becomes a matter of national security. For these reasons, absolute accuracy and completeness cannot be guaranteed as it was for my previous books. Having offered that disclaimer, I am still presenting this book as the most comprehensive reference work on the subject yet published. Using the same format as *Aviation Disasters*, all significant military losses from the earliest days of powered flight are reviewed. I have attempted to include every individual incident with at least 20 fatalities, although certain cases with a fewer number of casualties have also been recounted where they are particularly noteworthy. There are also some accounts of a few significant combat incidents involving heavy loss of life or aircraft. (Collisions between military and civil aircraft have also been included if a significant number of the fatalities were aboard the former, but major airline disasters falling into this category have previously been detailed in *Aviation Disasters*.) Some controversy is anticipated regarding my classification of a military air disaster, when considering that some of these were combat losses or occurred within a combat environment. Such losses should in no way detract from the success of a military operation. On the other hand, no wartime victory can totally overshadow the losses occurring therein. There may also be some disagreement as to exactly what is a military aircraft. In the former Soviet Union, for example, aircraft belonging to the airline Aeroflot were often used in military transport operations. In South America there exist several military branches that also perform civil aviation flights. Generally though, if either the operator or the operation were related to the military, they have been included, unless the incident has been dealt with in my previous book. As always, I shall be interested in hearing from readers, wherever they may be, who possess information that clarifies or corrects any of the material presented here, and who should contact me via the publishers.

David B. Gero

Acknowledgements and references

The author wishes to thank the following organisations and individuals for their assistance in the creation of this book:

Argentine Air Force. Contacts: Guillermo Raul Barreira and Mario Santamaria; Australian Archives. Contact: Elyse Boutcher; Australian Department of Defence. Contact: Wing Commander J. W. Kindler, David Wilson; Belgian Air Force. Contact: F. Mabeyt; Canadian Directorate of History and Heritage, National Defence Headquarters. Contact: Steve Harris; Dutch Ministry of Defence. Contact: Dr P. C. van Royen; French Ministry of Defence. Contact: Colonel J. F. Bodere; German Archives. Contact: Jansen; German Ministry of Defence. Contacts: Kunze, Dr Kruger Gorsdorf; German Naval Air Museum. Contact: Fritz Schroder; German War Archives. Contact: Dr Bernd-Rudiger Ahlbrecht; Israel Defence Force. Contact: Major Avital Margalit; UK Ministry of Defence Air Historical Branch. Contacts: L. R. Howard, E. A. Munday; US Air Force. Contacts: Colonel Donn Kearns, Rhonda M. Jenkins; US Air Force Inspection and Safety Center. Contacts: Louie F. Alley; Colonel Bernard Burklund, Colonel Rolland Moore, Vincent P. Murone; US Air Force Historical Research Center. Contacts: Alan Clair, Captain Christopher Cwynar, Lieutenant Robert Guentz, Daniel Haulman, Essie Roberts; A. T. Warnock; US Army Safety Center. Contacts: Lieutenant Colonels Thomas Johnson, Johnny Marshall and Marco Torres, and Major Joe Cole; US Coast Guard. Contact: W. K. Lowry; US Naval Historical Center; US Naval Safety Center. Contacts: G. T. Eccles, Lieutenant Commander Mark Enderson, H. W. Raines, and T. J. Tucker; US Navy Office of the Judge Advocate General. Contacts: Commanders R. N. Fiske, A. K. Llewellyn, J. B. Norman and G. C. Paad, and Colonel C. H. Mitchell (USMC); US National Archives. Contact: Mary J. Brooke.

Research services have been provided by Alan Cooper, Terry Denham, Ronan Hubert, Graham K. Salt and Kathryn Powers.

Translation services provided by: Global Language Services, Luis Gonzalez, Giorgio Isella, Piet Moeleker, Julio Puchalt and Claude Seywert.

Publications consulted included: *Aircraft Facts and Feats*, by Michael Taylor and David Mondey (Guinness Superlatives, 1984); Airclaims Loss Record; *Air Disasters*, by Stanley Stewart (Ian Allan Ltd, 1986); *Air Forces* magazine; *Airliner Production Lists*, by Tony Eastwood and John Roach (The Aviation Hobby Shop); *The Air War*, by Janusz Piekalkiewicz (Historical Times, 1978); *Alive: The Story of the Andes Survivors*, by Piers Paul Read (J. B. Lippincott, 1974); *The Anvil of the Gods*, by Fred McClement (J. B. Lippincott Co, 1964); *Aviation Letter* magazine; *Aviation Week and Space Technology* magazine; *The Battle for the Falklands*, by Max Hastings and Simon Jenkins (W. W. Norton, 1983); *Boeing Aircraft Since 1916*, by Peter M. Bowers (Putnam Books, 1989); *Boeing KC-135 Stratotanker* by Robert Hopkins III (Midland Publishing Ltd, 1997); *The Bomber Command War Diaries*, by Martin Middlebrook and Chris Everitt (Viking Press, 1985); *British Aerospace 748* (Air-Britain); *British Military Aircraft Accidents*, by David Oliver (Ian Allan Ltd, 1990); *The Concise History of Aviation*, by Paolo Matricardi (Arnoldo Mondadori Editore Spa, 1984); *Crash*, by Andrew Brookes (Ian Allan Ltd, 1991); *Esquire* magazine, July/August 1996 (Article Entitled *The Mystery of Flight F4J40*, by Christopher Hadley); *Falklands, The Air War*, by Rodney Burden, Michael Draper, Douglas Rough, Colin Smith and David Wilton (Arms and Armour Press, 1986); *Flight International* magazine; *Jane's Aerospace Directory*, by Bill Gunston (Jane's Publishing Co. Ltd, 1986); *Jane's All the World's Aircraft*; *Jet Tanker Crash*, by Cornelius Cotter (The

University Press of Kansas, 1968); *La Opinion* newspaper; *Lloyd's List* news-paper; *Lockheed Hercules Production List*, by Lars Olausson; *Los Angeles Times* newspaper; *Major Loss Record* (Airclaims Ltd); *Mighty Eighth War Diary*, by Roger Freeman (Jane's Publishing Co. Ltd, 1981); *Military Aircraft Serials of North America*, by A. Eastwood and S. Mitchell (The Aviation Hobby Shop); *New York Times* newspaper; *The Sky is Falling*, by Arthur Weingarten (Grosset and Dunlap, 1975); *Soviet Transports*, by Peter Hillman, Stuart Jessup and Guus Ottenhof (The Aviation Hobby Shop); *Target Berlin*, by Jeffrey Ethell and Alfred Price (Jane's Publishing Co. Ltd, 1981); *Target Germany* (Marshall Cavendish, 1974); *Times Atlas of the World*; *Times of London* newspaper; *World Aircraft Accident Summary* (Airclaims Ltd); *World Airline Accident Directory* (Civil Aviation Authority); and *The World Book Encylopedia*.

1908–1939

Loosely speaking, the first application of 'air power' was the day humans began throwing stones at one another. The first actual use of flying machines in combat is believed to have occurred in ancient China, when kites were employed as unmanned bombers. Soldiers took to the air for the first time in the mid-nineteenth century during the American Civil War when Union balloonists were used as forward spotters. True military aviation is a by-product of twentieth century technology, when governments first began using machines that were not bound by the whims of gravity or the wind. Even before its use in commerce, the aeroplane saw application during the First World War as a tool of conflict. During the same 'Great War', dirigibles also came into use as vulnerable though deadly offensive weapons. Following the Germans, the British, French and American military forces experimented with airships, with equal misfortune. Larger than today's jet transports and built with the highest hopes, many of these lighter-than-air craft, including the R.38, R.101 and *Akron*, ended their short careers with disastrous crashes. And with the explosion of the German commercial airship

The Wright biplane, carrying Orville Wright (in cap) and US Army Lt Thomas Selfridge, photographed prior to the demonstration flight that ended in tragedy. (Smithsonian Institution)

Hindenberg in 1937, aviation's affair with dirigibles ended altogether. Non-rigid airships, or blimps, were successfully used on patrol duties during the Second World War and saw a brief revival in the late 1950s, but that chapter also ended with a fatal crash. It is only now, using modern technology, that interest in such craft is being revived. The tremendous size of the early twentieth century airships accounts for their prominence in this section, which recounts major military air disasters prior to the Second World War.

Date: 17 September 1908 (c.17:20)
Location: Near Arlington, Virginia, US
Operator: Orville Wright
Aircraft type: Wright Type A

In what could be described as the first fatal military aeroplane accident, this crash occurred at Fort Myer, located just outside Washington, DC, during a demonstration flight for the US Army. The passenger, Lt Thomas E. Selfridge, suffered a fractured skull in the accident and died about three hours later, and pilot Orville Wright, who had made the first successful powered, heavier-than-air flight five years earlier, was seriously injured. The accident sequence began about four minutes after take-off, and at an estimated altitude of 150ft (50m)

above the ground, when a blade of one of the aircraft's two propellers broke, imbalancing the corresponding blade and causing the latter to tear loose one of the wires bracing the rudder-outriggers to the wing. Distortion of the rudder resulted in a loss of control, and as the pilot was attempting to land the biplane immediately fell to the ground from an approximate height of 75ft (20m).

Date: 9 September 1913 (c.18:30)
Location: North Sea
Operator: Kriegsmarine (Germany Navy)
Aircraft type: Zeppelin L.1

The first aviation disaster to result in double-figure fatalities would also be the first fatal one in a series of accidents and combat-related losses involving these huge German dirigibles. Flying in a thunderstorm, accompanied by rain and windy conditions, the airship was carried by an air current to a height of about 5,000ft (1,500m), then apparently encountered a severe down-draught and crashed some 20 miles (30km) north of the German island of Helgoland, killing 14 of the 20 men aboard. The survivors were rescued by surface vessels. On impact with the surface of the water, the envelope broke in two, and the control car sank immediately, drowning its occupants. A possible

The aftermath of the first fatal aeroplane crash, which occurred at Fort Myer, Virginia, on 17 September 1908. (Smithsonian Institution)

contributing factor in the accident, which occurred around dusk, was that the Zeppelin may have been overloaded.

Date: 17 October 1913 (c.10:30)
Location: Near Johannisthal, Germany
Operator: Kriegsmarine (German Navy)
Aircraft type: Zeppelin L.2

Aviation experienced its first major disaster, whose death toll doubled that of the worst previous one, with this fiery destruction of an airship just outside this suburb of Berlin. It was believed that highly-inflammable hydrogen gas being vented from valves on the underside of the hull was sucked into the forward engine and ignited. In seconds, the dirigible was enveloped in flames and exploded at an altitude of approximately 650ft (200m), falling into a field. All 28 men aboard were killed, including one who was removed from the burning hulk alive but died about eight hours later. The victims included both military personnel and representatives of the manufacturer. The accident occurred during a qualifying flight prior to the Navy's formal acceptance of the airship.

Date: 5 March 1915 (c.01:00)
Location: Near Tienen (Tirlemont), Brabant, Belgium
Operator: Kriegsmarine (German Navy)
Aircraft type: Zeppelin L.8

Attacked the night before by two British and two French aircraft, the dirigible crashed into trees about 25 miles (40km) east-south-east of Brussels as it was attempting to land in darkness. Among the 41 men aboard, 21 were killed and 17 injured.

Date: 3 September 1915 (c.15:20)
Location: Off Cuxhaven, Germany
Operator: Kriegsmarine (German Navy)
Aircraft type: Zeppelin L.10

Reportedly struck by lightning while valving off hydrogen gas in preparation for landing, the airship exploded during a thunderstorm and plummeted into the sea at the mouth of the River

Little remains of the German Zeppelin L.2, which crashed in flames near Berlin, killing all 28 men aboard. (US Library of Congress)

Elbe, in the vicinity of Neuwerk Island, killing all 19 men aboard.

Date: 28 July 1916 (time unknown)
Location: Near Jambol, Bulgaria
Operator: Imperial German Army
Aircraft type: Schutte-Lanz S.L.10

The crash of the dirigible, which occurred for unknown reasons in the vicinity of the Black Sea, claimed the lives of all 20 men aboard.

Date: 24 September 1916 (c.01:00)
Location: Near Billericay, Essex, England
Operator: Kriegsmarine (German Navy)
Aircraft type: Zeppelin L.32

Shot down in early morning darkness by a British fighter, the airship fell in flames some 10 miles (15km) north-east of London, and all 22 men aboard were killed.

Date: 1 October 1916 (c.23:45)
Location: Near Potters Bar, Hertford, England
Operator: Kriegsmarine (German Navy)
Aircraft type: Zeppelin L.31

All 19 men aboard were killed when the dirigible was shot down by a British aeroplane, falling in flames just outside the northern limits of London from an approximate height of 13,000ft (4,000m).

Date: 21 November 1916 (time unknown)
Location: Near Mainz, Germany
Operator: German military forces
Aircraft type: 'Super' Zeppelin

The airship reportedly crashed in a wooded area during a storm about 15 miles (25km) south-west of Frankfurt, and all but one of the 28 men aboard were killed.

Date: 28 November 1916 (c.23:45)
Location: Near West Hartlepool, Cleveland, England
Operator: Kriegsmarine (German Navy)
Aircraft type: Zeppelin L.34

Hit by British anti-aircraft artillery fire and attacked by British aeroplanes during a night raid, the airship fell in flames into the North Sea about 10 miles (15km) off shore, killing all 20 men aboard.

Date: 4 March 1917 (time unknown)
Location: Near Gent, Vlaanderen, Belgium
Operator: German military forces
Aircraft type: Dirigible

The entire crew of an estimated 20 men lost their lives when the airship caught fire in the air and crashed some 30 miles (50km) north-west of Brussels.

An early model Zeppelin-type airship, similar to those used by the German military to bomb England during the First World War. (US Library of Congress)

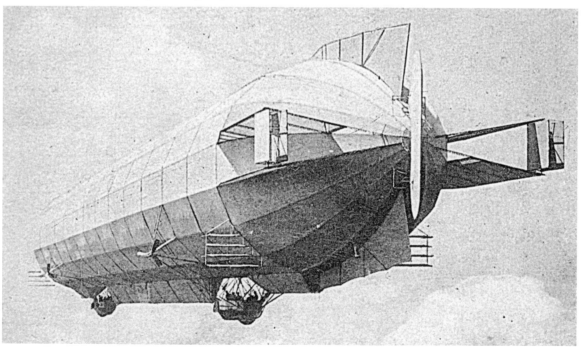

The remains of one of the many German dirigibles lost during World War I, which was shot down near London in the autumn of 1916. (UPI/Corbis-Bettmann)

Date: 30 March 1917 (time unknown)
Location: Off Northern Germany
Operator: Kriegsmarine (German Navy)
Aircraft type: Schutte-Lanz S.L.9

The dirigible caught fire in flight after apparently being struck by lightning and plunged into the Baltic Sea, killing all 23 men aboard.

Date: 14 May 1917 (c.05:15)
Location: North Sea
Operator: Kriegsmarine (German Navy)
Aircraft type: Zeppelin L.22

A British Naval Curtiss H.12 flying boat, firing tracer bullets, attacked the airship around dawn after observing it flying in a north-easterly direction at about 3,000ft (1,000m). Catching fire, the Zeppelin fell vertically in a tail-down attitude some 20 miles north-north-west of the Dutch island of Texel, with two members of its crew who were not wearing parachutes seen jumping out before it struck the water. There were no survivors among the 21 men aboard.

Date: 14 June 1917 (c.08:45)
Location: North Sea
Operator: Kriegsmarine (German Navy)
Aircraft type: Zeppelin L.43

As it was flying due north at an approximate height of 1,500ft (500m), the dirigible was attacked and shot down by a British fighter off the Dutch island of Vlieland. Hit by tracer bullets, the Zeppelin fell in flames, its wreckage continuing to burn on the surface of the water after crashing, and all 24 men aboard were killed.

Date: 21 August 1917 (c.07:00)
Location: North Sea
Operator: Kriegsmarine (German Navy)
Aircraft type: Zeppelin L.23

The dirigible was shot down by a British fighter off the western coast of Denmark, and all 18 men aboard were killed.

Date: 20 October 1917 (c.07:45)
Location: Near Luneville, Meurthe-et-Moselle, France
Operator: Kriegsmarine (German Navy)
Aircraft type: Zeppelin L.44

The airship was brought down by anti-aircraft artillery and crashed in flames about 15 miles (25km) south-east of Nancy, killing all 18 men aboard.

Date: 7 April 1918 (c.21:30)
Location: Strait of Otranto
Operator: Kriegsmarine (German Navy)
Aircraft type: Zeppelin L.59

Flying in darkness and clear weather conditions, with a visibility of 25 to 30 miles (40–50km), the airship plunged into the sea off the south-eastern coast of Italy, possibly after a mid-air explosion of unknown causes. All 23 men aboard were killed.

Date: 10 May 1918 (c.10:00)
Location: North Sea
Operator: Kriegsmarine (German Navy)
Aircraft type: Zeppelin L.62

Having been attacked and perhaps damaged earlier in the day by a British F.2 fighter, the dirigible crashed off the German island of Helgoland after an apparent in-flight explosion of an undetermined cause. There were no survivors among the 20 men aboard the airship.

Date: 5 August 1918 (c.22:30)
Location: North Sea
Operator: Kriegsmarine (German Navy)
Aircraft type: Zeppelin L.70

All 22 men aboard the dirigible were killed when it was shot down in darkness by a Royal Flying Corps aircraft, falling in flames from a height of around 17,000ft (5,200m) some 40 miles (65km) off shore from King's Lynn, Norfolk, England.

Date: 11 August 1918 (c.10:00)
Location: North Sea
Operator: Kriegsmarine (German Navy)
Aircraft type: Zeppelin L.53

During an air/sea battle between German and British forces, the airship was shot down by a Royal Flying Corps Camel fighter and fell in flames off the Dutch island of Ameland, killing all 19 men aboard.

Date: 24 August 1921 (c.17:40)
Location: Near Kingston upon Hull, Yorkshire, England
Operator: Royal Airship Works
Aircraft type: Royal Airship Works dirigible (R.38)

The hydrogen-filled airship plummeted into the River Humber 150 miles (250km) north of London after in-flight structural failure. All but five of its crew of 49 men, most of them British and American military personnel but also including four civilians, lost their lives in the disaster. Additionally, a 55-year-old woman on the ground reportedly died of 'shock' and scores of others suffered injuries, as did two of the survivors. At least two of the men aboard apparently tried to escape by parachute, but unsuccessfully. Most of the victims' bodies were subsequently recovered. Measuring 698ft (212m) long, the dirigible was on a trial flight prior to its planned take-over by the US Navy (as the ZR-2), and had been proceeding in a south-westerly direction at an approximate height of 1,200ft (350m). After initiating a sharp right turn at a speed in

excess of 60mph (100kph), its envelope fractured, with fire erupting in its front section, and the R.38 was then shattered by two explosions, the force of which broke hundreds of windows on the ground. The weather at the time was fair and apparently not a factor in the accident. The break-up would later be attributed to structural weakness, which was itself blamed on faulty design.

Date: 21 February 1922 (c.14:15)
Location: Near Norfolk, Virginia, US
Operator: US Army Air Service
Aircraft type: State Airship Factory dirigible *Roma*

The semi-rigid airship crashed in flames in the vicinity of Langley Field, where it had been based, killing 34 of the 45 men aboard, most of whom were American military personnel but also including several civilians. All but three of the survivors were injured. Built in Italy and measuring 410ft (125m) in length, the dirigible had been on a test flight and was proceeding at a speed of around 60mph (100kph) when it suddenly assumed a nose-down attitude at an approximate height of 600ft (180m) and plunged to earth. Its crew unable to recover from the uncontrolled descent, the *Roma* ultimately struck high-tension lines, and contact with their broken leads ignited the hydrogen gas in its envelope. According to the report of an Army investigative board, the accident was most likely precipitated by the flattening of the upper surface of the metal nose cap on the bow of the airship, which caused the nose-down condition. Resistance from the stern stabilisers would have produced overstressing that probably buckled the keel structure, completely disabling the elevator controls. Italian authorities disagreed with these findings, declaring that after the elevator cable had broken, the natural position of the control surfaces would have automatically caused the rear section of the dirigible to pitch upward, leading to the descent. Following this disaster, hydrogen was discarded as the lifting agent in American airships. The US Army also stopped experimenting with dirigibles, which would remain within the sole domain of the Navy.

Date: 23 December 1923 (c.02:30)
Location: Mediterranean Sea
Operator: Aeronavale (French Navy)
Aircraft type: Zeppelin *Dixmunde*

Originally built by Germany as the L.72 and taken over by the French after the First World War, this airship had been on a flight from its base near Toulon, France, to Algiers, Algeria, when it crashed in early morning darkness near Sciacca, Sicily, with 52 men aboard. One of the three bodies later found was that of the commander's; there were no survivors. In its last radio transmission, the hydrogen-filled dirigible was reported to have been nearly out of fuel and battling gale-force winds. Due to the charred condition of some of the recovered wreckage, an investigative commission concluded that it had been set afire by a lightning strike, then fell into the sea 5 miles (10km) off shore from an estimated height of 6,000ft (1,800m).

Date: 3 September 1925 (c.05:30)
Location: Near Caldwell, Ohio, US
Operator: US Navy
Aircraft type: Naval Aircraft Factory dirigible
  Shenandoah (ZR-1)

The helium-filled airship fell to earth in pieces around dawn some 80 miles (130km) south-south-west of Columbus, and 14 of the 41 American servicemen aboard were killed. All but two of those who survived escaped with little or no injury. Measuring 682ft (207m) in length, the ZR-1 had been on a publicity tour of the American Mid-west, the flight originating at Lakehurst, New Jersey, and was headed in a south-westerly direction when it encountered an area of thunderstorm activity. Inadvertently flying into a line squall, the dirigible rose to over 6,000ft (1,800m), then lost about half that height in a matter of only a few minutes, and subsequently suffered structural failure at an approximate altitude of 3,700ft (1,100m). Its control car broke away after the initial fracture, sending its

occupants, among them the commander, plunging to their deaths. The aft part of the airship, containing more than half of the survivors, and two other sections of the envelope descended to earth more slowly. The break-up was attributed to large aerodynamic forces against the dirigible which were produced by strong upward currents of air associated with the thunderstorm.

Date: 5 October 1930 (c.02:00)
Location: Near Beauvais, Val-d'oise, France
Operator: (British) Air Ministry
Aircraft type: Royal Airship Works dirigible R.101
  (G-FAAW)

During a trip from England to India, the airship crashed in darkness and adverse meteorological conditions about 40 miles (65km) north-north-west of Paris. Killed in the disaster were all but six of the 54 men aboard, including the six who had been designated as passengers on the flight. The survivors, five of whom were among the dirigible's crew of 42, suffered various injuries. Slightly more than 777ft (236m) in length, the R.101 had in fact undergone only one test flight prior to the long voyage that ended in tragedy. Flying on this Sunday morning just under a low overcast and in a south-westerly wind of around 35 to 45 knots, the dirigible was proceeding on a south-south-easterly heading at an approximate altitude of 1,000ft

Onlookers gather at the scene where one section of the US Navy dirigible Shenandoah *fell after the in-flight break-up of the airship during a thunderstorm.* (UPI/Corbis-Bettmann)

(300m) above the ground when it began to lose height. Levelling off briefly, it then descended into the ground, striking a ridge in a nose-down angle of 15 to 25 degrees before rebounding back into the air, and finally came to rest on the sloping terrain. Although the impact was not considered violent, fire erupted when the highly-inflammable calcium flares that were being carried aboard came in contact with the rain-drenched ground, leading to an explosion and a larger blaze that consumed the airship. Prior to the crash, some hydrogen gas had apparently been lost gradually, either through chafing or chattering of the valves, and considerably more was believed lost from at least one of the forward gas bags, possibly due to the ripping of the forepart of the envelope while still airborne. This condition and an encounter with a down-draught probably led to the uncontrolled descent into the ground. Another significant factor was the intentional reduction of engine power following the initial descent, in order to reduce the speed of the airship, and which would have further contributed to the loss of height. This disaster led to the end of Britain's dirigible industry.

The majestic R.101 was a true marvel of aeronautical engineering in its day, but its crash ended the British dirigible programme. (Air Ministry)

Completely burned out, the hulk of the R.101 rests in the French countryside following the tragedy that claimed 48 lives. (Air Ministry)

The US Navy's airship Akron *is photographed over Florida a few months before its disastrous crash off the New Jersey coast.* (UPI/Corbis-Bettmann)

A portion of the Akron *is raised from the Atlantic Ocean after it crashed in a thunderstorm early on the morning of 4 April 1933.* (UPI/Corbis-Bettmann)

Date: 4 April 1933 (c.00:30)
Location: Off Barnegat City, New Jersey, US
Operator: US Navy
Aircraft type: Goodyear-Zeppelin dirigible *Akron* (ZRS-4)

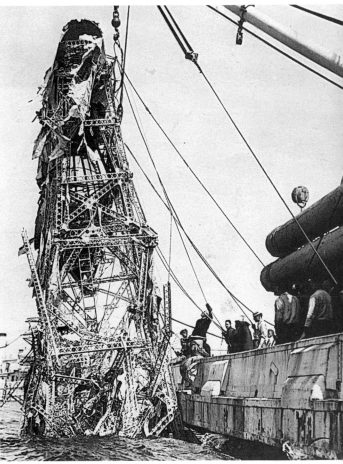

The helium-filled airship crashed in the Atlantic Ocean 20 miles (30km) east-south-east of the Barnegat lighthouse and approximately 70 miles (110km) south of New York City, killing 73 servicemen aboard. Except for a member of the US Army, one of seven occupants not part of the regular crew, the victims were all naval personnel. The three survivors, two Navy enlisted men and an officer, were rescued by a ship. Most of the victims' bodies were lost at sea, but a considerable amount of debris was recovered, and a marine research team located the main wreckage on the ocean floor, in water about 100ft (30m) deep, 53 years after the disaster. Flying in darkness through an area of thunderstorm activity, accompanied by heavy rain and high winds, the dirigible, which measured 785ft (240m) in length, apparently encountered a severe down-draught that could not be overcome by the crew's use of engine power, elevator controls or ballast release. Ultimately, it ploughed into the sea in a tail-down attitude and broke apart. Some 13 hours later, the US Navy blimp, J-3, which had been returning from the *Akron* rescue operations and was battling high winds, itself crashed just off shore from Beach Haven, New Jersey, and two of its seven crewmen lost their lives. Considered as contributory to the *Akron* disaster was an 'error of judgement' by its commander in flying into the storm despite the observance of lightning in its path. That no altimeter correction had been made to compensate for the drop in atmospheric pressure, which placed the airship about 600ft (180m) below its indicated height of around 1,000ft (300m), may have been an additional factor. Individual life preservers and rafts were later added to Navy dirigible operations and, perhaps as a result, in the loss of the *Akron*'s sister ship, the *Macon*, which crashed in the Pacific Ocean in 1935, all but two of the more than 80 men aboard survived. However, one additional casualty did result from the second accident, the American dirigible programme itself, which was disbanded.

A giant cloud of smoke rises above the grandstand seconds after the Colombian biplane crash, the first 'heavier-than-air' aviation disaster to claim more than 50 lives. (New York Times *Pictures*)

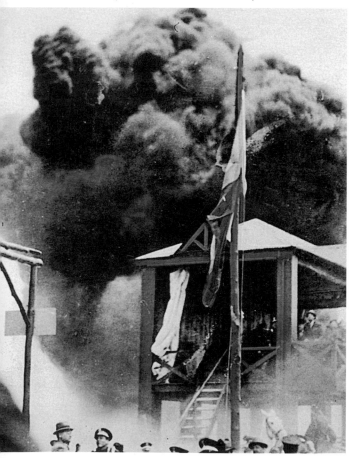

Date: 2 February 1938 (c.20:40)
Location: Off Southern California, US

First aircraft
Operator: US Navy
Type: Consolidated PBY-2 (0462)

Second aircraft
Operator: US Navy
Type: Consolidated PBY-2 (0463)

In the first 'heavier-than-air' disaster in the history of American military aviation to claim more than 10 lives, the two twin-engine amphibious patrol bombers collided in mid-air and plummeted into the Pacific Ocean south of San Clemente Island, 70 miles (110km) west of San Diego. The accident claimed the lives of 11 servicemen, while three others who managed to parachute from one PBY before it crashed were rescued with injuries. The two aircraft involved in the collision were part of a formation flying in darkness that had entered an area of intense rain, with the visibility reportedly reduced to zero.

Date: 24 July 1938 (c.13:00)
Location: Near Bogotá, Colombia
Operator: Ejército Colombiano (Colombian Army)
Aircraft type: Curtiss-Wright Hawk

As a squadron of the single-engine fighters were performing aerobatics before a crowd of about 50,000 at the Campo de Marte exercise field, one of them crashed into a grandstand, then plummeted into an area where other spectators were standing, and burst into flames. Killed in the disaster were 53 persons, including the pilot (and sole occupant) of the biplane, while more than 100 others on the ground suffered injuries. Though not officially reported, the crash may have resulted from an encounter with a gust of wind or a loss of control by the pilot during a looping manoeuvre.

Date: 8 May 1939 (c.12:00)
Location: Guayaquil, Ecuador
Operator: Fuerza Aérea Ecuatoriana (Air Force of Ecuador)
Aircraft type: Curtiss-Wright C-14 Osprey

The single-engine fighter was seen performing low-altitude aerobatics over the city before it crashed near a college. Among the 23 persons killed was the pilot (and sole occupant) of the aircraft; 60 others on the ground suffered injuries and numerous buildings and houses were destroyed or damaged. Following a loop, performed at an altitude of less than 500ft (150m) above the ground, the biplane apparently lost flying speed. It then clipped a tree before slamming into a street and erupting into flames.

1940–1949

Having relatively little significance during the First World War, the full power of military aviation was truly realised in the Second World War. The war not only saw fierce aerial combat, but also the deaths of millions of civilians to bombings, both conventional and, in two instances, with the use of nuclear weapons. A number of aircraft achieved immortality during this period: the Spitfire, P-51 Mustang, B-17 Flying Fortress, and the C-47. The latter, the famed Douglas transport, which had been originally designed as an airliner during the mid-1930s, was listed by the Allied Supreme Commander and future American President, Dwight Eisenhower, as one of the most important military tools of the Second World War. Air transport changed for ever the nature of ground warfare, making it possible to drop troops behind enemy lines. This technique paved the road to success in the Allied invasion of France in June 1944. Perhaps over-confident from their success at Normandy, the Allies stumbled three months later in Holland. Losses in men and aircraft in the war were heavy on both sides. In 1940, the Battle of Britain alone cost the Royal Air Force about 1,000 aeroplanes, mostly Spitfire and Hurricane fighters, together with 537 aviators. Total British air force losses were nearly 80,000 lives and some 22,000 aircraft. The loss figures were approximately the same for the US Army Air Force, which

Large, four-engine bombers such as the famed, American-built Consolidated B-24 saw wide action during World War II. (General Dynamics)

represented around one-fifth of the nation's war dead. About half of these fatalities were among members of the Eighth and Ninth Air Forces, which bore the brunt of the heaviest action in the European Theatre. A few of the more noteworthy combat losses are included in this section, but the majority of entries result from accidental causes.

Date: 10 May 1940
Location: Western Europe
Operator: Luftwaffe (German Air Force)
Aircraft types: Various (Total 304)

The heaviest losses experienced in a single-day airborne assault were suffered by German forces in their invasion of Belgium and The Netherlands. Aircraft losses included 157 Junkers Ju 52/3m trimotored transports, 430 in the entire operation. Nearly 600 Luftwaffe personnel were killed and more than 300 others reported missing, while losses among German airborne troops probably numbered several thousand in what was considered a highly successful campaign that would ultimately lead to the capture of most of Western Europe. Most of the losses were to ground fire or to Belgian, Dutch, French, Norwegian or British air forces.

Date: 20/21 May 1941
Location: Crete
Operator: Luftwaffe (German Air Force)
Aircraft types: Various (c.600)

During the invasion of the Greek island, some 270 Junkers Ju 52/3m transports and DFS 320 gliders were lost by German forces, either to hostile action or in accidents. In the air operation alone, a total of 3,748 men were killed or reported missing, and more than 2,600 others wounded. Despite the heavy casualties, Germany conquered Crete and forced the retreat of British forces from the island.

Date: 10 August 1941 (c.20:35)
Location: Arran, Strathclyde, Scotland
Operator: Royal Air Force
Aircraft type: Consolidated LB-30A Liberator (AM261)

All 22 persons aboard were killed when the four-engine transport crashed and burned on a ridge near Goat Fell, a mountain located on the island. The victims included both British and American military personnel, although two members of the crew of five were civilians. Impact occurred only about 75ft (20m) below the summit of the terrain, at an approximate elevation of 2,700ft (820m), 25 miles (40km) north-west of Ayr, from where it had taken off shortly before, on a transatlantic flight to Montreal, Canada. It was dark at the time, and the weather conditions were adverse, with rain and a

solid, low overcast. An apparent navigational error had placed the aircraft on a heading of 295 degrees, which at the time of the crash was 12 degrees, or some 10 miles (15km), north of the prescribed track. It was not, however, possible to determine what factors had led to this error.

Date: 14 August 1941 (c.20:40)
Location: Near Ayr, Strathclyde, Scotland
Operator: Royal Air Force
Aircraft type: Consolidated LB-30A Liberator (AM260)

The four-engine transport crashed and burned while on take-off from Heathfield aerodrome, killing all 22 persons aboard. Most of the victims were American and British servicemen, including the crew of four. Bound for Canada, the aircraft suddenly swerved off Runway 06, knocking over haystacks, hitting a hut and a telegraph pole and finally slammed into an embankment. It was dark at the time, but the weather conditions were good, with a broken overcast at 2,500ft (750m), a visibility of around 20 miles (30km), and a slight breeze out of the west.

Date: 1 July 1942 (c.12:00)
Location: Near Premier, West Virginia, US
Operator: US Army Air Forces
Aircraft type: Douglas C-49E (42-56093)

The twin-engine transport crashed and burned about 5 miles (10km) south-west of Welch, and all 21 American servicemen aboard, including the two-member flight crew, perished. Having taken off earlier from Battle Creek, Michigan, on a domestic flight to Florence, South Carolina, the aircraft was to have landed at Lunken Field, Cincinnati, Ohio, an en-route stop. Following three unsuccessful attempts, the C-49 began a fourth approach, at an excessive speed and with its flaps retracted, and as the pilot evidently tried to force the landing, it 'ballooned' about 20ft (6m) into the air, then dropped back on to the runway and bounced before power was applied. The aircraft then proceeded on towards its ultimate destination, which it never reached. Shortly before the crash, 42-56093 was observed flying in and out of a layer of low clouds in an area of thunderstorm activity, yawing with one power plant apparently surging. Plunging out of the overcast in a near-vertical dive, it then pulled up and levelled off at a height of approximately 800ft (250m) above the ground, at which time both wing tips and the outer sections of both ailerons broke off, followed by the starboard wing and engine and both stabilisers and corresponding elevators. The C-49 then went into a spin and plummeted into a wooded ravine. According to the investigative report, the pilot exercised 'very poor' flying technique and judgement in subjecting the aircraft to severe, abnormal shock loads in the baulked landing at Cincinnati, and then in continuing the flight without setting down to inspect for possible damage. Subsequently, he proceeded into questionable weather conditions, with turbulence, trying to fly visually and alternating to instrument procedures through an area where the ceiling was low. Prior to the accident, he apparently became lost and circled in the vicinity of Welch in an attempt to land or re-orientate himself. It was concluded that the transport had suffered damage at the wing root fittings and wing structure in both the initial hard landing and from the reversed loads experienced in the bounce. The surging power plant, which may have been related to carburettor icing, coupled with the turbulent air, which led to torsional vibration and created flutter, probably contributed to the failure of the wing that was ultimately overstressed during the pull-up manoeuvre. It was noted in the report that the atmospheric conditions were conducive to such icing, and that the carburettors installed on 42-56093 had shown potentionally dangerous characteristics if allowed to ice. Had the engine been subjected to a long period of surging, with backfiring and alternate cutting in and out of full power, it could have shifted the counterweight, creating a misalignment of the crankshaft, resulting in rough running or vibration that could have led to the in-flight break-up, particularly if combined with turbulence or mishandling by the crew. Heavy loading was an additional factor in the accident, and for that reason one of the recommendations made in the investigative report called for the specification of loading charts and rules for individual aircraft, a procedure that would later become a regular practice in transport flying.

Date: 25 August 1942 (c.14:00)
Location: Near Braemore, Caithness, Scotland
Operator: Royal Air Force
Aircraft type: Short Sunderland (W4026)

Prince George, the Duke of Kent, was among 14 military personnel killed in the crash of the four-engine flying boat, which took place 35 miles (55km) north-west of Inverness. Only the rear gunner, one of 11 crewmen assigned to the aircraft, survived. Having taken off earlier from the base at Invergordon, bound for Iceland, the aircraft was flying on the wrong track and at an insufficient height when it struck cloud-obscured Eagle's Rock, a hill rising to about 700ft (200m). There was no fire. One theory was that the accident resulted from an incorrect setting on the Sunderland's gyrosyn compass, then a relatively new piece of equipment, which placed the aircraft too far west. The crew then descended to a lower altitude in an attempt to make visual contact with the sea, over which they were thought to have been, resulting in the impact with the terrain.

Date: 1 October 1942 (c.09:30)
Location: Puerto Rico
Operator: US Army Air Forces
Aircraft type: Douglas C-39 (38-524)

The twin-engine transport crashed and burned in a mountainous region 15 miles (25km) north-

A Short Sunderland flying boat of the type flown by the RAF that crashed in Scotland, killing the Duke of Kent and 13 others. (Short Brothers Aircraft)

west of Caomo, while on an intra-island flight to the capital city of San Juan from Losey Field. All 22 persons aboard lost their lives, including three civilians; the rest of the passengers and the crew of five were American military personnel. Witnesses observed the aircraft making a wide right, descending turn from a north-easterly on to a south-easterly heading when over a small valley, then disappear into low overcast, its engines 'popping', or running roughly. Shortly thereafter, the C-39 slammed into a hill at high speed, about 200ft (60m) below the crest, and while flying on a heading of 150 degrees. Its throttles were found jammed in the closed position. The cloud layer in the area was some 4,000ft (1,200m) thick and extended to the tops of the hills. No information as to the probable or possible causes of the crash were released by military authorities.

Date: 15 January 1943 (time unknown)
Location: Near Paramarino, Dutch Guyana
Operator: US Army Air Forces
Aircraft type: Douglas C-54A (41-32939)

All 35 men aboard lost their lives when the four-engine aircraft, which was operated by the Air Transport Command (ATC) and bound for Africa from the US, crashed in a remote area along South America's Atlantic coast. The victims were both American military personnel and civilians, the latter including the transport's nine crewmen. No further details are known about the disaster or possible causes.

Date: 18 January 1943 (c.23:00)
Location: South Atlantic Ocean
Operator: US Army Air Forces
Aircraft type: Consolidated C-87 (41-1708)

Operated by the Air Transport Command (ATC) and on a transatlantic service from Accra, Gold Coast (Ghana), to Natal, Brazil, the converted B-24 bomber crashed at sea, probably between Ascension Island and its destination. Subsequently, two life rafts identified as belonging to the C-87 were recovered off the eastern coast of Brazil, but no survivors or bodies were found from the four-engine aircraft. The 26 Allied service personnel aboard included six American crewmen as well as 12 members of the Royal Air Force. It was dark at the time of the crash and the weather along the route of 41-1708 consisted of broken clouds and scattered rain showers.

Date: 18 February 1943 (c.12:30)
Location: Seattle, Washington, US
Operator: Boeing Aircraft Company
Aircraft type: Boeing XB-29 (41-3)

A trial flight of the second prototype of what was then the newest and largest American heavy bomber ended in a major disaster in a heavily urban area. With the intention of testing its power plant performance and cooling, propeller governing and two-engine capability, the XB-29 took off from Boeing Field, located at Renton. Less than 10 minutes later, a member of the crew radioed that

The famed Boeing B-29 Superfortress heavy bomber, whose early testing was marred by the disastrous crash in Seattle, Washington, US. (Boeing)

the aircraft was returning due to a fire in its No. 1 power plant, which had been brought under control using the engine fire-extinguishing system. A subsequent transmission reported it at a height of 2,400ft (730m) and descending, and that the same engine was ablaze and the corresponding propeller had been feathered. The radio operator also requested immediate landing clearance, and asked that emergency equipment to stand by, but stated that the trouble was not serious; his voice did not indicate any undue stress. But the situation deteriorated rapidly. In the final message from 41-3, the crewman advised the airport control tower, 'Have fire equipment ready. Am coming in with wing on fire.' Less than a minute later, and while on an approximately southerly heading, the four-engine aircraft struck a high-tension line and then slammed into a packing plant, bursting into flames on impact. Killed in the disaster were all 10 civilian crewmen of the aircraft, three of whom jumped out at a low altitude prior to the crash, and 20 persons on the ground. About a dozen others on the ground suffered injuries. The weather at the time, with a ceiling of around 8,000ft (2,500m) and a visibility of 5 miles (10km), was not considered a factor. The fire was thought to have originated from the leakage of fuel and/or oil into the engine nacelle, ignited by contact with the exhaust pipe or shroud, by the operation of electrical equipment, by the failure of the accessory section of the power plant, or a particular accessory. Gasoline that leaked into the leading edge, primarily around the filler neck cover and drain, could also have been ignited through contact with the heated nacelle skin or by fire through the nacelle firewall openings. The source of the gasoline was believed to have been overflow from the fuel tank filler necks, through vent holes, and subsequent leakage around the filler cover plates and their fastenings into the leading edge. (The location of the filler neck assembly in the leading edge of the wing, an area of greatly reduced air pressure, and the fact that the filler cap cover and the cap itself did not seal tightly could have allowed gasoline to be sucked out in this manner.) Flames then apparently spread to the leading edge of the port wing prior to the extinguishing of the nacelle fire, without the knowledge of the crew. Through the effect of gravity and the flow of ventilating air, the fire must have progressed through the leading edge to the inboard nacelle, wheel well and into the bomb bay. As the fire consumed a magnesium wing de-icer valve casting, the force of the air entering the leading edge caused an explosion that was observed by witnesses on the ground. This blast probably tore loose the No. 2 filler neck well and assembly, thereby releasing a large quantity of fuel, producing an inferno that must have led to the failure of both port engines. In the final seconds before the crash, the pilots probably abandoned any hope of reaching the airport, and the aircraft's

undercarriage was extended, possibly to allow members of the crew to escape or to throw out important records of the flight. As the cabin filled with smoke, visibility would have been reduced, preventing them from maintaining control of the bomber. One of the recommended changes in the B-29 made in the investigative report on this crash was a relocation of the filler necks outside of the leading edge and re-design of the caps to prevent the leakage of fuel. Considerable modifications were incorporated in the first production models of the aircraft, and thus the bomber that had such a tentative start would be given much of the credit for bringing an end to the war in the Pacific Theatre.

Date: 27 March 1943 (c.05:15)
Location: Near Brisbane, Queensland, Australia
Operator: Royal Australian Air Force
Aircraft type: Douglas C-47 Dakota (A30-16)

The twin-engine transport crashed and burned in a wooded area approximately 2 miles (3km) from Archerfield airfield, from where it had taken off shortly before, the accident occurring in pre-dawn darkness and conditions of poor visibility. All 27 military personnel aboard lost their lives; except for two American officers, the victims were Australian, including the crew of four. Although the cause was not determined with certainty, the crash probably resulted from power plant failure.

Date: 7 June 1943 (c.04:00)
Location: Near Red Springs, North Carolina, US
Operator: US Army Air Forces
Aircraft type: Douglas C-47A (42-23512)

All 20 American servicemen aboard were killed, including the crew of four, when the twin-engine transport crashed and burned 20 miles (30km) south-west of Fayetteville. The passengers were glider pilots, and the aircraft had been on an intrastate flight from Pope Field to Maxton Army Air Base when the accident occurred, in pre-dawn darkness. Proceeding on a southerly heading at a height of only about 200ft (c.60m), the C-47 had turned northward and then back towards the base, located 5 miles (10km) to the south-west, before it slammed to earth moments later in an area of thunderstorm activity. No casuative factors were given in investigative report on the accident.

Date: 1 August 1943 (c.15:00)
Location: Ploesti, Romania
Operator: US Army Air Forces
Aircraft type: Consolidated B-24

During the attack on Romanian oil fields, one of the bombers that had been hit by flak crashed into a women's prison, killing its 10 crewmen and 63 persons on the ground. Losses were heavy in this mission, designed to stall the German military machine, with 310 American airmen being killed, some on damaged aircraft that returned, and another 128 wounded. About 30 per cent of the B-24s dispatched on the mission, (54 of the 177 aircraft), were lost in combat or accidents, 41 being shot down by fighters or ground batteries over or on their way to the target.

Date: 1 August 1943 (c.16:00)
Location: St Louis, Missouri, US
Operator: US Army Air Forces
Aircraft type: Waco CG-4A (42-78839)

This Sunday afternoon demonstration to city officials of a locally-produced contribution to

Its right wing completely sheared off, the US Army Waco CG-4A glider is photographed during its plunge to earth. (St Louis Mercantile Library)

the American war effort ended in one of the worst peacetime glider accidents in the history of US military aviation. The glider involved was produced by the St Louis-based Robertson Aircraft Company, under contract to the principal manufacturer, Waco. Towed aloft by a C-47 transport, the CG-4A was to have landed on its own at Lambert Field. The two aircraft arrived over the airport from the south-east at an approximate height of 2,000ft (600m), but just after being released, the glider suffered catastrophic structural failure, its starboard wing folding up and separating from the fuselage completely, then plummeted to the ground, crashing in a grassy area adjacent to the runway. Ten persons aboard lost their lives, including St Louis Mayor William Dee Becker and three US servicemen, two of whom comprised the crew of 42-78839. There were no survivors. The local weather at the time, which was not considered a factor in the accident, consisted of scattered clouds at 2,500ft (750m), a visibility of 3 miles (5km) and light, variable winds. Examination of the wreckage indicated that the strut of the wing that failed was fractured at the point where it joined the fuselage. The military board investigating the crash expressed the opinion that the fitting that was welded on the lower end of the strut had too thin a wall thickness due either to erroneous specifications or faulty workmanship. Specifically, the machined dimensional limits of the fitting did not conform to the manufacturer's drawing with regard to the thickness of the wall between the inside diameter of the countersink in the fitting barrel and the outside diameter flat in the fitting shank taper. The wall thickness at the failed section was 1/16in (2mm), or only about 20 per cent of that specified, when considering a tolerance of 1/32in (1mm). It was obvious that the countersink had been drilled too deep. The failed section further showed evidence of deep tool marks, with both chattering, a surface flaw caused by vibration of the cutting tool, and gouging. Visual inspection would have easily detected these machining errors, while the thickness defect could have been found through the use of a micrometer or a caliper. According to the investigative report, these flaws indicated that there had been no inspection of the part by either the prime or sub-contractor, or by Army Air Force personnel. When the fitting broke, the wing was allowed to hinge upward as far as the wing root attachment fitting would permit, after which the unsupported spar snapped at a point approximately 1ft (300mm) from the fuselage. It was concluded that Robertson did not have a sufficient force of experienced personnel and did not exercise proper control over work produced by its sub-contractors, and that it could neither guarantee quality material nor workmanship or the quality of highly-stressed parts produced at some of its sub-contractors' plants. Also, the military inspector in charge was found to have insufficient help to properly exercise his duties with regard to the activities of the contractors. Subsequent to the accident, all gliders produced by Robertson were grounded until a complete inspection of highly-stressed parts used in them could be accomplished. A new inspection procedure was later introduced by the firm, and four civilian inspectors and the aforementioned military official were relieved of their duties.

Date: 10 September 1943 (c.16:00)
Location: Gulf of Mexico

First aircraft
Operator: US Army Air Forces
Type: Boeing B-17F (42-4621)

Second aircraft
Operator: US Army Air Forces
Type: Boeing B-17F (42-6031)

The two four-engine heavy bombers collided in mid-air, and both then crashed at sea 50 miles (80km) south-east of Galveston, Texas, US, killing 22 crewmen (11 aboard each one). There were no survivors. The two B-17s involved were among six bombers flying in a tight formation when the leading edge of the vertical stabiliser of 4621 contacted the trailing edge of the wing of 6031, after which the two aircraft slammed together with considerable force, the collision occurring in good weather conditions.

Date: 20 September 1943 (c.08:50)
Location: Near Maxton, North Carolina, US
Operator: US Army Air Forces
Aircraft type: Douglas C-53D (42-68729)

All 25 American service personnel aboard were killed, including four crewmen, when the twin-engine transport crashed in a wooded area about 35 miles (55km) south-west of Fayetteville after nearly colliding with another C-53 that was towing a glider. Immediately after it had taken off from Maxton Army Air Base, 42-68729 confronted the other two aircraft nearly head-on, at an approximate height of 300ft (100m), prompting an evasive manoeuvre. However, the crew was unable to recover from the steep bank and resulting stall, and the transport slammed to earth and burst into flames.

Date: 22 September 1943 (c.06:00)
Location: Near Calcutta, India
Operator: US Army Air Forces
Aircraft type: Douglas C-53 (42-6471)

The twin-engine transport crashed and burned slightly less than a mile (1.5km) north of Dum Dum Airport, from where it had taken off moments earlier. All 20 American servicemen aboard (15 passengers and a crew of five) were killed. The aircraft had struck trees following its departure from the north/south runway, the accident occurring around dawn and in meteorological conditions

The most famous bomber of the Second World War, the Boeing B-17 Flying Fortress, two of which, identical to the one shown here, were involved in a collision over the Gulf of Mexico. (Boeing)

consisting of a high overcast with scattered clouds at 2,000ft (600m), a visibility of 7 miles (11km) and a light wind. Whatever factors that caused or were factored in it were not divulged in the official investigative report on the crash.

Date: 19 October 1943 (time unknown)
Location: Near Joliette, Quebec, Canada
Operator: Royal Canadian Air Force
Aircraft type: Consolidated B-24

The four-engine bomber, which was on a flight to Montreal from a port on Canada's Atlantic coast, crashed 60 miles (100km) north of its destination, and all 24 Canadian service personnel aboard the aircraft were killed. Its wreckage and the remains of the victims were located nearly three years later.

Date: 22 October 1943 (c.20:20)
Location: Near Columbus, Georgia, US
Operator: US Army Air Forces
Aircraft type: Douglas C-47 (42-5677)

All 20 American servicemen aboard lost their lives, including a crew of five, when the twin-engine transport crashed and burned at Fort Benning, during a night parachute exercise. Shortly after 11 soldiers had successfully parachuted from it, the aircraft apparently stalled, then went into a

descending turn to the left at the prescribed drop altitude of 800ft (250m) and plummeted to earth.

Date: 8 November 1943 (time unknown)
Location: Poona, Maharashtra, India
Operator: Indian Air Force
Aircraft type: Unknown

The aeroplane crashed into the village located some 70 miles (110km) south-east of Bombay, striking huts and bursting into flames. Killed were 38 persons, including the pilot (and sole occupant) of the aircraft.

Date: 29 December 1943 (c.15:00)
Location: Near Lakeside, Utah, US

First aircraft
Operator: US Army Air Forces
Type: Consolidated B-24E (42-7183)

Second aircraft
Operator: US Army Air Forces
Type: Consolidated B-24E (42-7408)

A cross-country formation flight by five heavy bombers ended in tragedy when two of them collided in mid-air, then crashed and burned near the western shore of the Great Salt Lake, 70 miles (110km) north-west of Salt Lake City, killing 25 American servicemen. There were no survivors from

The wide use of the Douglas C-47 Dakota transport accounts for its involvement in so many accidents and combat losses during World War II. (McDonnell Douglas)

either aircraft, 12 aboard 7183 and 13 aboard 7408. The group had taken off earlier from Wendover Field, in Utah, bound for Pocatello Army Air Base, located in neighbouring Idaho, and proceeded normally until a point where 7183, which was in the No. 3 position, found itself too high and too far back from the formation. In trying to get back in place, it apparently got in the 'prop wash' of the lead aircraft, and was blown downward on top of 7408, which had been in the No. 4 position. In the ensuing collision, which occurred above the cloud layer at an approximate height of 11,000ft (3,400m), the latter's port wing outside of the No. 1 power plant was torn off, resulting in a loss of control, while the former was also badly damaged and went into a flat spin. Icing conditions existed in the area at the time within the clouds, the bases of which were down to about 700ft (200m). According to the official report, the accident was entirely attributable to the faulty flying technique displayed by the pilot of 7183.

Date: 6 March 1944 (c.13:00)
Location: Near Berlin, Germany

First aircraft
Operator: US Army Air Forces
Type: Boeing B-17 (42-31595)

Second aircraft
Operator: US Army Air Forces
Type: Boeing B-17G (42-31627)

Third aircraft
Operator: Luftwaffe (German Air Force)
Type: Messerschmitt Me410A

In what may have been an accident or an intentional act of ramming, the twin-engine fighter collided with one of the four-engine bombers, 31595, which itself then struck the second B-17, and all three aircraft crashed. Two German and 19 American airmen were killed; the sole survivor of the triple collision was the tail gunner of 31627. This incident occurred during a bombing of Berlin, which was one of the most costly missions of the Second World War, with 69 American bombers being destroyed in combat or from accidents, and more than 200 airmen losing their lives.

Date: 30/31 March 1944
Location: Germany
Operator: Royal Air Force
Aircraft type: Various (108)

The single costliest bombing mission in the history of the RAF was this night raid on Nuremberg, which claimed mostly Lancaster and Halifax bombers, and a Mosquito fighter on an intruder flight, the aircraft being lost due to both hostile action and accidents. A total of 545 airmen were killed in this operation.

Date: 6 June 1944 (c.01:15)
Location: Near Barneville, Manche, France
Operator: US Army Air Forces
Aircraft type: Douglas C-47A (42-93095)

Loaded with paratroopers and participating in the Allied invasion of Normandy, the twin-engine transport was believed shot down over the Cherbourg Peninsula, 25 miles (40km) north-west of Carentan while flying in darkness and meteorological conditions consisting of a broken overcast, with a visibility of 5 miles (10km). Including a crew of five, all 22 American servicemen aboard were killed.

Date: 6 June 1944 (c.01:30)
Location: Near Carentan, Manche, France
Operator: US Army Air Forces
Aircraft type: Douglas C-47A (42-101035)

During its participation in the Normandy invasion, the twin-engine transport was apparently brought down by anti-aircraft fire before it could drop its load of paratroopers. There were no survivors among the 22 American servicemen aboard the C-47, including a crew of four. Two of the paratroopers apparently jumped from the aircraft into the pre-dawn darkness before the crash were listed as 'missing in action'.

Date: 6 June 1944 (c.02:00)
Location: Near Flamanville, Manche, France
Operator: US Army Air Forces
Aircraft type: Douglas C-47 (42-100905)

The twin-engine transport, which was involved in the Normandy invasion, crashed about 10 miles (15km) south-west of Cherbourg, under unknown circumstances and about 5 minutes before the planned drop of its load of paratroopers. All 22 American servicemen aboard lost their lives, including a crew of four. It was dark at the time the aircraft went down, and the local weather consisted of scattered clouds, with a visibility of between 5 and 10 miles (10–15km).

Date: 26 July 1944 (time unknown)
Location: North Atlantic Ocean
Operator: US Army Air Forces
Aircraft type: Douglas C-54A (42-107470)

Operated by the Air Transport Command (ATC) and carrying 26 persons, the four-engine aircraft vanished while en-route from Iceland to Stephenville, Newfoundland, one segment of a scheduled transatlantic flight originating in England, with an ultimate destination of Long Island, New York, US. A thorough search failed to find any trace of the C-54 or its occupants, and it was concluded that whatever happened to it must have been sudden and without warning. The aircraft was last heard from shortly after 03:00 Iceland time, some three hours after its departure, when probably off south-eastern Greenland. The weather along the route taken was reported to have consisted of a broken overcast, with cloud tops of 6,000 to 7,000ft (1,800–2,000m). The passengers of the aircraft were all American service personnel and except for one, its six crew members were civilian employees of the US airline Transcontinental and Western Air (TWA), working under contract to the Army.

Date: 27 July 1944 (c.16:00)
Location: Near Westfrouegh, Argyllshire, Scotland
Operator: US Army Air Forces
Aircraft type: Douglas C-47A (42-93038)

All 22 military personnel aboard lost their lives in the crash of the twin-engine transport on the Island of Mull, in the vicinity of Port Logan. Except for one member of the Royal Air Force, the victims were Americans, including a nurse and the five members of the flight crew. The passengers comprised 13 men wounded in the Normandy invasion the previous month, who were being transported to the US, the C-47 had been en route to Prestwick from Filton aerodrome, near Bristol, and was proceeding under a low overcast at a minimal altitude so that a following aircraft could keep it in sight. Approaching land, 42-93038 initiated a climb, but did not gain sufficient height to clear a fog-shrouded cliff rising to more than 400ft (120m), which it struck only about 20ft (6m) from its crest,

bursting into flames on impact. The second aircraft barely avoided the terrain itself.

Date: 3 August 1944 (c.20:30)
Location: Near Naper, Nebraska, US
Operator: US Army Air Forces
Aircraft type: Douglas C-47A (42-23652)

The twin-engine transport, which was carrying as passengers Army Air Force pilots, was on an interstate flight from the air base located near Bruning, Nebraska, to one near Pierre, South Dakota, crashed and burned in a ravine 200 miles (320km) north-west of Omaha. All 28 American servicemen aboard, including a crew of four, were killed in the accident which occurred in darkness and during a thunderstorm. Both its power plants having failed after a severe lightning flash occurred nearby, the aircraft went into a steep dive, emerging from the cloud base before it disintegrated in the air, then apparently slammed to earth in an inverted attitude.

Date: 23 August 1944 (c.10:45)
Location: Freckleton, Lancashire, England
Operator: US Army Air Forces
Aircraft type: Consolidated B-24H (42-50291)

In the worst non-combat aviation disaster of the Second World War, the four-engine bomber crashed while attempting to land at Warton air depot, located around 7 miles (11km) west of Preston, striking the village school and an adjacent

Rescue workers sift through the remains of the village school and other structures struck by an American B-24 bomber at Freckleton, England. (US National Archives)

cafe, a pub and three houses and bursting into flames. Among the 61 persons killed were the three crewmen (and only occupants) of the aircraft, which had been on a test flight, and 38 children on the ground. About 30 others suffered injuries. The crash occurred during a thunderstorm, which was accompanied by heavy rain, a ceiling of 400ft (120m) and a horizontal visibility of less than 1,000ft (300m), with a northerly wind of approximately 25 knots and even stronger gusts. During its landing approach, the B-24 must have been forced down by the violent winds and down-draughts associated with the storm, and was unable to gain sufficient speed and altitude to prevent the crash.

Date: 28 August 1944 (c.01:00)
Location: Prestwick, Strathclyde, Scotland
Operator: US Army Air Forces
Aircraft type: Douglas C-54A (42-72171)

Having completed a transatlantic crossing, the four-engine transport crashed and burned in a residential area while attempting to land at Prestwick airport. All 20 service personnel aboard (14 passengers and a crew of six) and five persons on the ground, including a 6-year-old girl who had been sleeping in her home at the time of the accident, were killed. The crash occurred in early morning darkness and conditions of poor visibility, but no further information was released as to its cause or related factors.

Date: 18 October 1944 (c.15:40)
Location: Near Birkenhead, Merseyside, England
Operator: US Army Air Forces
Aircraft type: Consolidated B-24H (42-50347)

All 24 American servicemen aboard perished, including a crew of five, when the four-engine bomber crashed in the vicinity of Liverpool during a transtlantic flight. Its passengers were all airmen returning to their base in New York. Proceeding through an area of squally weather conditions, with heavy rain, a broken overcast of 1,000ft (300m), a visibility of 8 miles (13km) and a westerly wind of around 30 knots, the aircraft suddenly disintegrated at an estimated height of 6,000ft (1,800m) after either an explosion or a catastrophic structural failure, the cause of which could not be determined. Investigation revealed no evidence of pre-impact fire or mechanical failure.

Date: 19 November 1944 (c.15:10)
Location: Near Lewes, East Sussex, England
Operator: US Army Air Forces
Aircraft type: Douglas C-47A (43-15046)

The crash of the twin-engine transport, which occurred approximately 3 miles (5km) northeast of Brighton, claimed the lives of 25 servicemen

aboard the aircraft, including its entire crew of five. All the occupants were American except for two Frenchman, one of whom was among the five injured survivors. After it had flown into a low overcast, the C-47 struck the east slope of a hill at an approximate elevation of 600ft (180m), exploding on impact. Ten miles (15km) from the scene of the accident, the weather was characterised by a ceiling of only 300 to 400ft (100–120m), a visibility of about half-a-mile (0.8km), heavy, intermittent rain and a south-south-westerly wind of approximately 15 knots. The cause of the accident was not disclosed by US military officials.

Date: 2 February 1945 (c.10:15)
Location: Near Montieri, Grosseto, Italy
Operator: US Army Air Forces
Aircraft type: Douglas C-47 (41-18603)

Three Army nurses were among the 23 American service personnel aboard who were killed when the twin-engine transport, which was on an Italian internal flight from Florence to Rome, crashed and burned 60 miles (100km) north of its destination. Two passengers and the pilot, one of four crewmen assigned to 41-18603, survived with injuries. Proceeding on a south-westerly heading through a river valley, with hills on either side that were obscured by strato-cumulus clouds and mist, the C-47 encountered a fog bank, necessitating a transition by its crew from visual to instrument flight procedures. The pilot immediately initiated a climb to avoid rising terrain, but not at a sufficient rate to prevent the aircraft from hitting trees, whereupon it slammed to earth. At the time, the ceiling in the area was 2,000 to 3,000ft (600–1,000m), and the visibility reduced by the fog to less than 1 mile (1.5km).

Date: 6 February 1945 (c.10:05)
Location: Near Hunters Burgh, Sussex, England
Operator: Royal Air Force
Aircraft type: Douglas C-47 Dakota (KG630)

The twin-engine transport crashed and burned, killing all 23 British Commonwealth servicemen aboard (19 passengers and a crew of four). Flying too low in clouds, the aircraft struck a hill at an above-sea level elevation of around 500ft (150m), the impact shearing off the starboard wing, and the C-47 then plummeted into a wooded area.

Date: 13 February 1945 (c.06:30)
Location: Near Oakland, California, US
Operator: US Navy
Aircraft type: Douglas R4D-6 (50765)

All 24 American servicemen aboard were killed, including a crew of three, when the twin-engine transport crashed in San Francisco Bay shortly after

The fuselage section of the wrecked US Navy R4D transport is raised from San Francisco Bay following the crash that took 24 lives. (UPI/Corbis-Bettmann)

its departure from the Oakland airport. The main wreckage and the bodies of 17 victims were recovered from the water. Among the latter, the cause of death was divided by approximately half between traumatic injury and drowning. Ultimately bound for the US East Coast, the aircraft had taken off from Runway 27 and proceeded towards the west before making a right turn, whereupon its starboard wing struck the surface of the bay. Its undercarriage still extended, the R4D then slammed into the water. It was dark at the time, being before dawn, and the local weather consisted of a light drizzle, with a ceiling of 700ft (200m) and unlimited visibility under the clouds. The wind was out of the south-east at 5 knots. The aircraft's gyro horizon was found to be caged, or locked in a fixed position, and this could have been a factor in the crash. Because of this, it was recommended in the investigative report, that Navy transports be equipped with non-cageable gyro horizon units. Among the other recommendations was for a greater emphasis on the instrument training of pilots, specifically, in the use of rate-of-climb and turn-and-bank indicators, magnetic compass and clock.

Date: 20 April 1945 (c.06:40)
Location: Near Sweetwater, Texas, US
Operator: US Army Air Forces
Aircraft type: Douglas C-47 (41-18451)

The twin-engine transport crashed, exploded and burned in a pasture approximately 3½ miles (6km) south of the town, and all 25 American servicemen aboard were killed, including a crew of five. Having taken off earlier from Midland Army Air Field, also in Texas, on an interstate service to Nashville, Tennessee, the aircraft had been assigned to a cruising altitude of 5,000ft (1,500m) before it disintegrated while flying in an area of thunderstorm activity. The initial structural failure of its elevator was followed by a more general break-up of the C-47. Though not officially reported, severe turbulence was undoubtedly a factor in the accident.

Date: 5 May 1945 (22:26)
Location: Territory of New Guinea
Operator: US Army Air Forces
Aircraft type: Douglas C-54E (44-9043)

The four-engine transport crashed and burst into flames on Manus, one of the Admiralty Islands in the Bismarck Archipelago region, killing all 21 American servicemen aboard (15 passengers and a crew of six). Having taken off shortly before from the Sorido airstrip, on an intra-island flight, the C-54 slammed into a bluff at an approximate elevation of 500ft (150m). The accident occurred on a dark, moonless night, but the local weather conditions were otherwise good, with a ceiling of around 2,000ft (600m) and unrestricted visibility under the clouds. A slight breeze was blowing out of the north-west. Due to the complete destruction of the aircraft, it was not possible to determine the cause of the crash. However, its direction at the moment of impact indicated that the pilot did not make a turn away from the rising terrain as soon as he reached the minimum safe altitude for such a manoeuvre. Subsequently, the flight operations officer for the airfield issued a directory that aircraft departing on the same north-westerly heading as had 44-9043, initiate a left turn upon reaching a sufficient height and not more than 45 seconds after take-off. The investigative report also emphasized the importance of attaining a minimum altitude of 1,000ft (300m) before flap retraction in night operations of the C-54, which in this case was apparently not done.

Date: 6 May 1945 (12:54)
Location: Hindhead, Surrey, England
Operator: US Army Air Forces
Aircraft type: Curtiss-Wright C-46D (44-77839)

Loaded with litter patients being brought back from the Continent, the twin-engine transport crashed and burned after striking the tops of radar towers located on Gibbets Hill, 25 miles (40km) south-west of London. A total of 31 military personnel lost their lives in the crash, one of them a Canadian who was on the ground in a hut struck by falling debris and the rest aboard the aircraft; except for three British, the latter were all Americans, including the crew of five assigned to 44-77839. There were no survivors. Flying through a valley close to the terrain on account of a low overcast, with 8/10 cloud coverage at 600ft (180m) and a visibility of 3 miles (5km), the aircraft was bound for Newbury, Berkshire, England, when it hit the tops of the towers, which rose to 240ft (70m) above the ground, the impact shearing off the starboard wing. The accident was attributed to pilot error, specifically, his attempt to maintain contact (visual) flight rules in the instrument meteorological conditions. An additional factor may have been the absence of lights on the towers and the fact that the obstacles were not indicated on regional flight charts.

Date: 9 May 1945 (c.12:30)
Location: Near Roye, Somme, France
Operator: Royal Air Force
Aircraft type: Avro Lancaster (RF230)

Only about 12 hours after the end of hostilities in the European theatre, this prisoner-of-war transport flight ended in tragedy. All 31 servicemen aboard lost their lives when the four-engine bomber plummeted into a wooded area and caught fire 25 miles (40km) south-east of Amiens after going into an uncontrollable spin. The crash occurred during a flight to England from Brussels, Belgium; except for one American, the victims were British, including the crew of six. At the time, the weather conditions in the area consisted of scattered clouds above 10,000ft (3,000m) and high cirrus, with a visibility of between 5 and 10 miles (10–15km) and a slight, south-easterly breeze.

Date: 13 May 1945 (c.15:00)
Location: Netherlands New Guinea (West Irian)
Operator: US Army Air Forces
Aircraft type: Douglas C-47B (43-49788)

All but three of the 23 American military personnel aboard were killed when the twin-engine transport crashed and burned on a mountain at an approximate elevation of 7,000ft (2,000m). The injured survivors, who included a member of the Women's Army Corps (WAC), were found by a search party nearly two weeks later and taken back to civilisation. No official military report pertaining to the crash or its possible cause was released.

Date: 30 May 1945 (c.09:20)
Location: Near Sassandra, Ivory Coast
Operator: US Army Air Forces
Aircraft type: Douglas C-47B (44-76406)

Operated by the Air Transport Command (ATC), the aircraft had been on a scheduled flight from Accra, Gold Coast (Ghana), to Roberts

An RAF Avro Lancaster bomber, similar to the aircraft involved in the prisoners-of-war flight tragedy on 9 May 1945. (Philip Jarrett)

Field, serving Monrovia, Liberia. It carried 21 American service personnel, including three crewmen; its passengers were all members of the Women's Army Corps (WAC). Last reported cruising at an altitude of 8,000ft (2,500m), the C-47 sent out a Mayday distress message before it crashed in the Atlantic Ocean off Drewin. According to a native eye-witness, it plummeted into the water at an angle of approximately 45 degrees. Only an oil slick was found at the crash site; no survivors, bodies or wreckage were recovered.

Date: 15 June 1945 (c.07:50)
Location: Near Swanage, Dorset, England
Operator: Royal Air Force
Aircraft type: Consolidated LB-30A Liberator
 (JT985)

Flown by Transport Command, the aircraft crashed and burned on a hillside 10 miles (15km) south-south-west of Bournemouth, in conditions of poor visibility after experiencing engine trouble. All 27 persons aboard were killed, including the crew of five.

Date: 29 June 1945 (time unknown)
Location: Near Bangalore, Karnataka, India
Operator: Royal Indian Air Force
Aircraft type: Unknown

The aircraft crashed into a village where a 'jatra' celebration was taking place, killing both crewmen and 36 persons on the ground. About 20 others suffered injuries in the afternoon accident, while the impact explosion and ensuing fires destroyed or damaged numerous houses.

Date: 3/4 July 1945 (time unknown)
Location: North Atlantic Ocean
Operator: Royal Air Force
Aircraft type: Consolidated LB-30A Liberator
 (JT982)

Operated by Transport Command and carrying as passengers delegates returning from a conference in the US, the England-bound aircraft, which had last stopped at Montreal, Canada, vanished with 15 persons aboard. Among the occupants was a crew of six British, American and Canadian service personnel. Search for the transport was abandoned some two weeks later.

Date: 11 July 1945 (time unknown)
Location: Near Kisumu, Kenya
Operator: South African Air Force
Aircraft type: Douglas C-47 (6812)

All 28 South African servicemen aboard lost their lives, including a crew of four, when the twin-engine transport crashed into an inlet of Lake

Victoria. The accident occurred in early morning darkness shortly after the aircraft (its passengers all former prisoners-of-war returning home), had taken off, although the suspected cause was never released. Night flying from the airport was, however, temporarily suspended in the wake of the crash.

Date: 28 July 1945 (c.10:00)
Location: New York, New York, US
Operator: US Army Air Forces
Aircraft type: North American B-25D (43-0577)

This remains, even today, one of the best known military air disasters in history, due to its involvement with one of the most famous and, at that time, the tallest building in the world. The twin-engine bomber had been on a domestic inter-state flight originating at Bedford airfield, in Massachusetts, to New York City. It had been operating under a contact (visual) clearance only to La Guardia Airport, on Long Island, but upon reaching that point its pilot requested permission from the La Guardia control tower, and was so granted, to proceed on to Newark Airport, located across the Hudson River from Manhattan Island in New Jersey. Contained within that clearance were, however, instructions to return if the visibility fell below 3 miles (5km). Apparently becoming uncertain of his position, the pilot turned from a south-westerly to a southerly heading approximately over the Rockefeller Center, and while flying at too low an altitude. Ahead was the giant Empire State Building, towering to 1,250ft (380m), the top third of which was shrouded by fog, with an overcast of approximately 800ft (250m). Pulling up just before impact, the aircraft was in a near-vertical attitude when it struck the skyscraper at its 79th Floor, some 900ft (275m) above 34th Street. The crash resulted in an explosion and fire, with parts of the wreckage completely penetrating the building and dropping on to a near-by roof. Among the 14 persons killed were the three servicemen aboard the B-25 and the operator of an elevator in the Empire State Building, which plunged about 1,000ft (300m) into its basement after its support cable had been cut by the force of the impact; 25 others on the ground suffered injuries. But it could have been much worse. This was a Saturday, and many offices were closed, while others had reduced staffs. Also, several floors around the level of the crash were completely unoccupied. Although the clearance given him was considered a contributing factor, the Army primarily blamed the accident on an error in judgement on the part of the pilot for proceeding over Manhattan under the prevailing conditions. Subsequently, the US Civil Aeronautics Administration (CAA) raised the minimum altitude over lower Manhattan Island from 1,000ft (300m) above all obstructions to 2,500ft (750m) absolute.

Above *A North American B-25 medium bomber, used extensively during the Second World War and the type that struck the Empire State Building on 28 July 1945.* (US National Archives)

Right *The tremendous force of the impact of the B-25 is illustrated by the huge hole left in the side of the skyscraper.* (New York Times Pictures)

Date: 15 September 1945 (00:08)
Location: Near Kansas City, Missouri, US
Operator: US Army Air Forces
Aircraft type: Douglas C-47B (45-1011)

Flown by the Air Transport Command (ATC), the twin-engine aircraft crashed and burst into flames after its departure from Fairfax Field, located at Kansas City, Kansas. All but one passenger among the 24 American servicemen aboard were killed, including the crew of three, and the sole survivor was seriously injured. Bound for the US East Coast, the transport lifted off from Runway 35, but then failed to gain sufficient altitude. Initial contact was with trees located on the north bank of the Missouri River, which were about 30ft (10m) tall and approximately 1 mile (1.5km) beyond the end of the runway, with the impact shearing off both wings, and the C-47 then slammed to earth. The accident occurred in darkness and clear meteorological conditions, with a visibility of 10 miles (15km), and a slight breeze. Examination of the wreckage revealed one blade on the right propeller to be unbent, indicating a considerable reduction in power in the corresponding engine at the moment of impact. This suspected loss of power could have been related to one or a combination of the following factors: the aircraft's power plants had been fitted with spark plugs whose use was not recommended by the manufacturer; a possible misuse of the heat control by the crew due to dissimilarity with earlier models of the C-47, or excessive dilution and blow-by caused by a sudden increase in oil consumption during a preceding flight.

Date: 5 October 1945 (c.12:50)
Location: Near Elvetham, Hampshire, England
Operator: Royal Air Force
Aircraft type: Consolidated LB-30A Liberator (KG867)

The four-engine transport crashed and burned 2 miles (3km) south-west of Blackbushe airfield, from where it had taken off shortly before, bound for Prague, Czechoslovakia. All 23 persons aboard lost their lives, including a crew of five military personnel; the occupants were all Czech refugees returning home. Fire had erupted in the aircraft's No. 2 power plant nacelle, apparently resulting in a loss of control.

Date: 7 October 1945 (c.00:30)
Location: Near Rennes, Ille-et-Vilaine, France
Operator: Royal Air Force
Aircraft type: Short Stirling IV (LJ668)

Operated by Transport Command, the aircraft crashed less than a mile (1.5km) south of the city while attempting to land at the local airport, an en-route stop during a flight from London to Cairo, Egypt. All 26 British military personnel aboard (20 passengers and a crew of six) were killed. With its undercarriage extended, the four-engine transport lost height while in a turn and slammed to earth and caught fire as its crew attempted to break through the cloud base, which was down to about only 200ft (60m), the accident occurring in darkness.

Date: 13 October 1945 (c.20:45)
Location: Melsbroek, Brabant, Belgium
Operator: Royal Air Force
Aircraft type: Consolidated LB-30A Liberator (KL595)

The four-engine aircraft had been on a Transport Command trooping flight with an ultimate destination of India when it crashed and burned immediately after taking off in darkness from Melsbroek Airport, located about 5 miles (10km) north-east of Brussels. All 31 British military personnel aboard were killed, including a crew of six. Apparently failing to obtain sufficient flying speed, the Liberator had gained little height before it struck a small rise beyond the end of the runway.

Date: 16 October 1945 (c.11:30)
Location: Near Peking (Beijing), China
Operator: US Army Air Forces
Aircraft type: Curtiss-Wright C-46F (44-78591)

Following a flight from Hankou, in the Chinese province of Hubei, the twin-engine transport struck a commercial radio transmission tower while on a south-easterly heading as it approached for a landing at Nanyman airfield, which served the capital city, then crashed and burned. All 59 military personnel aboard lost their lives including four American crewmen; the passengers were all Chinese soldiers. At the time of the accident, the weather in the area was poor, with an overcast of about only 300ft (100m) and a visibility of approximately 1 mile (1.5km). As there were no radio beacon facilities in the area, the commercial broadcasting station was being used as a navigational aid.

A US Army Air Force Curtiss-Wright C-46 transport, two of which suffered major crashes in China during trooping flights in October 1945. (US National Archives)

But while the pre-flight pilot briefing mentioned the location of the antenna mast, some 15 miles (25km) west-north-west of the airfield, its height, which was 800ft (250m) above the ground and approximately 1,000ft (300m) above airfield elevation, had not been given.

Date: 30 October 1945 (c.19:15)
Location: Near Chihchiang, Hunan, China
Operator: US Army Air Forces
Aircraft type: Curtiss-Wright C-46A (43-47228)

The twin-engine transport, carrying a load of Chinese troops to Shanghai, crashed and burned on a hill about two minutes after it had taken off from the Chihchiang airfield, killing 45 servicemen. Four soldiers and the aircraft's co-pilot, one of the four American crewmen assigned to 43-47228, survived with injuries. The accident occurred in darkness, but the local weather conditions, with a ceiling of 12,000ft (3,700m), were not considered a factor. Prior to take-off, the co-pilot had noted that the right engine run-up and magneto checks were unsatisfactory, but in response to his questioning, the pilot stated that he knew the terrain very well and that he considered the power check satisfactory. A board of investigation expressed the opinion that a loss of engine power and the possibility of overloading of the aircraft, due to the fact that the troops had taken aboard with them some mortar ammunition that was not part of their regular equipment, had, in combination, contributed to the accident. A radiogram from Tenth Air Force headquarters had authorised this as a daylight operation, but this message was not received until two days after the crash. Subsequently, payloads were reduced and night flying abandoned in the Chinese troop transport flights.

Date: 1 November 1945 (c.15:30)
Location: Near Herrenalb, Germany
Operator: US Army Air Forces
Aircraft type: Douglas C-47A (42-93041)

The twin-engine transport crashed some 50 miles (80km) west of Stuttgart during a flight from England to an air base located near Munich. All but four of the 30 American servicemen aboard the aircraft lost their lives, including the entire crew of four, while the surviving passengers suffered serious injuries. In an apparent attempt to let the navigator check his position, the C-47 had descended through a low overcast, and witnesses stated that it then followed a river for several minutes before beginning to climb back into the clouds. It subsequently slammed into wooded mountainside and burned. According to a local observer, the meteorological conditions in the area at the time of the accident consisted of low stratus clouds that extended down to the hilltops, with a ceiling of around 1,300ft

(400m) and a visibility of 2 miles (3km) in light rain and haze. The underlying cause of the accident was that the pilot had been flying on instruments below a safe altitude. Responsibility was also placed on the navigator, who failed to warn the pilot of the high terrain in the area. As a result, the pilot had initiated a descent while uncertain of his position. And, after determining his location, he should have ascended using higher engine power settings. Still another factor was inadequate meteorological information provided to the flight crew, this due to the absence of weather stations in the area. For that reason, one recommendation made in the investigative report was to employ local residents with knowledge of or backgrounds in weather observation and forecasting.

Date: 3 November 1945 (c.02:00)
Location: Near Chhuka, Bhutan, India
Operator: US Army Air Forces
Aircraft type: Douglas C-54G (45-528A)

During an internal Indian flight to Karachi from Chabua airfield, located near Dibrugarh, Assam, the four-engine transport crashed into a mountain ridge in the Himalayas at an approximate elevation of 8,000ft (2,500m) and 50 miles (80km) south of Punakha. Although the wreckage of the aircraft was not located until the following month, all 44 American servicemen aboard (40 passengers and a crew of four) had perished in the crash. It was dark at the time of the accident, with no moon, but the meteorological conditions in the area, consisting of unlimited ceiling and visibility, were apparently not a factor. The location of the crash indicated that 45-528A had flown the direct route between the two cities and off the designated airway. An investigative board concluded that this action was probably deliberate on the part of the pilot-in-command, in violation of prescribed regulations, and placed the aircraft at an insufficient height to clear the terrain. Villagers reported seeing an aircraft, probably the C-54, proceeding east to west at a low altitude. Initial impact with trees tore off its starboard wing, after which the transport crashed, exploded and disintegrated.

Date: 8 November 1945 (c.20:00)
Location: Corpus Christi Bay, Texas, US

First aircraft
Operator: US Navy
Type: Martin PBM-3S Mariner (01710)

Second aircraft
Operator: US Navy
Type: Martin PBM-5 Mariner (69113)

The two twin-engine amphibious patrol bombers collided and crashed about 2½ miles (4km) north-north-west of Corpus Christi Naval Air

Station. Killed in the accident were 22 American servicemen, including all 12 occupants of 69113; the five survivors from 01710 suffered various injuries. Both aircraft were on training flights, 69113 having taken off from the water on a true heading of 150 degrees, while 01710 was making its approach to a different landing area and on a course of 165 degrees true. Despite taking off behind it, the former overtook the latter due to the differences in speed between the two models of the PBM, flying slightly to starboard but on an approximately parallel course. The tail lights on the Mariner were at best difficult to see, but when 01710 turned on its landing lights, 69113 pulled up and turned left in a futile attempt to avoid the collision, which occurred in darkness at an estimated height of 400ft (120m). The PBM-5 then plummeted straight down, exploding on impact with the water. At the time, the meteorological conditions in the area were good, with an unlimited ceiling and a visibility in excess of 10 miles (15km). An investigative report attributed the accident to error by the crew of 69113, primarily inattention on the part of its co-pilot, whose role would normally have been relegated to that of 'look-out' during instrument take-offs and landings. Other factors were the judgement displayed by its pilot in pulling up upon the sudden appearance of 01710, which was probably related to confusion on his part, when maintaining the same course could possibly have avoided the collision. It was determined that although the PBM-5 did establish radio contact with the control tower, there were no transmissions subsequent to the initial one. A board of inquiry considered it doubtful that as they were operating in an uncontrolled area, where pilots took off and landed at their own discretion, the crew had heard 01710 receive landing clearance, and also ruled that in its 'touch-and-go' exercise, 69113 had apparently proceeded too far in the traffic pattern before starting its down-wind turn.

Date: 9 November 1945 (c.20:00)
Location: Near Boccadi, Sicily, Italy
Operator: US Army Air Forces
Aircraft type: Douglas C-47A (42-24363)

Operated by the Military Air Transport Service (MATS) and on a scheduled flight to Naples from Athens, Greece, the twin-engine aircraft slammed into a mountain and burned near Palermo. The 24 persons killed in the crash included two civilian passengers and a British serviceman; the rest of the victims were American military personnel, among them the aircraft's four crewmen. The survivor, a US Army soldier riding as a passenger, was seriously injured. About an hour before the crash, the pilot radioed that he was lost. Some 20 minutes after its position had been re-established, 42-24363 flew over, then crashed approximately half-a-mile (0.8km) north of, Palermo airport. The crew

may have seen flares fired from the ground and initiated a climb just before the impact. It was dark at the time, and the weather in the area consisted of an almost solid layer of strato-cumulus clouds at about 2,000ft (600m) and broken fracto-cumulus at 1,000ft (300m), with a light rain and a visibility of around 3 miles (5km). The wind was out of the south-west at around 15 knots. According to the investigative report, the weather was undoubtedly the cause of the pilot becoming lost, which in turn led to the crash. The MATS division of the USAAF would subsequently discontinue night landings until the development of more sophisticated procedures and facilities.

Date: 11 November 1945 (c.12:00)
Location: Near Picinisco, Frosinone, Italy
Operator: US Army Air Forces
Aircraft type: Boeing B-17G (43-39197)

One of three bombers of the same type that had taken off earlier from Marignane airport, in France, bound for Athens, Greece, 43-39197 was last heard from when its pilot, in a radio transmission, reported heavy icing and requested permission to divert to Rome. A search failed to find any trace of the aircraft. The loss of the B-17 remained a mystery until the following May, when three shepherds came across its wreckage and the remains of the occupants about 75ft (20m) from the summit of Monte Meta, 65 miles (105km) east-south-east of the Italian capital. The aircraft had exploded and disintegrated on impact, and it was apparent that all 20 American servicemen aboard (16 passengers and a crew of four) had perished in the crash. Although the cause of the accident could not be determined, poor judgement on the part of the pilot or navigator coupled with the inclement weather encountered by the bomber, which consisted of cumulus clouds with bases of 4,000ft (1,200m) and tops at about 15,000ft (5,000m), with conditions conducive to icing, were suspected factors. In accordance with recommendations made in the investigative report, flight crews operating in the area would receive thorough briefings with regard to the dangers of icing and hazards associated with the mountainous terrain.

Date: 11 November 1945 (c.23:45)
Location: Near Castel Benito, Libya
Operator: Royal Air Force
Aircraft type: Short Stirling (PJ950)

Flown by Transport Command on a trooping flight, the four-engine aircraft crashed immediately after it had taken off from Tripoli. Including a crew of seven, all 29 British service personnel aboard were killed. Climbing slowly due to its heavy load, the aircraft reached an approximate height of 150ft (50m) before beginning to descend in a forced landing attempt, with one power plant afire. The

An RAF Short Stirling heavy bomber, which was also used as a transport aircraft, the type involved in the fatal crash in North Africa. (Short Brothers Aircraft)

Stirling then slammed to earth, disintegrated and burned, the impact occurring in darkness shortly before midnight.

Date: 15 November 1945 (time unknown)
Location: Territory of New Guinea
Operator: Royal Australian Air Force
Aircraft type: Douglas C-47A Dakota (A65-54)

All 28 Australian and Indian military personnel aboard were killed, including a crew of four, when the twin-engine transport crashed on New Britain Island in the Bismark Archipelago region. The site of impact was on a mountain rising to about 7,000ft (2,000m), the accident having occurred in adverse meteorological conditions shortly after the aircraft had taken off from the airfield near Jacquinot Bay.

Date: 22 November 1945 (c.10:00)
Location: White's Farm, Somerset, England
Operator: Royal Air Force
Aircraft type: Consolidated LB-30A Liberator (KH126)

Operated by the Transport Command and on a trooping flight with an ultimate destination of India, the aircraft crashed and burst into flames some 4 miles (6.5km) from the end of the runway at Merryfield air station, from where it had taken off shortly before. All 27 British and Polish service personnel aboard the four-engine transport (22 passengers and a crew of five) were killed in the accident. The pilot had initiated a left procedural turn before reaching the minimum terrain clearance altitude of 1,500ft (500m), and the aircraft subsequently crashed into Castle Hill approximately 800ft (250m) above airfield elevation, the accident occurring in cloudy weather conditions.

Date: 23 November 1945 (c.11:00)
Location: Dutch East Indies
Operator: Royal Air Force
Aircraft type: Douglas C-47 Dakota (KG520)

The twin-engine transport force-landed on an island in the South Pacific after power plant failure, and although its 25 occupants survived, all were subsequently killed by rebels.

Date: 3 December 1945 (c.13:30)
Location: Near Rochefort, Clarente-Maritime, France
Operator: Royal Air Force
Aircraft type: Consolidated LB-30A Liberator (KH125)

During a Transport Command trooping flight from India to Oakington, near Cambridge, England, the aircraft crashed in flames 20 miles (30km) south-east of La Rochelle. All 28 British servicemen aboard were killed, including a crew of five. Apparently due to severe turbulence, the left outboard wing section broke off as the four-engine transport was flying through a thunderstorm.

Date: 5 December 1945 (c.20:00)
Location: Off Florida, US
Operator: US Navy
Aircraft types: (5) Grumman TBM Avenger (23307) (45714) (46094) (46325) (73209) and (1) Martin PBM-5 Mariner (59225)

This multiple crash, which would later become the centre of the 'Bermuda Triangle' legend, began as a routine over-water navigational training flight out of the US Naval Air Station at Fort Lauderdale, located on Florida's eastern coast. The five torpedo bombers had been assembled into a

A formation of US Navy TBM Avenger torpedo bombers, identical to the aircraft lost off the coast of Florida in December 1945. (US Navy)

group designated as Flight 19. Its leader, Lt Charles Taylor, was a qualified instructor with recent combat experience; his students had between 350 and 400 hours in the air, more than 50 hours each in the type. Aboard the five aircraft were a total of 14 men, with one carrying two rather than the normal three-member crew. As part of the exercise, the group was to fly a triangular-shaped course over the Atlantic Ocean that would end back at the base. Following take-off, they proceeded almost due east for a distance of more than 100 miles (150km), with the initial leg including some low-level practice bombing at about the half-way point. The first hint of trouble came at around 16:00 local time, or some two hours into the mission, after the flight was to have turned left and continued on the second leg, on a heading of 346 degrees, when a radio conversation between two of its pilots was heard by the leader of another group of aircraft, indicating that they had become lost. Over a period of at least three hours, the group zigzagged over the sea, changing their direction several times, the flight leader trying to lead them to safety. Apparently

over the northern Bahamas, Lt Taylor, who had reported both his compasses inoperative, probably thought he had been over the Florida Keys, located off the southern tip of the state and with which he was more familiar. In the process, he disregarded the suggestions of his students to fly west, which, had he been obeyed, would have taken the aircraft out over the Gulf of Mexico, with no chance of reaching land. By using directional bearings obtained from different ground stations, the approximate position of the group was determined to have been in an area some 150 miles (250km) east of New Smyrna Beach, Florida. This information was relayed to the aircraft, but as attempts to contact them had been unsuccessful due to interference from Cuban radio broadcasting stations, static and atmospheric conditions, it probably never got through. An air/sea search that would continue for five days began after the bombers were reported in trouble, and during this operation a sixth aircraft was lost. The Mariner, with a crew of 13 men aboard, went missing after being dispatched from Banana River Naval Air Station, located near Merritt Island. At around 19:50, a crewman on a ship observed an aircraft, presumably 59225, burst into flames in the air, then plunge into the sea and explode at a position 30 miles (50km) west of New Smyrna Beach. The vessel reported passing through a pool of oil where the twin-engine amphibian had fallen, but recovered no survivors, bodies or solid pieces of debris from the water, which was about 80ft (25m) deep at the crash site. No trace was found either of the five TBM Avengers in what, to this day, remains as one of the biggest media-embellished incidents in the history of military aviation. The suspected causes were, however, far more mundane. An investigative report attributed the loss of Flight 19 to temporary mental confusion resulting in faulty judgement on the part of Lt Taylor, who allowed himself to become disorientated relative to the Florida peninsula, and his failure to use all the navigational facilities available to him. He also failed to take into account the strong winds that carried the aircraft farther east than expected, and did not switch to the emergency radio band, perhaps fearing that in changing frequencies, the pilots might lose contact with each other. Nor was there evidence that any of the pilots had used their ZBX homing devices designed to receive a special land-based transmitter. The aircraft would have exhausted their supply of fuel by 20:00, but the flight leader was heard to tell his fellow pilots that when any aircraft got down to 10 gallons (40l) of gasoline, they would all ditch together. But by then, darkness would have fallen, the sea was rough, and there could have been some unexpected development in the local weather, which as forecast, consisted of rain showers, with reduced visibility and a lower overcast within the areas of precipitation, and surface winds of 20 knots, gusting to more than 30. These factors and the relative inexperience of all but the lead pilot would have made a successful water landing unlikely. The apparent mid-air explosion of the Mariner, an aircraft that had become known as the 'flying gas tank' because of its fuel capacity, could have resulted from structural failure due to severe turbulence, power plant malfunction or the ignition of fumes by an electrical spark, or merely the lighting of a cigarette by a member of the crew in violation of smoking regulations. It was recommended in the report pertaining to the loss of the five Avengers that greater emphasis be placed on the importance of proper navigation and lost-aircraft procedures in such over-water flights.

Date: 9 January 1946 (time unknown)
Location: Changchun, Jilin, China

First aircraft
Operator: Chinese Air Force
Type: Unknown

Second aircraft
Operator: Chinese Air Force
Type: Unknown

The two transports, carrying as passengers army soldiers, collided in mid-air over the city. Among the 36 service personnel killed in the accident were six airmen, presumably the crews of the aircraft, while others were reported injured. One or both of the transports may have been Douglas C-47 or Curtiss-Wright C-46 models.

Date: 15 January 1946 (18:25)
Location: Near Marseilles, Bouches-du-Rhône, France
Operator: Royal Air Force
Aircraft type: Douglas C-47 Dakota (KN557)

Operated by Transport Command and returning British prisoners-of-war home from Sicily, Italy, the aircraft slammed into a hillside at an approximate elevation of 1,000ft (300m) some 5 miles (10km) south of Marseilles, the accident occurring in darkness and during a snow shower. All but two of the 25 servicemen aboard lost their lives in the fiery crash, including the four members of the aircraft's crew. Both survivors were injured.

Date: 5 February 1946 (time unknown)
Location: The Philippines
Operator: US Army Air Forces
Aircraft type: Douglas C-47

The twin-engine transport vanished in adverse weather conditions during an inter-island flight to Cebu from Iloilo, located on Panay. The wreckage was found in mountainous terrain on Negros more than seven months later. All 20 persons aboard the aircraft had apparently been killed in the crash. The passengers included nine American civilian entertainers; the rest of the victims being military personnel, including the crew of four. No information was made available regarding possible causative factors.

Date: 17 March 1946 (time unknown)
Location: Near Nanking, Jiangsu, China
Operator: Chinese Air Force
Aircraft type: Transport

At least one high-ranking Chinese official was among the 20 persons killed when the aircraft, on an internal flight from Shanghai to Nanking, crashed in mountainous terrain, reportedly during a low overcast. The aircraft may have been a Douglas C-47.

Date: 19 March 1946 (c.11:45)
Location: Near Hobart Mills, California, US
Operator: US Army Air Forces
Aircraft type: Douglas C-47B (45-1085)

The twin-engine transport crashed in the Sierra Nevada region, not far from the Nevada border, and all 26 American military personnel aboard (23 passengers and a crew of three) were killed. Having taken off earlier from Stockton Field in California, and stopped at McClellan Air Base, near the state capital of Sacramento, the aircraft had been en-route to Hill Field, located near Ogden, Utah, when it disintegrated at an approximate height of 7,300ft (2,200m) over Donner Summit. The separation of its right wing and empennage was followed by a more general break-up of the C-47 which scattered wreckage and bodies across the mountainous terrain over an area of some 2 square miles (3 sq km). No reason was given for the structural failure, but releasable findings of the investigation revealed no evidence of in-flight explosion or fire.

Date: 10 May 1946 (time unknown)
Location: Near Munson, Florida, US

First aircraft
Operator: US Navy
Type: Consolidated Vultee PB4Y-2 Privateer (59721)

Second aircraft
Operator: US Navy
Type: Consolidated Vultee PB4Y-2 Privateer

The two four-engine patrol bombers collided in mid-air and crashed in flames 35 miles (55km) north-east of Pensacola, killing all 28 military personnel aboard both aircraft. At the time, the two aircraft directly involved had been engaged in manoeuvres with a Grumman F-6F Hellcat fighter, which was making practice dives on them, and during a turn, one PB4Y struck the lead aircraft.

Date: 1 June 1946 (c.07:40)
Location: Off Amalfi, Avellino, Italy
Operator: US Army Air Forces
Aircraft type: Douglas C-54 (44-9078)

Operated by Air Transport Command (ATC), the four-engine aircraft had been en route to Ciampino Airport, serving Rome, from Payne Field, located near Cairo, Egypt, one segment of a flight originating in India, when fire of an undetermined origin erupted in the cockpit, to the left of the pilot's seat. An emergency bail-out by the occupants was initiated, but shortly thereafter the transport plummeted into the Gulf of Salerno, 30 miles (50km) south-south-east of Naples. Among the 38 men aboard, all US service personnel except for two civilians riding as passengers, only eight who parachuted from it were rescued, the survivors including four members of the crew of eight. The bodies of seven victims were retrieved from the water; the main wreckage of the aircraft sank and could not be recovered. Attempts to put out the blaze prior to the crash had been unsuccessful, and the flight crew was in fact forced from the cockpit by the smoke, fumes and gases produced by the fire extinguisher used in a small area, having left the C-54 on autopilot. Shortly afterward, the aircraft went into a flat spin. The passengers and most of the crew did not know how to use the British, quick-release-type parachutes that were provided. The meteorological conditions in the area, which were not considered a factor in the accident, consisted of scattered cumulus clouds, with bases of 2,000ft (600m), high cirrus and a visibility of 5 miles (10km).

A Douglas C-54 Skymaster transport, the type flown by the US Army Air Forces that crashed off the coast of Italy after an in-flight fire. (McDonnell Douglas)

Date: 9 June 1946 (c.13:15)
Location: Near Abeokuta, Nigeria
Operator: Royal Air Force
Aircraft type: Douglas C-47 Dakota (KG747)

All 18 persons aboard lost their lives when the twin-engine transport crashed about 60 miles (100km) north of Lagos, the accident occurring during an internal Nigerian flight from Kano to Ikeja. Other than four civilian passengers, the victims were British military personnel, including the crew of six. The C-47 had been flying too low while trying to avoid stormy weather conditions.

Date: 9 June 1946 (c.10:30)
Location: Taboga Island, Panama
Operator: US Army Air Forces
Aircraft type: Douglas C-54D (43-17231)

The four-engine transport crashed and exploded about 10 miles (15km) south of Albrook Field, located in the Canal Zone, near Balboa, where it was to have landed at the end of a flight from the US mainland. All 23 American service personnel aboard perished; except for one civilian passenger, the victims were American service personnel, including the crew of six. Executing a radio range instrument let-down procedure, the aircraft had been advised to remain above 1,000ft (300m). The subsequent crash occurred about 50ft (15m) below that height, near the summit of the island, after the crew reported being an estimated 5 miles (10km) south of the airfield. The local weather at the time consisted of a low overcast, with the clouds covering the top quarter of the island, and a visibility of about 300ft (100m) in a light drizzle. Significantly, no airway traffic control system existed in the area at the time to handle instrument flight operations.

Date: 9 July 1946 (c.20:10)
Location: Near Ware, Massachusetts, US
Operator: US Army Air Forces
Aircraft type: Boeing B-17G (43-39136)

All 25 persons aboard perished when the converted four-engine bomber crashed 8 miles (13km) north-west of Westover Field, where it was to have landed. This was an en-route stop during a flight originating in Labrador and ultimately bound for Mitchell Field, Long Island, New York, US. Except for one civilian, the occupants were US Coast Guard or service personnel, including the crew of four. Cleared to descend, but possibly not at the correct time, the aircraft struck a slope of Mount Tom at an approximate elevation of 1,000ft (300m), or some 200ft (60m) below its summit, bursting into flames on impact. It was dark at the time, and the local weather consisted of thunder-shower activity, with a ceiling of 3,000ft (1,000m) and a visibility down to around 5 miles (10km). The wind was out of the south at 10 knots.

Date: 20 July 1946 (c.12:15)
Location: Off Panama

First aircraft
Operator: US Army Air Forces
Type: Boeing B-17G (44-85624)

Second aircraft
Operator: US Army Air Forces
Type: Boeing B-17G (44-85626)

The two four-engine bombers were participating with another B-17 in a search for three missing P-47 fighters when they collided, and both then plummeted into the Pacific Ocean about 20 miles (30km) north of the Panamanian island of Coiba. Among the 20 crewmen, 10 aboard each aircraft, searchers recovered the bodies of five victims; there were no survivors. Due to deteriorating weather conditions, 85624 had closed in on the lead aircraft, 85626, while the third B-17 came into position on the leader's left wing. Suddenly, the leader and the No. 2 aircraft simultaneously sighted what appeared to be a life raft in the water and both then initiated a slight turn to the left, after which their wings interlocked. The collision, which occurred at an approximate height of 250ft (75m), severed the empennage of 85624 and the starboard wing of 85626. The exact cause of the accident could not be determined. However, in accordance with an earlier briefing, the sighting aircraft was supposed to have climbed to a higher altitude and circled to allow the others to fly lower and identify the object.

Date: 25 July 1946 (time unknown)
Location: Near Bassein, Burma
Operator: Royal Air Force
Aircraft type: Douglas C-47 Dakota (KN585)

The twin-engine transport crashed soon after taking off from Mingaladon, killing all 22 British military personnel aboard (18 passengers and a crew of four). Bound for Kanpur, India, the aircraft had been flying in adverse meteorological conditions when it plummeted into a swamp about 100 miles (150km) west of Rangoon after the structural failure of its left wing.

Date: 15 September 1946 (time unknown)
Location: Near Estevan, Saskatchewan, Canada
Operator: Royal Canadian Air Force
Aircraft type: Douglas C-47 Dakota (962)

All 21 Canadian and American servicemen aboard lost their lives when the twin-engine transport crashed and burned. Except for one, the victims of the morning accident were pilots. As it was approaching to land at Estevan Airport, with its

undercarriage extended, the pilot initiated a go-around manoeuvre, after which time the C-47 plummeted to the ground due to an apparent loss of control. There was an unconfirmed report that a control lock had not been removed from the aircraft's starboard elevator.

Date: 19 September 1946 (time unknown)
Location: Near Tripoli, Libya
Operator: Royal Air Force
Aircraft type: Avro Lancaster (NX690)

Flown by Transport Command and en route from St Mawgan, Cornwall, England, to Almaza airfield, near Cairo, Egypt, the four-engine aircraft plunged to earth in a steep angle about 5 miles (10km) west of Homs, in the province of Tripolitania, disintegrating on impact. All 25 British servicemen aboard (19 passengers and a crew of six) perished. The transport may have been hit by lightning.

Date: 6 October 1946 (c.07:30)
Location: Strait of Malacca
Operator: Royal Air Force
Aircraft type: Avro York (MW125)

For unknown reasons, the four-engine transport crashed approximately 100 miles (150km) south-west of Penang, Malaya. There were no survivors among the 21 British military personnel aboard the aircraft (15 passengers and a crew of six), which had been on a Transport Command flight originating in England, and searchers recovered none of the victims' bodies from the water.

Date: 7 October 1946 (c.11:20)
Location: Apeldoorn, Gelderland, The Netherlands
Operator: Marine Luchtvaartdienst (Royal Netherlands Naval Air Service)
Aircraft type: Fairey Firefly Mk 1 (PP526)

Having taken off on a solo flight from the Valkenburg air base, located near The Hague, the pilot proceeded without authorisation towards Apeldoorn, where his parents lived. Subsequently, PP526 was observed making low-altitude turns over the city, the pilot throttling his power plant in an apparent attempt to get the attention of those on the ground. Minutes later, the single-engine fighter suddenly lost height during a manoeuvre, its starboard wing hitting the roof of the main building at a high school as it tried to level off. The initial impact knocked off an external fuel tank, which fell atop the school gymnasium and ruptured, spreading its flaming contents over the building where 27 students and their instructor had just begun an exercise. The Firefly itself then crashed into some trees. In addition to the pilot, 22 teenaged boys on the ground lost their lives in the fiery holocaust, while about a dozen other persons suffered injuries.

An Avro York transport of the type flown by the RAF that crashed from unknown causes in the Strait of Malacca. (British Aerospace)

An additional indirect casualty of the crash was the mother of the young aviator, who died of a heart attack after watching her son crash to his death.

Date: 16 November 1946 (c.23:30)
Location: North Pacific Ocean
Operator: US Army Air Forces
Aircraft type: Douglas C-47

All 23 American military personnel aboard lost their lives when the twin-engine transport plunged into the sea, approximately 15 miles (25km) off Iwo Jima, in the Volcano Islands. The crash occurred in darkness, but no further details about it were known.

Date: 10 December 1946 (c.13:10)
Location: Near Osaka, Japan
Operator: US Army Air Forces
Aircraft type: Curtiss-Wright C-46F (44-78604)

The twin-engine transport crashed and burned approximately 3 miles (5km) south-west of Itami Air Base, from where it had taken off about two minutes earlier, killing all 24 persons aboard. Except for three American civilians travelling as passengers, the victims were US service personnel, including the crew of five. One of the victims was found alive in the wreckage but died nearly a week later. Having lifted off from Runway 28 on an internal Japanese courier flight that had originated at Tachikawa Air Base, near Tokyo, and ultimately destined for Konaya Air Base, the aircraft yawed to starboard, and after a shallow turn to the left, stalled, rolled back to the right and

finally slammed into a rice field, coming to rest inverted. The local weather at the time consisted of scattered clouds at 3,000ft (1,000m), a visibility of 15 miles (25km) and a westerly wind of around 20 knots. Examination of the wreckage revealed that the left propeller appeared to have been feathered at the moment of impact, but the cause of the power loss, if known, was not divulged in the report on the accident.

Date: 10 December 1946 (time unknown)
Location: Southern Washington, US
Operator: US Marine Corps
Aircraft type: Curtiss-Wright R5C-1 (39528)

The twin-engine transport, carrying 32 American servicemen (29 passengers and a crew of three), vanished during a domestic interstate flight originating at Miramar Naval Air Station, near San Diego, California, and destined for Sand Point Naval Base, at Seattle. In the last radio transmission from 39528, received at 16:16 local time, the pilot reported being at a position of 30 miles (50km) south of the airport serving the town of Toledo, about 30 minutes flying time from his destination and at a height of 9,000ft (2,700m). He also reported picking up ice, and asked permission to fly 500ft (150m) above the overcast. An attempt to contact the R5C 20 minutes later was unsuccessful. Darkness was falling at the time, and strong winds, in excess of 40 knots, would have been blowing out of the north-west at its cruising altitude. Despite an extensive search over the wooded, mountainous terrain, no trace of the aircraft was found, and due to the lack of evidence, no determination could be made as to the cause of its disappearance. Significantly, 39528 had not been equipped with de-icer boots.

Date: 14 January 1947 (c.09:00)
Location: Near Puebla, Mexico
Operator: Fuerza Aérea Mexicana (Mexican Air Force)
Aircraft type: Lockheed C-60 Lodestar (60-03)

All 21 Mexican servicemen aboard perished, including a crew of four, when the twin-engine transport crashed and burst into flames moments after it had taken off from a military base, on an internal flight to the city of Oaxaca. The passengers were all troops engaged in a practice manoeuvre. There were indications that the aircraft's right power plant had malfunctioned and that the pilot had lost control while trying to return to the airfield.

Date: 21 February 1947 (c.16:00)
Location: Near Chungking, Sichuan, China
Operator: Chinese Air Force
Aircraft type: Douglas C-47

The twin-engine transport, which was on an internal flight from Kunming, Yunnan, crashed while approaching to land, killing all 21 persons aboard. According to an unofficial report, the accident may have resulted from an encounter with severe icing conditions.

Date: 29 May 1947 (c.22:45)
Location: Near Atsugi, Kanagawa, Japan
Operator: US Army Air Forces
Aircraft type: Douglas C-54D (42-72553)

All 40 persons aboard perished when the four-engine transport crashed some 20 miles (30km) south-south-west of Tachikawa Air Base, where it was to have landed, and around 30 miles (50km) south-west of Tokyo. Except for four civilians, the victims were American military personnel, including the seven members of the aircraft's crew. As it neared the end of a flight from Kimpo Air Base, near Seoul, South Korea, 42-72553 was cleared for descent to 4,000ft (1,200m). Inexplicably, it assumed a north-westerly heading, and after initiating a right turn, struck a mountain at an approximate elevation of 5,000ft (1,500m), bursting into flames on impact. At the time of the crash, its heading was around 40 degrees, or some 10 degrees too far to the north of the correct course to its intended destination. The accident occurred in darkness, and the weather along the route was cloudy, with 3 to 6/10 cumulus clouds between 3,000 and 4,000ft (1,000–1,200m) and at about 8,000ft (2,500m) and broken alto-stratus above that, with a visibility of between 5 and 10 miles (10–15km). The

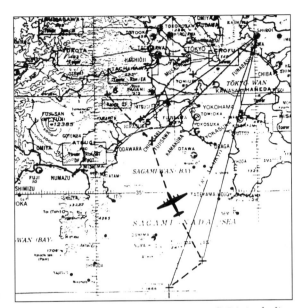

The route of the US Army Air Forces C-54, including the deviation in north-westerly direction that led to the disaster in Japan. (US Air Force)

winds in the vicinity of Tokyo and Nagoya were approximately 40 knots. Though the cause could not be determined with certainty, the crash apparently resulted from faulty navigation and poor piloting technique on the part of the crew, with the meteorological conditions considered as contributory.

Date: 31 July 1947 (time unknown)
Location: Near Yumen, Gansu, China
Operator: Chinese Air Force
Aircraft type: Douglas C-47

The twin-engine transport disappeared during an internal Chinese flight from Tihua (Urumqi), Xinjiang, to Lanzhou, Gansu, and its wreckage was later found 400 miles (650km) north-west of the destination with no survivors among the 26 persons aboard. Among the passengers were at least one American and one British civilian.

Date: 6 August 1947 (time unknown)
Location: North Pacific Ocean
Operator: US Navy
Aircraft type: Consolidated PBY-5A Catalina (34032)

During an intra-Alaskan flight from Kodiak to Dutch Harbor, located in the Aleutian Island chain, the twin-engine amphibian vanished with 20 American servicemen aboard (15 passengers and a crew of five). In its last radio message, the aircraft was reported at a position 150 miles (250km) from its destination and battling strong head winds.

A US Navy Consolidated Catalina amphibious patrol aircraft of the type lost over the North Pacific Ocean off the Alaskan coast. (General Dynamics)

Date: 31 October 1947 (time unknown)
Location: Near Srinagar, Jammu and Kashmir, India
Operator: Royal Indian Air Force
Aircraft type: Douglas C-47 (M1965)

The crash of the twin-engine transport claimed the lives of all 25 persons aboard the aircraft. No further details about the accident, including phase of flight and possible cause, are known.

Date: 28 November 1947 (c.14:10)
Location: Near Trappa, Cuneo, Italy
Operator: US Air Force
Aircraft type: Douglas C-47B (43-48736)

The twin-engine transport crashed and burned about 20 miles (30km) south-south-west of the city of Cuneo, killing all 20 persons aboard. Except for one civilian, the victims were all American military personnel, including the crew. As evidenced by the heavy clothing they were wearing and the use of makeshift medical applications, two men must have survived the impact, but one died soon thereafter, probably of shock, and the other apparently succumbed to exposure within eight hours of the crash. The wreckage and remains of the victims were not located until the following August. Bound for Frankfurt, Germany, the aircraft slammed into an eastern slope of Mount Carbone in the Maritime Alps, 150 miles (250km) west-north-west of Pisa, from where it had taken off earlier, and at a position approximately 30 miles (50km) off the prescribed route. Around the time of

the accident, the meteorological conditions in the area were adverse, with snowstorms, solid alto-cumulus clouds reaching all the way down to the mountaintops, and a 25-knot wind blowing from a west-south-westerly direction. Other pilots had reported strong south-westerly winds at an altitude of 2,000ft (600m), which were in excess of the forecasted 50 knots.

Date: 10 December 1947 (c.00:20)
Location: Near Goose Bay, Labrador
Operator: US Air Force
Aircraft type: Douglas C-54D (42-72572)

Operated by Air Transport Command, the four-engine aircraft crashed and burned 8½ miles (13.5km) north of Goose Bay Air Base, from where it had taken off shortly before, bound for Westover Field, Massachusetts, US. Of the 29 persons aboard the aircraft, all of whom were American military personnel except for one civilian, 23 lost their lives. The six servicemen who survived, all with injuries, included one member of the crew. About a minute after its departure, the crew requested an emergency landing, but the C-54 subsequently crashed into a wooded area in what appeared to be a 'power stall' attitude. It was dark at the time and the weather was overcast, with a ceiling of 2,500ft (750m) and a visibility of 10 miles (15km). Although it had stopped before 42-72572 took off, about ½ inch (12mm) of snow had fallen while the aircraft was on the ground, raising speculation as to its contribution to the accident.

Date: 11 December 1947 (c.18:10)
Location: Near Memphis, Tennessee, US
Operator: US Air Force
Aircraft type: Douglas C-47 (44-76366)

All 20 American service personnel aboard perished, including a crew of four, when the twin-engine transport crashed and exploded in a wooded area 3½ miles (6km) south-south-east of Memphis Municipal Airport, where it was to have landed at the end of a US domestic flight from Biggs Field, near El Paso, Texas. After beginning its let-down, in twilight conditions, the aircraft went into a right-hand spiral and plummeted to earth. Around the time of the crash, the weather conditions in the area consisted of an overcast of 1,700ft (520m) and a visibility of about 4 miles (6.5km) in smoke. The wind was from a north-north-easterly direction at approximately 10 knots. The reasons for the uncontrolled descent were unknown; there was, however, no evidence of pre-impact fire or explosion.

Date: 27 February 1948 (time unknown)
Location: Near Belem, Para, Brazil
Operator: Força Aérea Brasileira (Brazilian Air Force)
Aircraft type: Douglas C-47 (C-47.2040)

The twin-engine transport, its passengers comprising Brazilian service personnel and their dependents, crashed and burst into flames during a flight that had originated at Rio de Janeiro. The intended destination was Cayenne, French Guiana. Among the 26 persons aboard the aircraft, including a crew of six, there were only three survivors – an army man, a woman and a child. No further details about the crash, including the possible cause, were released.

Date: 17 January 1949 (c.09:50)
Location: Near Lochgoilhead, Argyllshire, Scotland
Operator: US Air Force
Aircraft type: Boeing B-29 (44-62276)

All 20 American servicemen aboard perished in the crash of the four-engine bomber, which occurred 30 miles (50km) north-west of Glasgow. One of two B-29s to have taken off earlier from Scampton, Lincolnshire, England, on a transatlantic flight to the US, 44-62276 had about half-an-hour before the accident requested, and been granted, clearance to ascend from 8,500 to 14,500ft (2,600–4,400m). At the time of the request, the aircraft was believed to have been encountering heavy icing conditions. Subsequently, the heavily-iced bomber slammed into a mountain at an approximate elevation of 700ft (200m), or about a third of the way to its summit, in a steep diving attitude and an air speed indicator reading of nearly 300mph (500kph). The surface weather, which was otherwise not a factor in the crash, consisted of rain, with an overcast of around 1,000ft (300m) and a visibility of about 1½ miles (2.5km). The wind was from a west-south-westerly direction at approximately 35 knots.

Date: 24 February 1949 (c.08:00)
Location: Near Cuzco, Peru
Operator: Cuerpo de Aeronautica del Peru (Air Arm of Peru)
Aircraft type: Douglas C-47

Operated by the Transportes Aereos Militares, the twin-engine aircraft crashed and burned as it was taking off from the city's airport, on an internal flight to Lima, killing 22 persons aboard. Two passengers, both of whom were seriously injured, and two members of the aircraft's crew of four military personnel, who escaped unscathed, survived the accident. Reportedly, one main undercarriage tyre on the C-47 had burst during the ground run, apparently resulting in a loss of control.

Date: 7 June 1949 (c.14:00)
Location: Near Florianpolis, Santa Catarina, Brazil
Operator: Força Aérea Brasileira (Brazilian Air Force)
Aircraft type: Douglas C-47B (C-47.2023)

The twin-engine transport, which was carrying as passengers Brazilian service personnel and their dependents, slammed into a mountainside and burned shortly after taking off from the city's airport. This was an en-route stop during an internal flight originating at Rio de Janeiro, with an ultimate destination of Porto Alegre. Including a crew of six, all 27 persons aboard were killed. The crash occurred in adverse weather conditions, which may have been a primary or contributing causative factor.

Date: 21 August 1949 (c.23:30)
Location: Near Bigstone Lake, Manitoba, Canada
Operator: Royal Canadian Air Force
Aircraft type: Consolidated Canso (11057)

During an internal mercy flight from Churchill to Winnipeg, the twin-engine amphibian crashed and burned in a wooded area 270 miles (435km) north-north-east of its destination, the accident occurring in darkness and adverse meteorological conditions consisting of thunderstorm activity, with rain and a low overcast. All 21 persons aboard perished. The passengers were civilians, the crew of seven being Canadian military personnel. No further details about the accident, including the possible cause, were released.

1950–1965

Simmering since the end of the Second World War, hostilities between the East and West reached boiling point when, on 25 June 1950, Soviet and Chinese-backed North Korean ground troops invaded South Korea. After three years of fighting, an American-led United Nations coalition managed to bring about an uneasy truce, one that exists to this day. The Korean War witnessed the first aerial dogfights between jet fighters and also extensive use, primarily in search-and-rescue and medical evacuation duties, of rotary-wing aircraft. This was also the period that multi-engine piston-powered transports reached the peak of their development. Their size accounted for their involvement in a number of major crashes, including the Korean airlift disaster of 1953, the first aviation catastrophe to claim more than 100 lives. The Cold War brought about the introduction of strategic nuclear forces, with such delivery systems as the 10-engine Convair B-36 and the famed eight-jet Boeing B-52. Of course, every aircraft has its own 'learning curve', which often means the loss of some in accidents before their optimum operational efficiency can be achieved. This section deals with incidents occurring during the Korean War and the height of the Cold War, from 1950 to 1965.

Date: 20 January 1950 (c.12:00)
Location: Near Vacas, Cochabamba, Bolivia
Operator: Fuerza Aérea Boliviana (Bolivian Air Force)
Aircraft type: Douglas C-47 (TAM-10)

The twin-engine transport, which was on an internal flight from Valle Grande to the city of Cochabamba, crashed in the Andes Mountains about 20 miles (30km) from its destination, during a thunderstorm. Including a crew of four, all 32 Bolivian military personnel aboard lost their lives; the passengers were soldiers. The weather undoubtedly factored in the accident, although the probable cause was not disclosed.

Date: 26 January 1950 (time unknown)
Location: Yukon Territory, Canada
Operator: US Air Force
Aircraft type: Douglas C-54D (42-72469)

Operated by the Strategic Air Command (SAC), the four-engine transport disappeared while flying between two air bases, from Elmendorf, near Anchorage, Alaska, to Great Falls, Montana, US, with 44 persons aboard, including a crew of eight. All were American military personnel except for two passengers, a civilian dependent and her infant son. In its last position report, transmitted shortly after 14:00 local time, the aircraft was in the vicinity of Snag; there were no indications of what could have happened to the C-54. The weather along the route ranged from clear to partly cloudy, except in the vicinity of Whitehorse, where there was a solid overcast at 7,500ft (2,300m), and a slight possibility of icing.

Date: 21 April 1950 (c.23:25)
Location: Near Atsugi, Kanagawa, Japan
Operator: US Air Force
Aircraft type: Douglas C-54D (42-72704)

All 35 persons aboard perished, including an eight-member crew of Air Force personnel, when the transport crashed and burned on Mount Tanzawa. The accident occurred about 20 miles (30km) south-west of Tachikawa Air Base, located on the western outskirts of Tokyo, where the aircraft was to have landed during a scheduled service originating from Clark Air Base in the Philippines, with en-route stops on Okinawa and O-shima Island. After he reported being over the O-shima radio range station, the pilot was cleared to proceed towards Tokyo and descend to 5,000ft (1,500m), and the C-54 was at approximately that altitude when it initially struck trees while on a north-easterly heading. It was dark at the time, with intermittent rain and stratiform clouds obscuring the mountains. Light to moderate turbulence within the clouds had been reported. Despite the pilot's position report of being over the radio range station, the aircraft was actually some 25 miles (40km) south-west of the navigational aid. Minutes before the crash, a radar facility other than the one responsible for its immediate control had observed it to have been to the left of the prescribed course and proceeding in an almost due northerly direction towards the high terrain. However, a subsequent transmission from the Tokyo control centre instructing 42-72704 to reverse its course and climb came too late. The cause of the apparent navigational error, if known, was not released by Air Force authorities.

Date: 23 July 1950 (c.10:20)
Location: Near Myrtle Beach, South Carolina, US
Operator: US Air Force
Aircraft type: Curtiss-Wright C-46D (44-77577)

The twin-engine transport crashed during a trooping operation, and all 39 American servicemen aboard, including a crew of four, perished. Following its take-off from Myrtle Beach Airport, on a US domestic flight to Nashville, Tennessee, and after it had turned eastward towards its point of departure, witnesses observed pieces fall from the aircraft. The C-46 then spiralled to the ground from an estimated height of 1,000 to 2,000ft (300–600m). It was determined that after the centre section of its left aileron had torn loose, the entire control surface had separated from the transport, and during the subsequent uncontrolled descent, both its wings failed due to overstressing. No distress message had been sent by the crew prior to the crash, and the weather, consisting of scattered clouds at around 5,000ft (1,500m) and a visibility of 10 miles (15km), was not considered a factor. The cause of the structural failure was not disclosed.

Date: 27 July 1950 (c.04:30)
Location: Off Japan
Operator: US Air Force
Aircraft type: Douglas C-47D (44-76439A)

The twin-engine transport crashed in the Pacific Ocean some 10 miles (15km) south of the Island of O-shima and about 65 miles (105km) south-south-west of Tokyo. Among the 26 persons aboard, including a crew of three Air Force personnel, only one passenger was rescued. Four of those killed were American civilian war correspondents. None of the victims' bodies was found, and the wreckage sank in water more than 5,000ft (1,500m) deep and was not recovered. Having taken off some 20 minutes earlier from Haneda Air Base, near the Japanese capital, and bound for the island of Kyushu, the C-47 had penetrated an overcast while climbing in pre-dawn darkness and was believed to have reached an altitude of about 3,500ft (1,050m) before its sudden and unexplained descent into the water. The army soldier who survived said that prior to impact the aircraft hit two moderate bumps, and that the cabin lights went dim, then went out, came back on and then dimmed again.

Date: 5 August 1950 (c.22:00)
Location: Near Fairfield, California, US
Operator: US Air Force
Aircraft type: Boeing B-29MR (46-87651)

This crash and subsequent explosion involving a four-engine bomber, which was operated by the Strategic Air Command (SAC), wreaked havoc at Fairfield-Suisan Air Force Base and the surrounding community, 40 miles (65km) north-east of San Francisco. The first hint of trouble came during the pre-flight run-up, when the two in-board propellers did not return to normal speed when the master control was decreased. The discrepancy was dismissed by the pilot and flight engineer as merely incorrect propeller settings. Nor did the aircraft commander express concern when his radio malfunctioned during the taxi phase, as the pilot was not experiencing the same difficulty. Take-off was then begun, but after the B-29 had used approximately three-quarters of Runway 21 and reached an indicated air speed of 125mph (200kph), the No 2 propeller started to overspeed. An attempt to correct the anomaly was unsuccessful, so the commander activated the feathering switch. The No. 2 propeller feathered just as the 46-87651 became airborne and, additionally, the aircraft's undercarriage would not retract. Soon afterward, the No. 3 propeller began to overspeed, but was brought under control through a reduction in manifold pressure. With the bomber unable to climb due to its configuration and reduced power condition, and with rising terrain ahead, the commander elected to make a 180-degree turn to the right, back towards the base. Upon completion of the turn, he experienced difficulty in holding up the left wing and asked the co-pilot for assistance with the controls. Shortly thereafter, the flight engineer advised the pilots that the No. 3 was running away again, and the aircraft began to shudder. Realising a crash was imminent, the commander allowed it to slide to the left to avoid a trailer park directly in its path, and the B-29 finally stalled and slammed into the ground along the boundary of the military installation. Impact was at a speed of around 120mph (190kph), with the left wing slightly down and the nose raised, upon which the aircraft broke apart and caught fire. Some 25 minutes later, after crash personnel and equipment had arrived on the scene, the load of bombs being carried aboard 46-87651 detonated. A total of 19 American servicemen were killed in the disaster,

A scene of devastation is left by the crash and subsequent explosion of the Boeing B-29 bomber at Fairfield-Suisan Air Force Base. (Wide World Photos)

including 12 of the 20 who had been aboard the aircraft. About 180 others suffered injuries, among them the eight survivors of the crash and several dozen civilians. Numerous trailer caravans and vehicles were damaged, as the second explosion threw debris and burning gasoline over an area of some 2 square miles (3 sq km). It was dark at the time, but the weather conditions were not considered a factor. It was of the opinion of personnel investigating the accident that a fault existed in the electrical circuit of the undercarriage that prevented the gear from being retracted, but the nature or identity of the problem could not be determined. Significantly, the radio trouble experienced prior to take-off could have been a manisfestation of this fault. It was further ruled that the No. 2 propeller may have oversped due to the improper adjustment of the propeller control brush block assembly. Brush tracks revealed they had been rubbing against one side of the slip ring separators. Examination also revealed badly burned decrease, feather and common slip rings, with the automatic decrease ring indicating the worst damage. As the No. 3 engine/propeller assembly had been destroyed, no similar examination on it was possible. However, in view of the condition of the No. 2 slip rings, the same condition may have also brought about its malfunction. An important operational factor in the crash was the failure of the pilot to follow standard operating procedures in the event of a runaway propeller, in that he left the propeller selector switch in the automatic position. Had he placed it in the fixed position, it would probably not have run away a second time. Alternatively, his placement of the No. 2 feathering

switch in the off position could have had similar adverse consequences by allowing an increase in propeller rotation commensurate to the increase in air speed. He probably could have maintained control of that propeller by intermittently actuating the switch, instead of letting it feather completely. Following this accident, an order was issued requiring all aircraft equipped with Curtiss Electric propellers, as was 46-87651, to be test flown after any corrective maintenance. The same B-29 had experienced overspeeding of the No. 2 propeller only five days earlier, and as a result the ground crew had been instructed to install new contactor leads. There was no way of knowing whether this had been done, as the same crewmen were killed in the crash. In accordance with another recommendation made in the accident report, the number of persons allowed aboard on any B-29 flight operation was reduced to 16. Overloading of men, baggage and equipment and an insufficient number of safety belts probably factored in the loss of life, since 10 of the occupants killed had been trapped in the rear cabin section. Also killed was the aircraft and base commander, Brigadier General Robert F. Travis. The installation where the disaster occurred on that summer night in 1950 was later re-named in his honour, becoming Travis Air Force Base.

Date: 20 September 1950 (c.05:20)
Location: North Pacific Ocean
Operator: US Navy
Aircraft type: Douglas R5D-3 (56496)

The four-engine transport crashed at sea and exploded about three minutes after taking off from the US naval air station on Kwajalein, one of the Marshall Islands, an en-route stop during a flight from Hawaii to the Far East. There were no survivors among the 26 American military personnel aboard which included a crew of seven; among the passengers were 11 Navy nurses. Sharks were later observed molesting the bodies of victims in the water. Four unidentified female victims were recovered and debris was found floating in the general vicinity of the crash, approximately 1½ miles (2.5km) from the easterly end of Runway 07, which the aircraft had used. Due to the depth of the ocean in the area, the main wreckage could not be salvaged. An investigative board was unable to determine the specific cause of the crash, which had occurred in pre-dawn darkness. Possible causes listed in the accident report, in the order of probability, were as follows: a) The pilot-in-command experienced vertigo at a time when the co-pilot's attention was directed to shifting radio frequencies or something else in the cockpit and away from monitoring the flight instruments; b) The malfunctioning of instruments that resulted from the improper intermediate positioning of the vacuum selector control; c) A sudden loss of power in one engine and the unintentional feathering of the propeller of another power plant on the same side; d) The inadvertant engagement of an unaligned autopilot by a member of the crew other than the pilots at the controls; e) A loss of lateral control due to an asymmetric wing flap condition resulting from the malfunction of either the flap's interconnecting or operating mechanism; f) Malfunctioning of one or more of the primary flight controls; g) Partial structural failure leading to the loss or misalignment of a certain component, such as the outer wing panel or a part of the empennage, or h) Any reasonable combination of the aforementioned items. The weather was not a factor. Among the recommendations appearing in the report was one designed to improve the manner in which maintenance information on a particular aircraft is collected and made available, and one that called for a review of search-and-rescue (SAR) procedures. The latter was in response to what the investigative board considered as an unreasonable delay in the dispatch of SAR aircraft, with the first surface vessel not reaching the scene until more than 80 minutes after the R5D had gone down. It was noted in the report, however, that since the impact with the water was apparently non-survivable, this delay did not cost any lives in this particular instance.

Date: 26 September 1950 (c.01:00)
Location: Near Kita-Kyushu, Fukuoka, Japan
Operator: US Air Force
Aircraft type: Douglas C-54D (42-72457)

Bound for Kimpo Air Base, near Seoul, South Korea, the four-engine transport crashed in the

Korea Strait, off the island of Kyushu, shortly after taking off from Runway 30 at Ashiya Air Base. Killed in the accident were 23 of the 51 American military personnel aboard, including five members of its crew of eight. All of the survivors suffered injuries. The crash occurred approximately 1 mile (1.5km) from the end of the runway which the aircraft had used, in darkness and meteorological conditions consisting of a high overcast, with a visibility of 2 miles (3km) in ground fog. Military authorities did not release the findings as to the probable cause of the accident.

Date: 19 December 1950 (c.07:30)
Location: Near Kabayan, Benguet, the Philippines
Operator: US Air Force
Aircraft type: Douglas C-54G (44-9096)

Operated by the Military Air Transport Service on a scheduled service between two US air bases, from Naha, on the island of Okinawa, to Clark, located near Angeles, the Philippines, the aircraft crashed on Luzon 30 miles (50km) north-east of Baguio and about 100 miles (150km) north of its destination. Its burned wreckage was located two days later on Mount Tabayoc, with no survivors among the 38 persons aboard; except for two Filipino passengers, the victims were all American servicemen, including the crew of seven. Proceeding under instrument flight rules, the aircraft was probably in and out of clouds at its assigned height of 8,000ft (2,500m) prior to impact, although natives had reported a solid overcast at the time and location of the crash. The C-54 had struck the mountain at that altitude, or some 1,500ft (500m) below its peak. No details as to the cause or suspected cause of the disaster were released by US Air Force officials.

Date: 28 January 1951 (c.08:40)
Location: Near An-tung, Taiwan
Operator: Royal Air Force
Aircraft type: Short Sunderland (PP107)

The four-engine flying boat crashed in mountainous terrain during a flight to Hong Kong from Iwakuni, Japan. The burnt wreckage was later found at an approximate elevation of 5,000ft (1,500m) with no survivors among the 16 British servicemen aboard, including a crew of five; two of the victims were not on the original manifest. The cause was probably related to the bad weather conditions in which the accident occurred.

Date: 22 March 1951 (c.23:50)
Location: North Atlantic Ocean
Operator: US Air Force
Aircraft type: Douglas C-124A (49-244)

Although the exact circumstances of this disaster could not be determined, a mid-air explosion

The size of the Douglas C-124 Globemaster accounted for its involvement in several major crashes in the early 1950s, including the North Atlantic disaster. (McDonnell Douglas)

or catastrophic structural failure was suspected in the loss of the four-engine transport, which in its last position report had been 750 miles (1,200km) west of Limerick, Ireland. Searchers recovered pieces of floating wreckage from the aircraft approximately 600 miles (965km) off Ireland's south-western coast. Of the 53 American servicemen aboard (40 passengers and a crew of 13), no survivors were found. Operated by the Strategic Air Command, the C-124 had last stopped at Loring Air Force Base, near Limestone, Maine, during a transatlantic flight originating at Walker Air Force Base, near Roswell, New Mexico. Its ultimate destination was Mildenhall Air Force Base, Suffolk, England. The aircraft had been flying in darkness, and the weather along the route consisted of extensive formations of cumulus clouds, with bases of 2,500 to 3,000ft (750–1,000m) and tops generally at 7,000 to 8,000ft (2,000–2,500m), with scattered build-ups to 13,000ft (4,000m), the latter being accompanied by showers. Examination of the recovered debris revealed that a post-crash blaze had occurred, although no further conclusions could be made.

Date: 8 April 1951 (c.11:35)
Location: Near Charleston, West Virginia, US
Operator: US Air Force
Aircraft type: Douglas C-47D (43-48298)

The transport crashed about 5 miles (10km) north-east of Kanawha County Airport, which served Charleston, where it was to have landed. Including a crew of three, all 21 American service-

men aboard were killed; one of the passengers succumbed to his injuries nine days later. Most of the victims had been on their way from Godman Air Force Base, in neighbouring Kentucky, to attend a funeral for a fellow flier killed in a previous crash. In his last radio message, the pilot reported being on the outbound track and making a procedural turn during the automatic direction finder (ADF) instrument procedure approach to Runway 23. Subsequently, the C-47 struck a wooded hillside at an approximate elevation of 1,200ft (350m), the impact with the trees shearing off both its wings, and burst into flames. The local weather at the time consisted of an overcast estimated at 1,000ft (300 m), with scattered clouds down to 200ft (60m), a visibility of 3 miles (5km) and a west-south-westerly wind of 10 knots. The cause of the accident was not revealed by military authorities. Significantly, the aircraft's instrument landing system indicator was reported by the pilot to have been inoperative, which would have prevented him from making a precision approach.

Date: 6 May 1951 (c.12:30)
Location: Near Albuquerque, New Mexico, US
Operator: US Air Force
Aircraft type: Convair B-36D (49-2660)

The 10-engine strategic bomber crashed at Kirtland Air Force Base, killing 23 of its 25 crewmen. Both survivors, who had been seated in the rear part of its fuselage, were injured. A lack of lateral control was an apparent factor in the accident, which occurred as the aircraft attempted to land on Runway 08 during a 30-knot east-south-easterly wind, with gusts of up to 35 knots, and a visibility of 8 miles (13km) in blowing dust. The pilot appeared to have difficulty maintaining the correct flight path, making constant corrections to keep the wings level and remain aligned with the runway centreline. Passing over the threshold with its wings level but to the left of the centreline, the B-36 banked to the right for correction, whereupon its starboard jet pod and No. 6 propeller struck the pavement some 500ft (150m) down the runway. Following the initial impact with the ground, which tore off the propeller blades of the piston power plant, the pilot undoubtedly decided to go around. The aircraft climbed to about 200ft (60 m) above airfield elevation with the No. 6 engine afire, then slammed to earth on a northerly heading and in a right wing-down attitude and burst into flames, its undercarriage extended at the time of the crash. A C-54 four-engine transport, a twin-engine Lockheed Lodestar and a single-engine Beechcraft Bonanza that had been parked at the air base were damaged by flying debris and/or fire.

Date: 27 October 1951 (c.19:00)
Location: Near Flores, Peten, Guatemala
Operator: Fuerza Aérea Guatemalteca (Guatemalan Air Force)
Aircraft type: Douglas C-47

Its passengers comprising Guatemalan radio stars who had been touring the country, the twin-engine transport crashed and burst into flames in a jungle area some 170 miles (270km) north-north-east of Guatemala City, the accident occurring in darkness shortly after it had taken off from the local airport. All but two of the 27 persons aboard were killed, including the entire crew of five military personnel, and both survivors suffered serious injuries. Though not reported officially, authorities initially suspected that one of the passengers may have started a fire in the aircraft's cabin with a cigarette.

Date: 13 November 1951 (c.13:00)
Location: Near Besse-St-Anastaise, Puy-de-Dome, France
Operator: US Air Force
Aircraft type: Fairchild C-82A (45-57801A)

All 36 American servicemen aboard (32 passengers and four crew members) perished in the crash of the twin-engine transport. Wreckage was located two days later, about 25 miles (40km) south-west of Clermont-Ferrand. The aircraft was en route from Rhein-Main Air Base, near Frankfurt, West Germany, to Bordeaux, France, when it struck a mountain peak at an approximate elevation of 5,600ft (1,700m), exploded and burned. Around the time of the accident, the meteorological conditions at Clermont-Ferrand consisted of a low ceiling, with 6/8 cumulus clouds at around 3,000ft (1,000m), a visibility of 25 miles (40km) below the overcast and a west-south-westerly wind of 12

The flaming wreckage of the US Air Force C-47, which crashed during an attempted landing at Charleston, West Virginia, US. (UPI/Corbis-Bettmann)

A US Air Force Fairchild C-82 transport, identical to the aircraft that crashed into a mountain in France. (Fairchild Aircraft)

knots. Winds of up to 30 knots had been forecast in the area from Dijon to Bordeaux. The pilot had been operating under an instrument flight rules (IFR) clearance with an assigned cruising height of 6,000ft (1,800m) when the C-82 crashed about 60 miles (100km) to the left of the proposed route. However, no details as to the suspected cause of the deviation were released by the US Air Force.

Date: 30 December 1951 (c.15:40)
Location: Near Roosevelt, Arizona, US
Operator: US Air Force
Aircraft type: Douglas C-47D (47-76266)

The transport crashed and burned on a mountain 70 miles (110km) north-east of Phoenix, and all 28 American military personnel aboard were killed, including four crew members. Most of the passengers were army cadets returning to the US Military Academy at West Point, New York. The aircraft was to have landed at Williams Air Force Base, located about 25 miles (40km) south-east of Phoenix, while en route from California to Texas, one segment of the transcontinental flight. Cleared down to 6,000ft (1,800m) during the instrument let-down, the crew had last reported leaving 7,000ft (2,000m), which was the approximate elevation of the crash site. The local weather at the time was overcast, with a ceiling of 6,000ft and a visibility of 15 miles (25km) under the cloud base, and a south-westerly wind of 13 knots. Military authorities did not disclose any information as to the possible cause of the accident.

Date: 26 August 1952 (c.07:00)
Location: Near Khewra, West Pakistan
Operator: Royal Pakistan Air Force
Aircraft type: Bristol 170 (G783)

The twin-engine transport crashed and burned, killing all 18 persons aboard, 100 miles (150km) north-west of Lahore, from where it had taken off earlier. Except for one civilian, the victims were all Pakistani military personnel. The aircraft had been on an internal flight to Peshawar when it plummeted into hilly terrain, possibly after a power plant malfunction, although no cause was given officially.

Date: 6 September 1952 (c.15:40)
Location: Near Aldershot, Hampshire, England
Operator: de Havilland Aircraft
Aircraft type: de Havilland 110 (WG236)

As it was performing at the Farnborough air show, the jet fighter disintegrated about 1½ miles (2.5km) from the public enclosure area, and one of its two engines then plummeted into a crowd of spectators. Killed in the disaster were a total of 30 persons, including both crewmen of the aircraft; about 60 others on the ground suffered injuries. The accident sequence began with a supersonic dive from an approximate height of 40,000ft (12,000m). After civilian test pilot John Derry levelled off and made a low pass along the runway, the aircraft circled in a tight left-hand, high-speed bank. As it returned to level flight from this turn and then began an upward roll, the break-up occurred at an approximate height of 500ft (150m) above the ground and an estimated speed of 650mph (1,050kph). An examination of the distribution of the wreckage, which was supported by the analysis of an amateur motion picture taken of the accident, showed that the starboard outer wing failed first, followed by the separation of the port outer wing section. The subsequent rapid pitch-up of trim caused a more general disintegration, with the aircraft's cockpit section, power plants and tailplane breaking away due to abnormal gravitational forces. The initial failure was believed to have resulted from heavy 'suction' loading on the upper and lower wing surfaces, combined with vibration or wing 'flutter'. (It was noted in the investigative report that intermittent wing vibration had been noted previously in both flying prototypes of the de Havilland 110.) Considerable modification was made on the type, including thicker ribs and reinforced stringers in the wing, before its acceptance as a carrier combat jet. A new set of rules was also introduced to guarantee greater safety in exhibition flying events taking place in the UK and since that occasion, no member of the public has been killed at a British air show.

Date: 16 October 1952 (time unknown)
Location: Off Kangnung, Kangwon-do, South Korea
Operator: US Air Force
Aircraft type: Curtiss-Wright C-46D (44-77538)

The twin-engine transport crashed in the Sea of Japan with 25 American servicemen aboard, including a crew of four. A massive search failed to locate any trace of the aircraft, and only two bodies were found, one, which had washed ashore, being identified as a passenger; both victims wore life vests. There were no survivors from the crash, the circumstances of which were unknown. Having taken off from a military base shortly before 01:00 local time, on an internal South Korean flight that should have lasted about 40 minutes, the C-46 was last observed by the control tower operator as it climbed into the early morning darkness. The weather along the route was clear, but the winds were believed to have been strong at higher altitudes.

Date: 7 November 1952 (c.03:00)
Location: Near Summit, Alaska
Operator: US Air Force
Aircraft type: Fairchild C-119C (51-2560A)

During an intra-territorial Alaskan flight from Elmendorf Air Force Base, near Anchorage, to the town of Big Delta, the twin-engine transport crashed in the vicinity of Mount McKinley, some 150 miles (250km) south-west of Fairbanks. The wreckage was located about a week later at an approximate elevation of 12,000ft (3,700m), with no survivors among the 19 American military personnel aboard (14 passengers and a crew of five). Occurring in darkness and local weather conditions consisting of an overcast of 5,000ft (1,500m), a visibility of 15 miles (25km) and a gentle breeze from a north-north-westerly direction, the accident apparently resulted from a navigational error. The course deviation that led to the crash may have resulted from the confusion between two radio

A spectator's snapshot captures the moment of impact of a section of the de Havilland 110, the crash of which killed both crewmen and 28 persons on the ground. (Associated Press)

range stations associated with precipitation static. A possible contributing factor was the absence on the aircraft of an additional automatic direction finder (ADF) or a high-frequency receiver, which could have been used for obtaining immediate fixes, coupled with insufficient navigational aids on the ground.

Date: 14 November 1952 (c.14:45)
Location: Near Songch'on-ni, Kyonggi-do, South Korea
Operator: US Air Force
Aircraft type: Fairchild C-119C (51-2551A)

All 44 American servicemen aboard (37 passengers and a crew of seven) were killed in the crash of the twin-engine transport, which took place some 20 miles (30km) east of Seoul. En route from Ashiya Air Base in Japan, the aircraft struck a mountain and burned while approaching to land at a US military base, designated K-16, using ADF instrument procedures. Its undercarriage still retracted, the C-119 was on a westerly heading and flying level longitudinally, though banked slightly to the right, when it crashed at an elevation of about 2,000ft (600m). The base weather at the time of the accident was overcast, with solid coverage at approximately 3,000ft (1,000m) and scattered clouds down to around 1,500ft (500m), which obscured the tops of the surrounding mountains,

A US Air Force C-119 transport, two of which crashed fatally in Alaska and a third in South Korea during the month of November 1952. (Fairchild Aircraft)

including the one hit by 51-2551A. The visibility was about 7 miles (11km). The Air Force investigation revealed no evidence of inaccuracy in the aircraft's pressure altimeter reading or any indication of power plant failure; the suspected cause of the crash was, however, not disclosed.

Date: 15 November 1952 (time unknown)
Location: Territory of Alaska
Operator: US Air Force
Aircraft type: Fairchild C-119C (51-2570)

One in a formation of five aircraft on an intra-territorial flight from Elmendorf Air Force Base, near Anchorage, to Kodiak Naval Air Station, the twin-engine transport vanished with 20 American military personnel aboard (15 passengers and five crewmen). The search for 51-2570 was finally abandoned one month later. The C-119 had been cruising at 8,000ft (2,500m) under an instrument flight rules clearance. A radar plot of an aircraft, probably 51-2570, was established on a course parallel to the airway until 12:16 local time, while the targets of the other transports in the group were tracked approximately on course. The error had been detected by air defence surveillance radar, but reports received from the pilot stating that he was on course led to the assumption from the Elemendorf air-traffic controller monitoring the flight that the echo had been that of another aircraft. The loss of 51-2570 was believed to have resulted from precipitation static that caused confusion between two different radio range stations. Subsequent to this and the previous C-119 accident, the US Civil Aeronautics Board agreed to replace the low-frequency facilities extensively used in Alaska with more reliable very-high-frequency omni-directional range (VOR)installations.

Date: 22 November 1952 (c.20:15)
Location: Territory of Alaska
Operator: US Air Force
Aircraft type: Douglas C-124A (51-107A)

All 52 American servicemen aboard (41 passengers and a crew of 11) perished when the four-engine transport, which was bound for Elmendorf Air Force Base, near Anchorage, struck the south slope of Mount Gannett 50 miles (80km) east of its destination. The aircraft was being flown by the Military Air Transport Service (MATS) on a service from McChord Air Force Base, in Washington state, when it crashed at an approximate elevation of 9,000ft (2,700m), or about 1,000ft (300m) below the top of the mountain, disintegrated and burned. Located a few days later and subsequently identified, its wreckage lay buried in snow, and neither it nor the remains of the victims could be recovered. It was dark at the time of the accident, and the weather conditions in the area consisted of an indefinite ceiling of 600ft (180m), with a visibility of 2 miles (3km) in fog. The cross-winds encountered by 51-107A following its passage of Middleton Island may have been between 60 and 80 knots, more than double that forecast. Under the circumstances, the course correction made by the pilot would have been insufficient to compensate for the northward drift of the aircraft, which would account for its deviation from the proper track by some 30 miles (50km). The crew had been operating under an instrument flight rules clearance, but static and terrain features could have interfered with signals from the Elmendorf radio range station, and the crew had also faced icing conditions. Subsequently, the minimum height along the portion of the route where the disaster occurred was raised from 9,000 to 11,000ft (2,700–3,400m).

Date: 28 November 1952 (c.00:50)
Location: Near Tacoma, Washington, US
Operator: US Air Force
Aircraft type: Douglas C-54G

The four-engine aircraft, which was on a MATS flight from Alaska and carrying American servicemen and their dependents, crashed in early morning darkness and conditions of poor visibility, with fog and a low overcast, killing 37 persons aboard. Among the fatalities were the seven members of the crew, all Air Force personnel. Two passengers, including an 8-year-old boy whose family was killed, survived with injuries. After abandoning a ground-controlled approach to land at McChord Air Force Base due to the weather, the pilot announced his intention to proceed to Great Falls, in neighbouring Montana, but the aircraft's No. 3 power plant failed. Subsequently, the C-54 struck trees, slammed into a clearing approximately 1 mile (1.5km) south-west of the airfield and burst into flames.

Date: 20 December 1952 (c.06:30)
Location: Near Moses Lake, Washington, US
Operator: US Air Force
Aircraft type: Douglas C-124A (50-100)

Operated by the Tactical Air Command (TAC) and on a joint operation to carry personnel on Christmas leave to US air bases in Texas, Tennessee, South Carolina and Florida, and to pick up a helicopter and aircraft parts, the four-engine transport crashed and burned at Larson Air Force Base about a minute after it had taken off. Killed in the disaster were 87 of the 115 American servicemen aboard; among the survivors, which included five members of the aircraft's crew of 10, all but six suffered injuries. The crash occurred in pre-dawn darkness and as a light snow was falling. The sky was overcast, with an indefinite ceiling of 500ft (150m) and a visibility of 2 miles (3km), and the

The aftermath of the disastrous C-124A accident at Larson Air Force Base, which claimed the lives of 87 servicemen. (Wide World Photos)

wind blowing out of the north at 13 knots. It was determined that the aircraft's rudder and elevator gust locks, designed to keep these control surfaces fixed in windy conditions while on the ground, had not been disengaged by the crew prior to take-off (the activating handle only having been advanced enough to release the throttle and aileron locks). This would have prevented free movement of the flight controls and thus the transport from gaining height after becoming airborne, accounting for the fact that it never got higher than approximately 100ft (30m) above the ground. Following the accident, a directive was sent out to all US Air Force commands flying the C-124 emphasizing strict compliance with the existing requirement that pilots take steps to assure free movement of the control surfaces before taking off.

Date: 15 January 1953 (c.04:50)
Location: Mediterranean Sea

First aircraft
Operator: Royal Air Force
Type: Vickers Valetta Mk 1 (VX562)

Second aircraft
Operator: Royal Air Force
Type: Avro Lancaster (TX270)

The twin-engine transport and the four-engine bomber collided at an approximate altitude of

1,500ft (500m), and both then crashed some 100 miles (150km) north-west of the island of Malta. A total of 26 British service personnel lost their lives in the accident, including the Lancaster's seven crewmen; there were no survivors from either aircraft. The Valetta, carrying 16 passengers and a crew of three, had been en route from Malta to England and the Lancaster was on an anti-submarine exercise at the time of the collision, which occurred in pre-dawn darkness and thunderstorm activity, with heavy rain and hail having reduced the visibility to zero.

Date: 9 February 1953 (c.19:00)
Location: Near Cairo, Egypt
Operator: Egyptian Air Force
Aircraft type: Curtiss-Wright C-46 (1001)

During an internal flight from Al 'Arish to Almaza Airport, near Cairo, the twin-engine transport crashed into a hill east of its destination, the accident occurring in darkness and during a sandstorm. Of the 40 Egyptian military personnel aboard, 29 were killed, the survivors suffering various injuries. Though not officially reported, the accident may have been related to mechanical failure.

Date: 18 March 1953 (04:10)
Location: Random Island, Newfoundland, Canada
Operator: US Air Force
Aircraft type: Convair RB-36H (51-13721A)

Operated by the Strategic Air Command, the 10-engine strategic reconnaissance bomber had been on a simulated combat mission that originated in the Azores and was to have terminated at Rapid City Air Force Base, in South Dakota, US, when it crashed and burned near Smith Sound, and its 23 crewmen perished. Operating under instrument flight rules, the aircraft had flown at a low altitude over the Atlantic Ocean and was to have initiated a climb 20 miles (30km) from land. However, position reports received from the crew and known changes in the weather indicated that it encountered unexpected tail-winds during the last half of the leg and reached landfall about 1½ hr before the navigator's estimated time of arrival. The resulting accident occurred in darkness and during a low overcast, with a ceiling estimated at only 50 to 100ft (15–30m), which was accompanied by sleet, freezing drizzle and fog, conditions that had reduced the horizontal visibility of from less than 700ft (200m) to zero. Its ground speed estimated to have been around 230mph (370kph), 51-13721A was in level flight when it struck a hill at an approximate height of 800ft (250m), only about 100ft (30m) below its crest, the initial impact shearing off the left wing. Later that same day, a US Air Force B-29 that was searching for the missing RB-36 itself crashed in St

Georges Bay, between Nova Scotia and Cape Breton Island, and its 10 crewmen were also killed. The installation where 51-13721A had been based was later named in honour of its then-commanding officer, Brigadier General Richard Ellsworth, one of the victims of the RB-36 accident.

Date: 18 June 1953 (c.16:30)
Location: Near Kodaira, Japan
Operator: US Air Force
Aircraft type: Douglas C-124A (51-137A)

The first aviation disaster known to have claimed more than 100 lives occurred near the end of the Korean War during the movement of troops back to duty status following a five-day leave in Japan. Including a crew of seven, all 129 American servicemen aboard were killed when the four-engine transport crashed 25 miles (40km) west of Tokyo and approximately 3½ miles (6km) north-east of Tachikawa Air Base, from where it had taken off earlier. Originally bound for Kimpo Air Base, near Seoul, South Korea, the aircraft had turned back toward its departure point, the pilot reporting that its No. 1 power plant was shut down and the corresponding propeller feathered. Giving his height as 1,200ft (350m), he then accepted an offer for a ground-controlled approach; later, the tower controller heard over the radio the pilot, in intra-cockpit conversation, excitedly request 'More power, more power'. The C-124 was on the downwind leg of the airfield circuit and proceeding in a due northerly direction when it faded from the radar scope. At the time and location of the accident, the weather consisted of a broken overcast at around 1,000ft (300m), a visibility of 1 mile (1.5km) and a south-easterly wind of 6 knots. There was fog and light rain in the immediate area, with broken clouds down to only 400ft (120m). The power plant failure that indirectly led to the disaster was attributed to a sheared generator shaft, but the subsequent crash was blamed on the crew's premature application of full flaps during the three-engine let-down, which apparently resulted in a loss of flying speed. Its undercarriage still retracted, the aircraft plummeted into a field in a nose and left wing-down attitude, on a heading of 140 degrees and with no forward velocity, exploded and burned. The flight had lasted about 5 minutes.

Date: 17 July 1953 (c.23:15)
Location: Near Milton, Florida, US
Operator: US Navy
Aircraft type: Fairchild R4Q-2 (131663)

The twin-engine transport crashed and burned about 20 miles (30km) north-north-east of Pensacola, moments after it had taken off from Whiting Naval Air Station, on a domestic US flight to the Norfolk naval base in Virginia. All but two of

The first known aviation disaster to claim more than 100 lives was this crash of a US Air Force C-124A near Tokyo, Japan, on 18 June 1953. (UPI/Corbis-Bettmann)

the 46 American servicemen aboard lost their lives in the accident, while the survivors, one a passenger and the other a member of the aircraft's crew of six, suffered injuries. Its undercarriage and flaps fully retracted, the R4Q slammed into a wooded area in a wings-level attitude approximately 4,000ft (1,200m) from the departure end and to the left of the extended centreline of Runway 31, which it had used. The crash occurred on what was described as an 'extremely black' night, and there were patches of fog in the area despite an unlimited ceiling and a visibility of 10 miles (15km). The co-pilot, who was flying the aircraft at the time of the take-off, must have been unable to visually denote obstacles in his flight path or adequately discern his attitude owing to the absence of both a distinguishable horizon and reference lights in his forefront, and had apparently failed to maintain a sufficient rate of climb during the crucial phase of operation after becoming airborne. A retired Marine aviator with experience in the type later noted that the faster accelleration of such aircraft as the R4Q affected its gyros and could result in an instrument indication opposite to what was happening, ie climbing instead of descending, which led pilots to change procedures during instrument take-offs. It was not known, however, whether this factor contributed to the crash of 131663.

Date: 17 December 1953 (c.06:50)
Location: Guam, Mariana Islands
Operator: US Air Force
Aircraft type: Boeing B-29MR (44-87741)

Flown by Strategic Air Command, the bomber crashed into an officer's housing area at Anderson Air Force Base, located near the tip of the island 15 miles (25km) north-east of Agana, while attempting an emergency landing with one of its four engines out. Among the 19 persons killed

The correct circling approach path (large silhouette) and the course taken by the B-29 bomber (small one) that crashed at Anderson Air Force Base on Guam. (US Air Force)

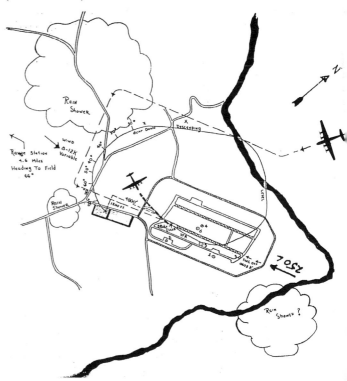

were five of the 16 American servicemen aboard the aircraft and eight civilians on the ground, six of them children. Eight others suffered injuries, four of whom were survivors from the B-29. About 15 minutes after 44-87741 had taken off from the island of Kwajalein, its No. 2 power plant developed high oil and cylinder temperatures and was smoking and throwing sparks from around the cowl flaps; the power plant was then shut down and the crew diverted to Guam. As it was turning left on the base leg of the circuit, the B-29 overshot the final approach course to Runway 07-Right. Its bank angle increased to about 80 degrees, whereupon the bomber stalled, plunged into the residential area and exploded. The weather, which at the time consisted of a broken overcast at 800ft (2,500m), with a visibility of 8 miles (13km) and a west-south-westerly wind of 8 knots, was apparently not a factor as the aircraft had been under the clouds while in the traffic pattern of the base.

Date: 6 January 1954 (c.17:20)
Location: Near Aldbury, Hertfordshire, England
Operator: Royal Air Force
Aircraft type: Vickers Valetta (WJ474)

All but one of the 17 British servicemen aboard were killed, including the entire crew of four, when the twin-engine transport crashed in a wooded area 30 miles (50km) north-west of London. The surviving passenger was seriously injured. The accident occurred in darkness and during a snow shower, with an estimated visibility of

All but one of the 17 occupants lost their lives in the crash of the RAF Valetta transport, which took place on 6 January 1954. (UPI/Corbis-Bettmann)

only 100ft (30 m), about 4 minutes after the aircraft had taken off from Bovingdon airfield on a communications flight to the Thorney Island facility, located near Portsmouth. For unknown reasons, the aircraft had lost height and descended into the ground, with no evidence being found of power plant or other mechanical failure.

Date: 1 February 1954 (c.13:50)
Location: Off Hokkaido, Japan
Operator: US Air Force
Aircraft type: Curtiss-Wright C-46D (44-78027A)

Operating on a scheduled internal Japanese service originating at Tachikawa Air Base, near Tokyo, and carrying 35 American servicemen (30 passengers and a crew of five), the twin-engine transport had last taken off from Misawa, the second of two en-route stops, bound for its ultimate destination of Chitose Airport, located near Sapporo. It had nearly completed this last leg of the flight when the pilot reported a fire in the cargo compartment, and that he may have to ditch. Two minutes later, in his last message, he radioed, '... I've lost control of the aircraft ... we're going in!' The C-46 crashed in the Pacific Ocean, approximately 20 miles (30km) south of Tomakomai, and in meteorological conditions consisting of a low overcast, with scattered clouds at 2,000ft (600m), a visibility of about 10 miles (15km) beneath them and a wind out of the north at 5 knots. Searchers recovered the bodies of two victims; there were no survivors.

Date: 4 March 1954 (c.14:30)
Location: Near St Étienne-de-Tinée, Alpes-Maritimes, France
Operator: US Air Force
Aircraft type: Douglas C-47A (42-24096A)

The transport crashed in the Alps 60 miles (100km) north of Nice, and all 20 American servicemen aboard, including the two pilots, were killed. Proceeding on a heading of about 305 degrees while on a flight with an ultimate destination of Hahn, West Germany, which had originated at Wheelus Field, near Tripoli, Libya, and last stopped at Rome, Italy, the aircraft struck a mountain at an approximate elevation of 8,000ft (2,500m), disintegrated and burned. Much of the wreckage was then carried down the slope in an avalanche. Only receiving an oral briefing about the weather, the pilot had not requested a cross-sectional forecast for the intended route. The subsequent accident occurred in instrument meteorological conditions, with falling snow and a low overcast. Only winds of 60 to 75 knots, twice that reported by pilots flying the same route on the day of the crash, could account for the distance that 42-24096A had drifted off the prescribed course. The required velocity would have been slightly less had no wind drift correction been made.

Date: 19 March 1954 (c.22:30)
Location: Near Lothian, Maryland, US
Operator: US Air Force
Aircraft type: Fairchild C-119F (51-7993)

All 18 American servicemen aboard (12 passengers and a crew of six) were killed in the crash of the twin-engine transport, which took place 15 miles (25km) west of Andrews Air Force Base, and just east of the Potomac River. The aircraft, on a domestic US flight from Oklahoma to Mitchell Field, on Long Island, New York, slammed to earth and burned about 20 minutes after its departure from Bolling Air Force Base, near Washington, DC, which was an intermediate stop. Prior to the crash it had been circling over a radio beacon under visual flight rules (VFR) procedures, awaiting an IFR clearance before proceeding on towards its destination. Factors apparently contributing to the accident were: a) an attempt to maintain VFR flight at night and in rain (although the exact weather conditions at the time and scene of the crash were not known), and b) possible crew fatigue.

Date: 2 July 1954 (c.12:00)
Location: Near Salvador, Bahia, Brazil
Operator: Força Aérea Brasileira (Brazilian Air Force)
Aircraft type: Lockheed C-28 (C.28-2901)

After completing an internal flight from Fortaleza, Ceara, the twin-engine transport crashed while attempting to land at the Salvador military base, killing all 20 persons aboard. The passengers included some civilian dependents, five of them children; the rest of the victims were military personnel, among them the aircraft's four crewmen. Though not officially reported, the accident was believed to have resulted from power plant failure, which occurred during the landing approach, after which the C-28 plummeted to earth and burst into flames.

Date: 27 August 1954 (c.22:10)
Location: Near Rapid City, South Dakota, US
Operator: US Air Force
Aircraft type: Convair RB-36H (51-13722)

Having already completed five landing approaches to Ellsworth Air Force Base, using

A giant, 10-engine Convair B-36 bomber of the US Air Force, similar to the aircraft that crashed near Ellsworth Air Force Base in South Dakota. (General Dynamics)

plan-position indicator (aerial mapping) procedures, the strategic reconnaissance bomber, operated by Strategic Air Command, was making a sixth when it crashed and burned about 2 miles (3km) north-north-west of the military installation. All but one of the aircraft's 27 crewmen lost their lives, including two who succumbed within five days of the accident; the survivor was seriously injured. Configured with its undercarriage retracted and flaps set at 20 degrees, the RB-36 was on a south-south-easterly heading towards Runway 12 when it slammed into the ground some 9,000ft (2,700m) from its threshold and approximately 200ft (60m) to the right of its extended centreline. The impact point was on a bluff around 150ft (50m) above airfield elevation. It was dark at the time, although the weather conditions were good, with the sky cloudless and a visibility of 15 miles (25km). The wind was out of the south at 6 knots. No information regarding the possible cause of the accident was disclosed by Air Force authorities.

Date: 24 October 1954 (c.17:50)
Location: Near Limone Piemonte, Cuneo, Italy
Operator: US Air Force
Aircraft type: Douglas C-47A (43-16044)

The transport was bound for Lyon, France, from Rome, Italy, when it crashed in the Maritime Alps near the border of the two countries. The wreckage was located nearly a week later, with no survivors among the 21 American servicemen aboard (18 passengers and a crew of three). An error in planning on the part of the pilot proved to be the primary factor in this accident. Specifically, the instrument flight plan he had filed indicated a cruising height that was lower than the authorised minimum altitude on the portion of the route wherein the accident occurred. The flight plan also

contained a bearing error of 13 degrees, possibly resulting from confusion between the Poretta radio beacon and Bastia, which is also located on the island of Corsica but some 15 miles (25km) farther north. Proceeding in darkness on a north-westerly track at a height of 8,500ft (2,600m), the C-47 slammed into the mountainous terrain and disintegrated. There was no post-impact fire. The weather at Lyon, about 175 miles (280km) north-west of where the crash occurred, was forecast to have consisted of broken cloud layers at 8,000ft (2,500m) and at 2,000ft (600m), with a visibility of around 5 miles (10km) in light rain. The winds encountered by the aircraft, which may have been an additional contributing factor in the accident, were blowing from a south-westerly direction and may have reached a velocity of 45 knots.

Date: 30/31 October 1954 (time unknown)
Location: North Atlantic Ocean
Operator: US Navy
Aircraft type: Lockheed R7V-1 (128441)

The four-engine transport had taken off from Patuxent River Naval Air Station, in Maryland, US, bound for Kenitra (Port Lyautey), Morocco, with a planned stop in the Azores. Most of the 42 persons aboard were American service personnel, including 21 on and off-duty crew members, although the passengers also included seven civilian dependents, nearly all of them children. Proceeding in darkness and 'intermittent' instrument meteorological conditions, the aircraft was last heard from when at a position of approximately 300 miles (480km) east of Ocean City, Maryland. Within 90 minutes of that radio transmission, sent at 23:30 local time, a possibly sudden and catastrophic event of an unknown nature claimed 128441 and its occupants. A search by aircraft and ships, which

A US Navy Lockheed RV7-1, a military version of the Super Constellation airliner and the type lost during a transatlantic flight. (US Navy)

began after the transport was reported overdue, went on for four days, but failed to find any survivors, bodies or wreckage.

Date: 16 November 1954 (time unknown)
Location: Near Huayllay, Pasco, Peru
Operator: Fuerza Aérea del Peru (Peruvian Air Force)
Aircraft type: Douglas C-47 (403)

Operated by the military airline Transportes Aereos Militares and on a domestic passenger flight to Lima from Pucallpa, Loreto, the aircraft disappeared over the Andes Mountains with 24 persons aboard, including a crew of three military personnel. No survivors were found at the crash site, which was located four days later, about 100 miles (150km) north-east of the transport's destination.

Date: 11 January 1955 (c.21:00)
Location: North Atlantic Ocean

First aircraft
Operator: Royal Air Force
Type: Avro Shackleton Mark 2 (WG531)

Second aircraft
Operator: Royal Air Force
Type: Avro Shackleton Mark 2 (WL743)

Both four-engine patrol aircraft were on training flights out of St Eval air base, in Cornwall, England, when lost with a total of 18 crewmen aboard (nine assigned to each). Though never proven, there was speculation that they had collided in darkness and possibly during a rain shower. The accident could have happened less than five minutes after the last radio message from one of them. More than a decade later, the No. 4 power plant identified as belonging to WL743 was inadvertently found by fishermen off the southern coast of Ireland, between the Skelligs and Bull Rock.

Date: 22 March 1955 (c.02:00)
Location: Oahu, Territory of Hawaii
Operator: US Navy
Aircraft type: Douglas R6D-1 (131612)

All 66 persons aboard perished when the four-engine transport crashed and burned in the Waianae Mountain range, some 15 miles (25km) north-west of Honolulu. Most of the victims were American servicemen, including the nine members of the crew, although the passengers included two civilian dependents – the wife and 3-year-old daughter – of a Navy enlisted man who was also on the aircraft. Operated by the Military Air Transport Service and originally bound for Travis Air Force Base, in California, the R6D was returning to land at Hickam Field, where it had taken off from earlier, because its high-frequency radio transmitters were inoperative. Communications were not affected when the aircraft came within close proximity to the islands. Cleared for landing, the transport was last reported descending out of

An RAF Avro Shackleton patrol bomber, two of which were lost off the coast of England during training manoeuvres. (British Aerospace)

3,000ft (1,000m) before it slammed into the slope and exploded at an approximate elevation of 1,200ft (350m), or some 750ft (230m) below the peak of the mountain. Just prior to impact, its landing lights were turned on and it had banked to the right in what might have been an evasive manoeuvre. Due to apparent navigational miscalculations by the flight crew as to their position and direction, the transport was at the moment of the crash some 8 miles (13km) north of the proper approach pattern and flying at an insufficient height to clear the terrain. It was dark at the time, and the meteorological conditions in the area, which were considered a contributing factor in the disaster, consisted of scattered clouds and rain showers, with a visibility of around 7 miles (11km). The wind was calm. No deficiencies were found in the Honolulu radio range or very-high-frequency omni-directional range (VOR) stations or other facilities.

Date: 11 August 1955 (c.14:20)
Location: Near Edelweiler, West Germany

First aircraft
Operator: US Air Force
Type: Fairchild C-119G (53-3222)

Second aircraft
Operator: US Air Force
Type: Fairchild C-119G (53-7841)

The two aircraft involved in this disaster were members of a flight of nine 'Flying Boxcar'

Top *The diagram illustrates the formation of C-119 transports, indicating the two involved in the disastrous mid-air collision on 11 August 1955.* **Bottom** *A soldier stands guard at the crash site of one Flying Boxcar.* (US Air Force and Associated Press)

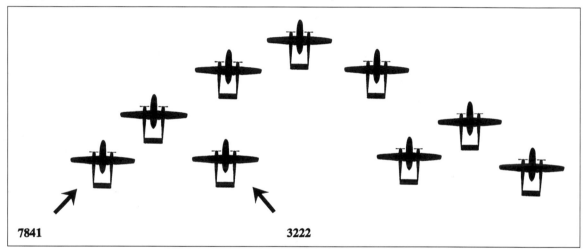

7841   3222

transports participating in a joint US military exercise out of Echterdingen Air Base, located near Stuttgart, their passengers all army soldiers. Proceeding in a westerly direction in good meteorological conditions, with a visibility of more than 10 miles (15km) and layers of scattered clouds at 3,000ft (1,000m) and at 20,000ft (6,000m), the group had begun a left turn back towards the east at a height of 4,000ft (1,200m), or about 2,000ft (600m) above the terrain, when 3222 reported losing its left power plant and that it was leaving the formation. Shortly thereafter, that C-119 collided with 7841. Both transports then plummeted to the ground 30 miles (50km) west of the city of Stuttgart, disintegrated and burned. A total of 66 American servicemen perished in the accident, 46 aboard 7841 and 20 aboard 3222; 10 of the victims were Air Force personnel, the two five-member crews assigned to each aircraft. There were no survivors. After its final message had been acknowledged by the lead aircraft, which then cleared it to a heading of 80 degrees, 3222 started a descending turn to the left, but as it was passing under 7841, the latter inexplicably also began to descend in a left bank, resulting in the collision. The underside of the nose section of 7841 struck the left vertical stabiliser of 3222, the impact severing the latter's starboard boom and tail section. The collision could have rendered the controls of 7841 inoperative, and/or sent flying debris into the cockpit, incapacitating the two pilots. Falling into a spin, 3222 crashed into a wooded area in a flat attitude, while 7841 continued straight-and-level for a few seconds before going into a right turn, finally crashing into a field in a steep nose-down, inverted attitude. Whereas 3222

used the correct procedures in exiting the group, 7841 had failed to maintain its position in the formation.

Date: 17 February 1956 (c.13:45)
Location: Near Niles, California, US
Operator: US Marine Corps
Aircraft type: Douglas R5D-2 (39116)

All 40 American servicemen aboard (35 passengers and a crew of five) perished when the four-engine transport crashed about 20 miles (30km) south-east of Oakland. Operating under an instrument flight rules clearance, the aircraft had been en route from El Toro Marine Air Station, in Southern California, and was to have landed at Alameda Naval Air Station, located on the east side of San Francisco Bay. After receiving instructions from Oakland approach control to maintain at least 1,000ft (300m) above the clouds, it entered a holding pattern and circled for about half-an-hour before being cleared for a straight-in radio range approach from the Newark fan marker beacon. It was observed by a ground witness proceeding in a westerly direction under a low overcast and in a level or slight nose-down attitude and to disappear into the clouds. Moments later, and while on a magnetic heading of approximately 270 degrees, the R5D slammed into Sunol Ridge at an approximate elevation of 1,500ft (500m), or almost 200ft (60m) below the crest of the hill, exploded and burned. The cloudy conditions in the area were accompanied by occasional squalls, containing light to moderate rain, one of which obscured the terrain struck by 39116. Examination of the wreckage

The crash of the US Marine Corps R5D into a ridge claimed 40 lives during a landing approach to Alameda Naval Air Station in California. (UPI/Corbis-Bettmann)

revealed no evidence of material failure in the aircraft, or any indication of altimeter mis-setting. The accident was attributed to the non-adherence of the flight crew to the holding pattern, and to their departure from the radio beacon and let-down in an unprescribed manner. These irregularities may have resulted from one or more of the following factors: improper instrument procedures; misinterpretation of radio-navigational signals; an incorrect automatic direction finder indication; miscalculation of time while on the final outbound leg of the circuit, or an attempt to proceed in the instrument meteorological conditions under visual flight rules (VFR) procedures. Apparently unable to descend in a standard four-minute pattern to 3,500ft (1,050m), the specified final approach initiation altitude, the pilots extended the outbound leg of the circuit in order to reach the Newark radio beacon at that height. This took the aircraft to an area where the ground was visible, which must have been misidentified as the flat terrain in the vicinity of Niles and nearby Irvington, located to the west of its actual position. The descent continued to 1,500ft, with the R5D flying in and out of the clouds, the pilots firmly convinced they would clear all obstacles at this height as they proceeded towards the Oakland radio range station (their belief would have been reinforced by the high background signals of the navigational aid that they would have been receiving at this location). It was also possible that the aircraft had been in or near the correct pattern and that the crew elected to make an unprescribed left-hand turn back to the Newark homing beacon, when VFR conditions were observed to the south-east. It was noted in the

investigative report that the area where the crash took place had a history of pilot disorientation and several major accidents. The standard instrument approach chart used by pilots flying into the Alameda base lacked an annotation with regard to the minimum altitude at the point of the final approach fix, which was actually 2,000ft (600m) higher than that indicated, and a procedural change was one of the recommendations made in the report.

Date: 13 July 1956 (c.15:35)
Location: Near Browns Mills, New Jersey, US
Operator: US Air Force
Aircraft type: Douglas C-118A (53-3301A)

This scheduled Military Air Transport Service (MATS) flight ended in disaster shortly after the aircraft had taken off from Runway 24 at McGuire Air Force Base, located on the grounds of the Fort Dix Military Reservation, some 20 miles (30km) south-west of Lakewood. Bound for Harmon Air Force Base, Newfoundland, Canada, the first segment of a transatlantic service with an ultimate destination of England, the four-engine transport had been airborne for approximately 2 minutes before it slammed into a wooded area some 2 miles (3km) from the end of the runway and shattered into pieces, although there was no post-impact fire. The crash claimed the lives of 46 persons, including all but two of the aircraft's 10 Air Force crew members; though mostly comprised of US military personnel, the passengers included six American and British civilians who were among those killed. All 20 survivors suffered serious

A Douglas C-118A transport of the type that crashed after taking off from McGuire Air Force Base on a MATS flight. (McDonnell Douglas)

injuries. Shortly before the accident, the weather in the area consisted of thunderstorm activity, with 'sheets' of rain, a ceiling of about 2,000ft (600m) and scattered clouds at 500ft (150m), and a visibility of 1 mile (1.5km). The wind was blowing out of the west at 10 knots, gusting to almost 30. Severe down-draughts were believed to have been present, and although no official cause was announced by Air Force authorities, an encounter with one or more of these vertical air currents apparently led to the uncontrolled descent of the aircraft into the ground. The fact that the C-118 had rear-facing passenger seats may have saved lives in this crash.

Date: 10 October 1956 (c.22:00)
Location: North Atlantic Ocean
Operator: US Navy
Aircraft type: Douglas R6D-1 (131588)

Operated by MATS, the aircraft had taken off from Royal Air Force Lakenheath, Suffolk, England, with an ultimate destination of McGuire Air Force Base, New Jersey, US. It was carrying 59 American servicemen, including a crew of nine Navy personnel; all the passengers were members of the US Air Force. With a planned stop at Lajes Air Base, in the Azores, the four-engine transport was on the first segment of the transatlantic flight when it met with disaster, the circumstances of which will probably for ever remain a mystery. Its last known position report was sent at 20:55 local time, at which time, and in accordance with its flight plan, the aircraft would have been cruising in darkness at an approximate height of 15,000ft (5,000m). A search that began after it was reported missing failed to find any survivors or victims' bodies. Subsequently, wreckage identified as belonging to the R6D, a life raft and a main under carriage gear leg, with the two wheels still attached, were recovered 250 miles (400km) south-west of Land's End, England, and examination of the tyres revealed traces of post-impact fire. Two aircraft that had flown the same course before and after 131588 described the weather along the route as consisting of a scattered to broken overcast, with cloud tops at around 5,000ft (1,500m). With regard to the possibility of a malicious act, it was noted in the investigative report that normal security measures had been in effect at the Lakenheath air base before the departure of the transport.

Date: 28 October 1956 (c.22:00)
Location: Mediterranean Sea
Operator: Egyptian Air Force
Aircraft type: Curtiss-Wright C-46

The twin-engine transport, its passengers including both military personnel and civilians, vanished in darkness during a flight to Cairo from Damascus, Syria, with 23 persons aboard.

The wreckage of the US Air Force C-118 is scattered among the trees following the crash that occurred in a thunderstorm. (Wide World Photos)

Date: 30 November 1956 (c.22:00)
Location: Near Ballico, California, US
Operator: US Air Force
Aircraft type: Boeing RB-52B (52-8716)

The worst-ever B-52 crash involving a single aircraft occurred about a year and a half after the first of the eight-engine jet bombers had entered service with the Strategic Air Command. A little less than 3 minutes after it had taken off from Castle Air Force Base, on a combat training mission, 52-8716 plunged to earth and disintegrated in a fiery explosion some 15 miles (25km) north-north-west of Merced, and all 10 crewmen were killed. The accident occurred in darkness, but the weather was clear, with a slight breeze out of the west. At the moment of impact, the cleanly-configured aircraft was descending at an angle of about 5 degrees from the horizontal, in a slight right wing-down attitude and on an almost due northerly heading. Investigation revealed no evidence of in-flight fire, explosion or structural failure, and that the crash apparently resulted from an abnormal nose-down trim condition which the pilots could not

A US Air Force Boeing RB-52B, serial number 52-8716, the same aircraft that crashed during a night training flight in November 1956. (Boeing)

or did not correct due to an unknown malfunction or distraction. Subsequent to this accident, the minimum altitude for flap retraction in B-52 operations was raised to 1,000ft (300m), and pilots flying the type would also receive expanded training to include the importance of maintaining a positive rate of climb when retracting the flaps.

Date: 11 January 1957 (c.09:00)
Location: Near Buenos Aires, Argentina
Operator: Fuerza Aérea Argentina (Argentine Air Force)
Aircraft type: Vickers Viking 1B (T-11)

Operated by the military airline Lineas Aéreas del Estado (LADE) on a scheduled domestic passenger flight bound for Mar del Plata, with an ultimate destination of Mendoza, the twin-engine transport crashed and burned immediately after taking off from Jorge Newbury Airport. The accident claimed the lives of 18 persons, one of whom was on the ground and the rest aboard the aircraft. Among the 16 injured survivors was the co-pilot, one member of the transport's crew of four military personnel. With the operation out of this airport by an aircraft the size of a Viking judged 'critical' even under normal circumstances due to runway length, T-11 had been attempting to take off during a cross-wind that exceeded the maximum allowed, apparently resulting in a loss of control.

Date: 22 February 1957 (c.20:00)
Location: Near Yanggong-ni, Kyonggi-do, South Korea
Operator: US Air Force
Aircraft type: Douglas C-124A (51-141A)

Heavily laden with passengers, the four-engine transport had taken off from Runway 32 at Kimpo Air Base, bound for Japan. After reaching a height of about 800 to 1,000ft (250–300m), the No. 3 power plant backfired, and an emergency was then declared. As it was returning to the airfield, the same engine exploded, with flying debris disabling the No. 4 power plant and tearing a hole in the fuselage. Despite the application of maximum power on the two port engines, level flight could not be maintained, and the C-124 continued descending until finally touching down, with its undercarriage still retracted, in a channel of the Han River, about 10 miles (15km) north of the base and 25 miles (40km) north-west of Seoul, coming to a stop on an ice-littered sand bar. Among the 159 American service personnel aboard, 22 lost their lives, including three of the aircraft's 10 Air Force crew members, one of them the co-pilot. The survivors, 24 of whom suffered varying degrees of injury, were evacuated from the crash scene by helicopter. Fire, which had erupted in the wing areas an estimated 15 minutes after the crash, eventually consumed most of the wreckage. The cause of the initial power plant failure was not disclosed by military authorities. The resulting forced landing was carried out in darkness, but the meteorological conditions in the area were good, with the sky clear and a visibility of more than 10 miles (15km).

Date: 5 March 1957 (c.11:00)
Location: Drayton, Berkshire, England
Operator: Royal Air Force
Aircraft type: Blackburn Beverley C Mark 1 (XH117)

Operated by Transport Command, the four-engine aircraft crashed about half-an-hour after it had taken off from Abingdon airfield, located 75 miles (120km) north-west of London. All

An RAF Blackburn Beverley transport, the type that crashed following multiple power plant loss linked to faulty maintenance. (British Aerospace)

but three of the 18 British servicemen aboard plus two persons on the ground were killed in the accident; one other civilian and the three survivors from the aircraft, including two members of the crew of five, suffering injuries. Originally bound for Cyprus, the transport had turned back after the crew detected a serious fuel leak near the No. 1 power plant, which was feathered. During the let-down procedure, the corresponding gauge indicated an unusual loss of fuel from the No. 2 tank, and so the fuel cocks and boosters for that tank were turned off. The cocks and boosters for the No. 1 tank remained on. When power was increased on the remaining three engines, the No. 2 failed to respond, and with the loss of power, the aircraft began to lose height and air speed until the point that it became uncontrollable, striking power lines and trees before it ploughed into two farm buildings

The remains of the Beverley beside one of the badly damaged farm buildings it struck in Drayton, Berkshire, England. (UPI/Corbis-Bettmann)

and caught fire. The base weather around the time of the crash consisted of a low overcast, with 8/8 cloud coverage at around 500ft (150m), a visibility down to less than 1,000ft (300m) and easterly winds of nearly 10 knots. The four fuel tanks on the port side of the Beverley were designed to feed into a collector box, from which gasoline would be provided to both left-hand engines. Investigation revealed that on XH117, the non-return valve between the No. 1 tank and the collector box been fitted in reverse, and that the No. 2 power plant malfunctioned due to fuel starvation resulting from this maintenance error, to the fact that the fuel supply from the other main tank had been turned off after the No. 1 engine was feathered, and because the fuel supply from the two smaller port tanks had been turned off throughout the flight. The latter action, which was that of the pilot's, did not conform to proper handling of the aircraft's fuel system. However, it was noted in the investigative report on the accident that as the amount of fuel in the two smaller tanks was not large, he would have had no reason to believe that the two port engines could not operate satisfactorily off the two main tanks alone. As a result of this accident, an RAF mechanic was court-martialled for negligence, but his punishment was later reduced to only a reprimand. Additionally, a requirement was implemented requiring that tests be carried out after this type of maintenance had been performed on an aircraft.

Date: 17 March 1957 (c.01:30)
Location: Near Asturias, Cebu, the Philippines
Operator: Philippine Air Force
Aircraft type: Douglas C-47

Ramon Magsaysay, the President of the Philippines, was among 24 persons killed when the twin-engine transport crashed and burned on a jungle-covered mountain on the island of Cebu, about 20 miles (30km) north-west of the city of Cebu, from where it had taken off shortly before, on an internal flight to Manila. The victims also included the aircraft's five crewmen, all military personnel. One seriously injured passenger survived the accident, which occurred in early morning darkness. Prior to the crash the pilot had reported no difficulties and that the weather conditions were clear, although no information as to the possible cause was released by the Philippine Air Force.

Date: 22 March 1957 (c.01:00)
Location: North Pacific Ocean
Operator: US Air Force
Aircraft type: Boeing C-97C (50-702A)

The aircraft was on a scheduled Military Air Transport Service flight from Travis Air Force Base, in California, US, to Tokyo, Japan, with three en-route stops, the last of these on Wake Island, when it vanished during the final segment of the transpacific crossing. Except for three civilians, including a female dependent, the 67 persons aboard were American servicemen, including the crew of 10. Operating under an instrument flight rules clearance, with a cruising altitude of 8,000ft (2,500m), the four-engine transport was last heard from around 00:40 local time, or about 20 minutes before the unexplained disaster was believed to have occurred, at an approximate location of 200 miles (320km) south-east of its intended destination. Search was abandoned eight days later, with no trace of it having been found. The pilot of a commercial airliner, who had flown the Wake Island-to-Tokyo route some 30 minutes ahead of the C-97, reported cloudy weather in the area where the latter was believed lost, with bases of 5,000ft

A US Air Force Boeing C-97, virtually identical to the aircraft that vanished during a MATS transpacific flight from California to Japan. (Boeing)

(1,500m) and tops at 10,000ft (3,000m), light icing and light-to-moderate turbulence. He also observed lightning in the night sky some distance to the north of his position.

Date: 17 April 1957 (c.08:30)
Location: Near El Quweira, Jordan
Operator: Royal Air Force
Aircraft type: Vickers Valetta C.Mk 1 (VW832)

The twin-engine transport crashed and burned 25 miles (40km) north-east of Aqaba, from where it had taken off about 5 minutes earlier. All 27 British servicemen aboard (24 passengers and a crew of three) were killed. As the aircraft was proceeding in a north-easterly direction through a mountain pass, its left wing snapped, and evidence indicated that the structural failure resulted from the imposition of loads that exceeded its designed strength. It was considered probable that the break-up was precipitated by a loss of control in conditions of clear-air turbulence and the attempted recovery from the resulting high-speed dive.

Date: 23 December 1957 (c.16:00)
Location: North Pacific Ocean
Operator: US Navy
Aircraft type: Lockheed WV-2 (143197)

A simulated emergency led to a real disaster about 30 miles (50km) north of Kakuku Point, on Oahu, one of the Hawaiian islands, in this first major crash of one of the early warning/radar intelligence aircraft designed to protect US coastlines. The WV-2 was on a training syllabus flight and had descended beneath a low overcast when the aircraft commander and designated check pilot instituted the drill, a simulated fire in the forward cargo compartment. As part of this exercise, he instructed the pilot to turn off the aileron boost during the drill, then to return his aileron booster control to the 'on' position. In attempting to regain elevator boost, however, one of the men in the cockpit, the pilot, check pilot or one of the two flight engineers, moved the emergency shut-off levers in the wrong direction, to the 'blast air, fuel and hydraulic off' position. This error deprived all four engines of their fuel supply, resulting in a total loss of power. Its propellers windmilling, 143197 rapidly descended from an approximate height of 1,000ft (300m) and finally slammed into the water with its undercarriage and flaps in the retracted position and with its nose and left wing slightly low, breaking into at least two major sections on impact. Fire then erupted and burned for a while on the surface of the ocean. Among the 23 crewmen, four injured survivors were rescued, including the commander. Searchers recovered only two bodies, but several of those killed were known to have survived the impact. Around the time of the accident, the cloud base was down to less than 1,000ft (300m) and the visibility only about half-a-mile (0.8km) in the area where it had been raining, higher outside those areas. With the wind blowing from an east-north-

An RAF Vickers Valetta transport, one of which crashed in Jordan after turbulence-related in-flight structural failure. (Martin W. Bowman)

easterly direction at 15 to 25 knots, the sea was rough. It was ruled that the check pilot had failed to initiate remedial action when the WV-2 began to lose altitude and while at the relatively slow indicated air speed of around 180mph (290kph) during the fire drill, and also failed to exercise authority when a real emergency developed. Neither did he activate the emergency warning bell when the ditching was imminent.

Date: 1 February 1958 (c.19:15)
Location: Norwalk, California, US

First aircraft
Operator: US Air Force
Type: Douglas C-118A (53-3277A)

Second aircraft
Operator: US Navy
Type: Lockheed P2V-5F (127723)

The two aircraft collided at an approximate height of 3,000ft (1,000m), scattering wreckage over residential and business areas of suburban Los Angeles. Killed in the disaster were a total of 47 American military personnel, all 41 aboard 53-3277A (35 passengers and six crew members) and six of the eight crewmen of 127723, one of whom died on the way to hospital, plus one civilian on the ground who was struck by a piece of falling debris outside her house. The two Navy men who survived suffered serious injuries. Operated by the Military Air Transport Service, the C-118 had taken off from Long Beach Municipal Airport about 5 minutes before the accident, on a domestic transcontinental flight with a destination of McGuire Air Force Base, in New Jersey. Although it was to have continued under instrument flight rules upon reaching its cruising altitude of 17,000ft (5,200m), the four-engine transport had been cleared to climb to that height under visual flight rules (VFR) procedures. Meanwhile, the twin-engine patrol bomber had been on an instrument training exercise, also being conducted under VFR. At the moment of the collision, 53-3277A was on an easterly heading and banked to the right, and 127723 northbound, and the former then burst into flames. Its empennage fell atop a service station and the main portion of its wreckage crashed in the near-by parking lot of the Norwalk Sheriff's Department sub-station, with some 30 civilian or patrol vehicles being destroyed or damaged in the impact or ensuing fires. The P2V fell into a rock quarry about 2½ miles (4km) to the north of the C-118 crash site. It was dark at the time of the accident, although the meteorological conditions were good to excellent, with a high, thin ceiling and a visibility of 15 miles (25km). In accordance with civil air regulations, when two aircraft are on crossing paths, the one on the right (in this case the P2V), would have had the right-of-way.

Date: 20 February 1958 (c.05:35)
Location: North Atlantic Ocean
Operator: US Navy
Aircraft type: Lockheed WV-2 (141310)

In the early years of the Cold War, before satellites and sophisticated ground-based systems, WV-2 early warning aircraft played an important role in the defence of the US coastline. This particular aircraft, with 22 crewmen aboard, which was part of the so-called 'Atlantic Barrier' fleet, vanished for reasons unknown while flying along a rhumb line oriented on a true heading of 113 degrees that stretched from Argentia, Newfoundland, Canada,

A US Navy Lockheed P-2V Neptune, similar to the aircraft involved in the collision with a MATS transport over suburban Los Angeles. (Lockheed Martin)

The empennage of the US Air Force C-118 and the badly damaged service station following mid-air collision with the Navy patrol bomber. (UPI/Corbis-Bettmann)

to Lajes Air Base, on the island of Terceira, in the Azores. A Navy board of inquiry concluded that 141310 had been 'suddenly and catastrophically' destroyed approximately 100 miles (150km) west of Corvo, another island in the Azores, in such a manner as to prevent any distress message from being transmitted. It was dark at the time, but there were no indications of any thunderstorm activity or other adverse weather conditions in the area. Numerous conjectures were considered by the Navy as to the cause of its disappearance, among them catastrophic material failure and the clandestine action of a foreign aircraft, but the following were considered the most likely: a) A strike of lightning or a static discharge causing total electrical failure; b) The explosion of an accumulation of fuel vapor in some part of the aircraft; c) A loss of a single propeller or an entire blade, or d) A loss of control resulting from an error or failure by the crew. There was, however, evidence that seemed to contradict some of these theories. One endorsement to the investigative report noted that the operating history of the WV-2 and its close relative, the R7V-1 transport, did not support the probability of an in-flight explosion, and that such an event would be expected to distribute some buoyant items that searchers should have found floating on the surface of the ocean. And a fire in the aircraft should have afforded the crew ample time for an emergency radio transmission. It was also noted that the loss of

an entire propeller or individual blade, though not unknown to piston-engine aircraft, would probably be progressive in nature and not result in an instantaneous loss of control. Nevertheless, some six months after the loss of 141310, a Super Constellation airliner, very similar to the WV-2, crashed off the coast of Ireland, the sudden nature of which prevented the crew from sending a distress message, and an investigative board concluded with a degree of high probability that the disaster resulted from the overspeeding of an outer propeller.

Date: 7 March 1958 (c.19:45)
Location: Off Okinawa, Ryukyu Islands

First aircraft
Operator: US Marine Corps
Type: Fairchild R4Q (128741)

Second aircraft
Operator: US Marine Corps
Type: Douglas AD-6 Skyraider (135350)

Both propeller-driven aircraft had flown from Subi Point, in the Philippines, the twin-engine 'Flying Boxcar' transport actually escorting the single-engine attack bomber because of the former's superior navigational equipment. After having entered a holding pattern, both were descending in darkness through a broken to solid layer of clouds when they collided and plummeted into the Philippine Sea 4 miles (6.5km) from the south end of one runway at Naha Air Base, where they were to have landed, and slightly to the left of its extended centreline. A total of 26 American servicemen lost their lives in the accident, including the transport's crew of six and the pilot (and sole occupant) of the bomber. There were no survivors. Searchers were able to recover all of the victims' bodies and the main wreckage of the two aircraft from the water, which was about 50ft (15m) deep at the crash site. Investigation revealed that the initial contact was between the left side of the fuselage of 135350 and the right wing tip of 128741, after which time the former's propeller struck the latter's starboard power plant. The collision apparently resulted from the failure of the AD-6 pilot to maintain his correct position as wing man in a formation during a descending left-hand turn due to several factors, either alone or in combination with others: a) Disorientation on his part while manoeuvering through moderate turbulence; b) Loss or impairment of visibility because of the clouds, aggravated by the darkness; c) Possible vertigo caused by these conditions, aggravated by flashing navigational lights; d) Moderate fatigue and slight hypoxia affecting the pilot. However, a board of inquiry did not totally discount the possibility that the pilot of the transport had himself become disorientated and executed a manoeuvre that was too sudden for successful evasive action by the smaller aircraft. He also erred in failing to request clearance to make a visual flight rules (VFR) procedure let-down earlier or, having elected to remain above the overcast, in failing to break formation and, utilising available navigational aids and ground radar, penetrate the clouds separately. It was recommended in the investigative report that except in emergency situations, such joint flights as the one here be permitted only in VFR conditions and daylight hours, and that the aircraft involved maintain a horizontal separation of 1,000ft (300m) at all times. The Commanding General of the Marine Corps' Pacific and Atlantic fleets was requested to ensure that their standard operating procedures relative to the transport escort of tactical aircraft be clear and consise in matters related to safety.

Date: 27 March 1958 (c.16:15)
Location: Near Bridgeport, Texas, US

First aircraft
Operator: US Air Force
Type: Douglas C-124C (52-981A)

Second aircraft
Operator: US Air Force
Type: Fairchild C-119C (49-195A)

Both operating under instrument flight rules and cruising along designated airways, the two transports collided over a very-high-frequency omni-directional range (VOR) station 40 miles (65km) north-west of Fort Worth, and both crashed in farmland, with the wreckage of 52-981A burning after ground impact. A total of 18 American servicemen were killed in the accident, with no survivors from either aircraft. The four-engine C-124 had been on a north-north-easterly heading and en route from Kelly Air Force Base, near San Antonio, Texas, to Tinker Air Force Base, in neighbouring Oklahoma, and carrying five passengers and a crew of 10, while the twin-engine C-119 was on a south-easterly heading and on an intra-state flight from Sheppard Air Force Base, near Wichita Falls, to Carswell Air Force Base, near Fort Worth, with three crewmen aboard. The collision was determined to have occurred at an approximate height of 6,000ft (1,800m), in the midst of an overcast, with a visibility of around 5 miles (10km) but down to zero within the clouds. There was also haze and fog in the area. Whereas 52-981A had been cleared by the Fort Worth air-traffic control centre to maintain 7,000ft (2,000m), the height at which it collided with 49-195A, which had been assigned to 6,000ft, indicated that it was in fact flying at the wrong altitude at the time of the accident.

Date: 22 May 1958 (c.13:15)
Location: Near Middleton, New Jersey, US
Operator: US Army
Aircraft type: Douglas Nike-Ajax (8)

Ten persons were killed, four of them civilians and the rest servicemen, in a massive explosion that destroyed the eight anti-aircraft missiles at Battery B of the AAA Missile Battalion, an army launching facility located 25 miles (40km) south-south-east of Newark. Three others suffered injuries in the blast, which occurred as a team of civilian ordnance specialists, aided by several soldiers, was installing a new arming mechanism on one of the missiles (the modification involving the removal of the warhead). According to an investigative report, the most probable cause of the disaster, the worst in the history of US military rocket forces, was the rupturing of a detonating cap. New safeguards were announced for the next generation of anti-aircraft missile, the Nike Hercules.

Date: 27 June 1958 (c.00:30)
Location: Near Chicopee Falls, Massachusetts, US
Operator: US Air Force
Aircraft type: Boeing KC-135A (56-3599A)

Taking off from Runway 23 at Westover Air Force Base, on an attempted record-breaking transatlantic flight to London and then back to the US, the Strategic Air Command jet tanker crashed just north of Springfield. All 15 men aboard perished, including six journalists and two other civilians riding as passengers; the seven members of the crew were Air Force personnel. Since mission requirements called for the maximum permissible fuel load, surface air temperature and its effect on the aircraft's take-off performance were critical. Through calculations made by both the mission and the aircraft commander, it was determined that a flap setting of 40 degrees would provide for a take-off roll of the desired length. There would be a penalty in decreasing the ground roll, however, namely a shallower climb-out path. It was suspected that the pilots had concentrated on monitoring their air speed and failed to detect that the KC-135 had gone into a slight descent after becoming airborne, initially striking tree tops with its left wing and engines, at a point some 4,000ft (1,200m) from the end of the runway. The tanker then cut several power cables and finally slammed to earth in a near-vertical left bank and burst into flames, scattering wreckage across the Massachusetts Turnpike. It was dark at the time of the crash, and the meteorological conditions consisted of a high overcast, with scattered clouds at 700ft (200m) and a runway visual range of 1½ miles (2.5km) in fog. The wind was from a south-westerly direction at 9 knots. Investigation ruled

Right *The blackened area near the top of the photograph marks the scene of the multiple Nike-Ajax explosion at a US Army missile launching facility.* (UPI/Corbis-Bettmann)

Below *A US Air Force Boeing KC-135, the first jet tanker/transport, which suffered its first major accident during an attempted record-breaking flight.* (Boeing)

out in-flight fire or pre-impact structural failure, power plant or other mechanical malfunction. It was therefore concluded that the accident must have resulted from complications in aircraft handling technique, associated with the high gross weight and the marginal weather and night-time visibility conditions, which were compounded by flight instrument limitations.

Date: 2 September 1958 (c.06:10)
Location: North Pacific Ocean
Operator: US Air Force
Aircraft type: Douglas C-124C (52-1081A)

Operated by the Military Air Transport Service, the aircraft crashed approximately 35 miles (55km) west of Agana Naval Air Station, on the island of Guam, where it had taken off from earlier, on a cargo flight to Clark Air Base, in the Philippines. Around four hours later, floating wreckage was spotted and, subsequently, the bodies of two victims were recovered, but none of the 19 American servicemen aboard (12 passengers and a crew of seven) survived. There were indications of an in-flight fire, the origin of which remained undetermined. Airborne around dawn, the four-engine transport had been cleared to its cruising altitude of 8,000ft (2,500m) prior to the crash, which occurred some 20 minutes after its take-off. The weather in the area at the time was good, with a high overcast and scattered cumulus clouds at around 1,200ft (350m), and a visibility of at least 5 miles (10km).

Date: 2 September 1958 (c.14:00)
Location: Near Talin, Armenia, USSR
Operator: US Air Force
Aircraft type: Lockheed C-130A-II (56-0528)

All 17 American servicemen aboard were believed to have perished when the highly-modified four-engine turboprop transport crashed and burned about 35 miles (55km) north-west of Yerevan. Some three weeks later, the remains of six airmen were returned to American authorities in Turkey; these were reportedly the only victims found in the wreckage. The US later released the recording of a conversation among Soviet fighter pilots as they attacked the unarmed aircraft, which it was claimed had strayed off course while ostensibly being used to study the propagation of radio waves transmitted by US broadcast stations, at a reported height of 10,000ft (3,000m). More than 30 years later, the true nature of the mission came to light with the release of previously-classified documents. The C-130 had in fact been sent to identify Soviet radar defences and test their capabilities, and must have been located and shot down not long after passing into Soviet airspace at 22,000ft (6,700m).

Date: 8 September 1958 (c.19:20)
Location: Near Airway Heights, Washington, US

First aircraft
Operator: US Air Force
Type: Boeing B-52D (56-661)

Second aircraft
Operator: US Air Force
Type: Boeing B-52D (56-681)

This remains as the worst disaster in the history of the US Strategic Air Command's jet bomber operations. Both aircraft had been on pilot proficiency flights and were preparing to land on Runway 23 at Fairchild Air Force Base when 681 was advised to pull up and break to the right after dropping below the glide path during a ground-controlled procedure approach. After being advised by the control tower of what the other B-52 was doing, 661 radioed back, 'Roger tower, tell him to turn the other way', and the latter then banked to the right. Seconds later, the bombers collided at an approximate above-ground height of 900ft (275m) some 2½ miles (4km) north-east of the base and about 5 miles (10km) west of Spokane, and both then plunged to earth and exploded. Killed in the accident were a total of 13 airmen, eight from 661 and five from 681. Among the three survivors, who bailed out with three others that did not survive, one crewman from 661 was slightly injured, while one of the co-pilots assigned to 681 suffered serious injuries and that aircraft's tail gunner escaped unscathed. The collision occurred at dusk, and the weather conditions in the area consisted of a broken overcast at 10,000ft (3,000m), with a visibility under the clouds of 20 miles (30km) and a slight breeze from a north-north-easterly direction. Prior to the collision, the instrument flight rules clearances of both aircraft had been cancelled.

Date: 9 October 1958 (c.18:25)
Location: Near New Plymouth, Idaho, US
Operator: US Air Force
Aircraft type: Fairchild C-123B (55-4521A)

The twin-engine transport crashed and exploded on flat terrain some 7 miles (11km) east of Payette, and all 19 persons aboard were killed. Except for two civilian passengers, the victims were all American servicemen, including the crew of five. Operated by the Tactical Air Command and designated as the support aircraft for the 'Thunderbirds', the US Air Force precision flying team, 55-4521A had been en route from Hill Air Force Base, in Utah, to McChord Air Force Base, near Tacoma, Washington, one segment of a transcontinental flight originating in North Carolina, when it apparently stalled at an approximate height of 500ft (150m) above the ground, apparently after experiencing uncontrolled phugoid, or 'porpoising' motions. At the time of the accident, around dusk, the local weather was good, with an estimated ceiling of 9,000ft (2,700m) and a visibility of 30 miles (50km). The wind was calm. A loss of control or the incapacitation of one of the pilots may have factored in the accident.

Date: 15 October 1958 (time unknown)
Location: Near Villa Montes, Tarija, Bolivia
Operator: Fuerza Aérea Boliviana (Bolivian Air Force)
Aircraft type: Douglas C-47A (TAM-03)

Operated by the military airline Transportes Aereos Militares on a non-scheduled domestic passenger flight from Fortin Campero to the city of Tarija, the aircraft was reported missing at 17:30 local time, possibly having been diverted by bad weather conditions. Wreckage was later found on a mountain about 100 miles (150km) north-east of its destination, with no survivors among the 20 persons aboard, which included a crew of four military personnel.

Date: 30 June 1959 (c.10:35)
Location: Okinawa, Ryukyu Islands
Operator: US Air Force
Aircraft type: North American F-100D (55-3633A)

A fire and having been abandoned by its pilot, the jet fighter crashed in a residential area in the village of Ishikawa, located 40 miles (65km) north-east of Naha, exploding on impact and hurling debris into a school compound. Five of the 17 persons killed on the ground were children, as were most of the other 169 who suffered injuries. The aircraft, which

was on a functional check flight following a time compliance technical order (TCTO) modification, had taken off from Kadena Air Base, and after climbing to an approximate height of 1,200ft (350m) and accelerating to nearly 300mph (480kph) with the afterburner on, the power plant compartment fire warning light illuminated. The pilot then jettisoned two empty fuel tanks and a bomb rack, which fell into the sea, and retarded power, whereupon the light went out. After turning back and while approaching to land, he initiated a go-around for reasons that were not disclosed, but at that instant an explosion occurred in the aircraft. Although it was headed toward an unpopulated area when he ejected, the fighter subsequently veered to the right, and following the accidental deployment of its drag chute and a second explosion, it slammed into some houses. The pilot landed safely by parachute, without injury. In all, 27 dwellings were destroyed or badly damaged. The local weather at the time consisted of scattered clouds at 1,000ft (300m), with a visibility beneath them of 40 miles (65km) and a slight breeze from the west.

Date: 26 February 1960 (c.13:00)
Location: Rio de Janeiro, Brazil

First aircraft
Operator: US Navy
Type: Douglas R6D-1 (131582)

Second aircraft
Operator: Consorcio REAL Aerovias Nacional
Type: Douglas DC-3 (PP-AXD)

Both aircraft were approaching to land, the military transport at Galeao Airport and the

A North American F-100 Super Sabre, the US Air Force's first operational supersonic jet fighter and type that crashed into the village on Okinawa. (AP/Wide World Photos)

Brazilian airliner at Santos-Dumont Airport, when they collided in mid-air, and both then plummeted into Guanabara Bay. The disaster claimed the lives of 61 persons, all but three passengers among the 38 American servicemen aboard the R6D, including the crew of seven, and all 26 aboard the DC-3 (22 passengers and four crew members). Among the victims from the former aircraft were members of a US Navy band that was to have played for the visiting American President, Dwight D. Eisenhower. Operating under instrument flight rules, the military transport was en route from Buenos Aires, Argentina, and the commercial one, operating under visual flight rules, near the end of a scheduled domestic service from Vitoria, Espirito Santo. The local weather at the time consisted of a broken layer of strato-cumulus clouds at about 2,300ft (700m) and a solid overcast at approximately 10,000ft (3,000m). As it converged with the eastbound DC-3, the northbound R6D was believed to have emerged from a cloud just before the accident, which did not give its crew sufficient time to initiate evasive action. The airline pilots probably never saw the Navy aircraft. In the subsequent collision, which occurred at an estimated altitude of 5,000ft (1,500m) and some 2½ miles (4km) south of

Diagram showing the flight paths of the US Navy transport and the Brazilian airliner that collided over Guanabara Bay. (International Civil Aviation Organisation)

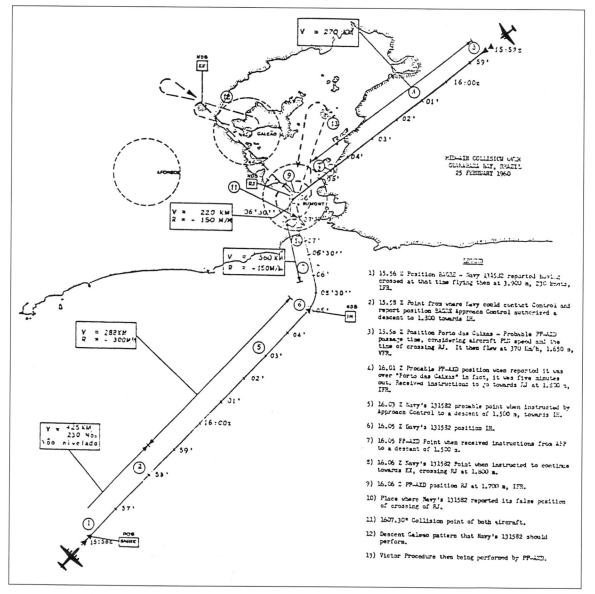

Santos-Dumont Airport, both the right wing of PP-AXD and the aft fuselage section of 131582 were severed. The three men who miraculously survived without serious injury were in the rear-facing seats in that part of the R6D, which dropped into the water in an oscillating motion similar to a falling leaf. Most of the wreckage from the two aircraft was subsequently recovered from the bay, as were the bodies of those killed. Brazilian authorities attributed the disaster to 'improper piloting procedure' by the crew of the military transport, who reportedly disobeyed the instructions of approach control to descend before reaching the Ilha Rasa non-directional beacon. Conducting its own investigation, the US Navy came to a different conclusion, blaming the actions of the air-traffic controller, specifically, his uncertainty as to the original position of the commercial flight; under-estimation of time factors, including that related to aircraft reaction, and a lack of appreciation of communications difficulties and the increasing seriousness of the situation, which it said created the conditions that ultimately led to the collision. Other factors that it said could have played a role in the accident included the absence of modern navigational aids and air-traffic control facilities on the ground, and the role of language differences. With regard to the latter, Naval authorities noted that while English was used in air/ground communications, pilots and controllers often had difficulty understanding one another because of their accents. Furthermore, in this particular case, the controller's instructions to PP-AXD were given in Portuguese, preventing the American crew from determining the height and anticipated flight path of the airliner. According to the Navy report, its conclusion reportedly based on his own testimony,

the controller believed that the R6D was considerably higher than the DC-3 and intentionally reversed his earlier instructions, ie, for the former to descend and the latter to remain at 6,000ft (1,800).

Date: 6 July 1960 (c.14:30)
Location: Off New Jersey, US
Operator: US Navy
Aircraft type: Goodyear ZPG-3W (144242)

The helium-filled blimp crashed in the Atlantic Ocean about 10 miles (15km) east of Barnegat City, killing 18 men. Three other members of the crew, all of whom suffered injuries, were rescued. Searchers later recovered the bodies of 13 victims, all but one of whom had drowned, and most of the airship's wreckage, which had sunk in water some 75ft (20m) deep. According to a Navy investigative report, the accident resulted from the failure of a seam in the envelope, which was apparently related to some factor that degraded the cement adhesion, and the subsequent shearing of the stitching of the fabric. Starting at the top of the envelope, the tear occurred about a third of the way from the front, and after its forward section collapsed, the blimp plunged nose-first into the ocean from an approximate height of 800ft (250m). The weather, which at the time consisted of a broken overcast, a visibility in excess of 10 miles (15km) and a south-south-easterly wind of around 15 knots, was not considered a factor. Just over 400ft (120m) long, 144242 had been delivered to the Navy less than six months earlier, one of the ZPG-3W class airships designed for the mission of airborne early warning, and at the time of the accident it was searching for two missing

A US Navy airship of the Goodyear ZPG-3W class, one of which was lost off the New Jersey coast on 6 July 1960. (UPI/Corbis-Bettmann)

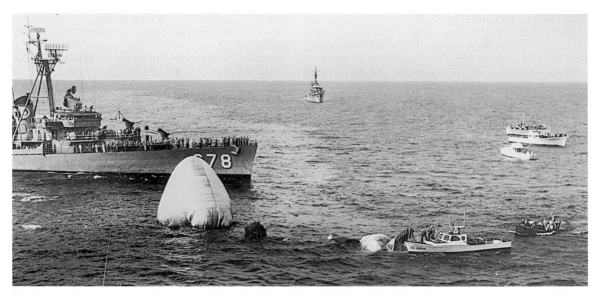

Surface craft converge on the scene where the Navy blimp fell into the Atlantic Ocean after envelope failure, killing 18 crewmen. (UPI/Corbis-Bettmann)

yachts, both of which were later found safe. Lighter-than-air operations in the US Navy would end soon afterwards, with the rest of its blimps being retired the following year.

Date: 11 July 1960 (c.11:45)
Location: Near Quito, Ecuador
Operator: US Air Force
Aircraft type: Douglas C-47E (45-1109A)

Its passengers comprised mostly of American military dependents and Ecuadorean civilians, the twin-engine transport crashed and burned on Mount Pichincha about 10 miles (15km) west of the Ecuadorean capital, where it was to have landed during a flight from Bogotá, Colombia. All 18 persons aboard, including four US Air Force crewmen, were killed. The aircraft struck the volcano at an approximate elevation of 13,000ft (4,000m). Although the meteorological conditions in the area were generally good, the Pinchincha Pass was heavily overcast, with one patch of rain, and the mountain itself cloud-obscured. Although the Air Force did not disclose its findings as to the probable cause of the crash, the investigative report did note, significantly, that at the time the crew had been operating under visual flight rules.

Date: 19 July 1960 (c.13:45)
Location: Near Goma, Kivu, Belgian Congo (Zaire)
Operator: Force Aérienne Belge (Royal Belgian Air Force)
Aircraft type: Fairchild C-119G (CP-36)

The twin-engine transport crashed and burned on a mountain north of Lake Kivu, and all but four of the 41 Belgian military personnel aboard were killed, including the crew of four. All of the survivors suffered injuries. Flying from Belgium, the aircraft had experienced the failure of a power plant, and considering the mountainous terrain and high temperature factor, it was unable to maintain altitude on the remaining engine. Contributing to the accident were the adverse weather conditions, with clouds obscuring the terrain.

Date: 17 August 1960 (c.23:45)
Location: Near El Kelaa, Morocco
Operator: Aeronavale (French Naval Aviation)
Aircraft type: Avro Lancaster 1 (WU-26)

All 20 French servicemen aboard were killed in the crash of the four-engine bomber, which occurred in darkness 100 miles (150km) south of Casablanca. The aircraft had been en route to Agadir, Morocco, from Istres, France, the final segment of a flight originating at Le Bourget Airport, near Paris, when the pilot reported one power plant was afire and that he had turned back in an attempt to reach Casablanca.

Date: 22 September 1960 (time unknown)
Location: North Pacific Ocean
Operator: US Marine Corps
Aircraft type: Douglas R5D-3 (56541)

The four-engine transport, carrying 29 American servicemen (23 passengers and a crew of six), had been en route from the naval base near Atsugi, Japan, to the installation at Subi Point, in the Philippines, when it sent a radio message reporting a fire in the No. 3 power plant and that it was diverting to Okinawa. In its last transmission, sent shortly after 14:00 local time, the aircraft was reported maintaining a height of 6,500ft (1,980m) and on a heading of 339 degrees, and also requested air/sea rescue assistance. Less than two hours later, floating debris was sighted from the air, the R5D having crashed at sea approximately 180 miles (290km) south of Naha, the capital of the island. Some 770lb (350kg) of wreckage from 56541 was subsequently recovered, much of it showing signs of flash burning, but no survivors or bodies were found. An investigative board could not determine the cause of the crash with certainty. According to available evidence, the most probable sequence of events was that the blaze reported in the No. 3 engine nacelle had been extinguished, but that a residual fire continued to burn, igniting one or both tyres on the right main undercarriage leg, and that one or both then exploded, rupturing the adjacent integral wing fuel tank. Fuel from the breached tank could then have created a combustible fuel/air mixture, resulting in a second explosion that either led to the break-up of the aircraft or significantly affected its airworthiness. The R5D probably disintegrated when it struck the surface of the water, with a flash fire possibly occurring on impact. The in-flight blaze was believed to have originated from an unidentified electrical or mechanical malfunction or from the detonation of an incendiary device that had been planted aboard prior to take-off. No unusual weather conditions were known to have existed along the route taken by 56541.

Date: 11 December 1960 (c.19:50)
Location: Near San Andres de Giles, Buenos Aires, Argentina
Operator: Fuerza Aérea Argentina (Argentine Air Force)
Aircraft type: Avro Lancastrian IV (T-102)

Operated by the Correo Aereo Militar al Exterior (CAME) courier branch on a passenger/mail service to the city of Buenos Aires from Lima, Peru, the four-engine transport crashed and exploded 100 miles (150km) west-north-west of its intended destination, the accident occurring around dusk and during a heavy rain and low overcast. All 31 persons aboard, including a crew of eight military personnel, were killed. The primary cause of the crash was pilot error, specifically, the continuation under visual flight rules (VFR) procedures into the adverse meteorological conditions, coupled with instrument failure. A contributing factor was considered to be the weather itself.

Date: 17 December 1960 (c.14:10)
Location: Munich, West Germany
Operator: US Air Force
Aircraft type: Convair C-131D (55-291)

Nearly all of the passengers on this flight to England were American college students, the children of American military personnel, who had been returning to their families for the Christmas holiday. Bound for Royal Air Force, Northolt, London, the twin-engine transport had been airborne for only about a minute when the co-pilot radioed that it was returning to Riem Airport, serving Munich, from where it had taken off, its left propeller having been feathered. Shortly thereafter, in response to a request by the radar controller to ascend to 3,000ft (1,000m), the same crewman reported that the aircraft, then at a height of 2,200ft (670m), was unable to climb. His voice sounding excited, he also requested the airport crash crew to stand by. Subsequently, and while on an approximate heading of 320 degrees and at a height of about 470ft (140m) above the ground, 55-291 struck, with its port wing, a steeple of St Paul's Cathedral church, plummeted into a business section of the city, crashing in an almost inverted, left wing-low attitude, then exploded and burned. The disaster claimed the lives of 33 persons on the ground, nearly half of whom had been riding in a

A US Air Force Convair C-131 transport, the type involved in the disastrous Munich crash on 17 December 1960, which claimed 53 lives. (General Dynamics)

The wrecked German streetcar continues to smoulder after being struck by the crashing American military aircraft. (AP/Wide World Photos)

streetcar that was struck by an engine and gutted by fire, and all 20 occupants of the aircraft. Among the latter, one passenger and the seven crew members were American military personnel. About a dozen others suffered injuries. At the time, the weather in the area was characterised by an indefinite ceiling of 100 to 150ft (30–50m), with a visibility of approximately half-a-mile (0.8km) and a 7-knot wind from an east-north-easterly direction. And with the temperature below freezing, the conditions were conducive to carburettor icing, which could have caused a power loss. Significantly, examination of the power plant that was reported to have malfunctioned revealed a collection of water in the inlet side of the left fuel tank booster pump, and disassembly of the pump disclosed even more water. It was further noted in the investigative report that difficulty had been experienced in starting both engines. However, the exact cause of the crash was not disclosed by military authorities.

Date: 26 January 1961 (time unknown)
Location: North Atlantic Ocean
Operator: US Air Force
Aircraft type: Douglas C-118A (51-17626)

Operated by the Military Air Transport Service, the aircraft crashed while en route from the Azores to the air base at Argentia, Newfoundland, Canada, one segment of a transtlantic flight origi-

nating at Kenitra (Port Lyautey), Morocco, with an ultimate destination of Norfolk Naval Air Station, in Virginia, US. The crew of another American military aircraft flying in the area reported seeing a mid-air explosion in the pre-dawn darkness, at around 03:30 local time, about 25 miles (40km) north-east of Argentia, but a subsequent search found no trace of the four-engine transport or any of the 23 persons aboard, most of whom were American servicemen, including a crew of 10 Navy personnel. Due to certain classified aspects of this particular operation, no further details were released concerning the loss of 51-17626.

Date: 25 March 1961 (time unknown)
Location: Near Natal, Rio Grande do Norte, Brazil
Operator: Força Aérea Brasileira (Brazilian Air Force)
Aircraft type: Douglas C-47 (C-47.2055)

The twin-engine transport crashed as it was attempting to land at the local airport, and 22 persons aboard were killed, including the two-member flight crew, both military personnel. Seven other passengers survived the accident, which occurred during an internal flight from Rio de Janeiro to Belem.

Date: 6 April 1962 (c.15:00)
Location: Near Villavicencio, Meta, Colombia
Operator: Fuerza Aérea Colombiana (Colombian Air Force)
Aircraft type: Douglas C-47 (FAC-563)

The twin-engine transport, which had last stopped at Araracuara during an internal flight originating at Bogotá, crashed on a mountain about 60 miles (100km) from the Apiay military base, located near Villavicencio, where it was to have landed. All 31 persons aboard perished, including a crew of five military personnel; the passengers included prison officials and five inmates on parole. The wreckage of the aircraft was located the following day at an approximate elevation of 11,500ft (3,500m). Proceeding in adverse meteorological conditions, the C-47 was some 10 degrees off the prescribed course at the time of impact, the deviation probably attributable to the easterly winds it had encountered. An additional significant factor was the absence of ground navigational aids along the route.

Date: 8 May 1962 (time unknown)
Location: Eastern Burma
Operator: Union of Burma Air Force
Aircraft type: Douglas C-47 (UB-BG707)

All 32 persons aboard lost their lives when the twin-engine transport crashed and burned in a ravine about 400 miles (650km) north-east of

Rangoon and approximately 5 miles (10km) north-west of Mong Pa Liao, from where it had taken off shortly before, on an internal flight with an ultimate destination of Mandalay. The passengers included 11 civilians; the rest of those killed in the afternoon accident were Burmese military personnel, including the four members of the aircraft's crew. According to a military source, power plant failure was suspected as the cause of the crash.

Date: 22 May 1962 (c.11:40)
Location: Near Markt Schwaben, West Germany
Operator: US Navy
Aircraft type: Lockheed WV-2Q (131390)

The four-engine radar intelligence aircraft, which was on a navigational training exercise, crashed and burned about 10 miles (15km) east of Munich, after experiencing catastrophic structural failure. All 26 American servicemen aboard, including four Army personnel designated as observers, perished. Departing earlier in the morning from Rhein-Main Air Base, near Frankfurt, the WV-2 had last acknowledged ascending out of flight level 170 before twice broadcasting the message, 'Munich, 131390 … Request emergency landing at your field, immediately! Over'. The aircraft began to disintegrate at an approximate altitude of 18,000ft (5,500m), the break-up, which was almost instantaneous, involving the separation of the empennage, followed by the left wing and all but one power plant. Major components were scattered over an area of approximately 10 square miles (15 sq km), although the dispersal of classified documents that were being carried aboard it extended more than 40 miles (65km). It was of the opinion of an investigative board that the initial fracture in the fuselage of 131390 resulted from a combination of a large sized force imposed on the aft section at a time the cabin had been substantially pressurised. This led to an explosive decompression and the more general disintegration of the aircraft. The nature of the emergency that occurred prior to the break-up, and which prompted the distress message, could not be determined, but was definitely not related to a control system malfunction. Possible reasons for the original emergency included an in-flight fire in the forward fuselage area, or an uncontrollable propeller. It was noted in the accident report, however, that the latter would be expected to have caused some internal damage to the power plant, which should have been evident upon examination. The weather was not a factor. In the recommendations portion of the report, it was noted that administrative procedures of the squadron that operated the WV-2 were considered lacking to assure the required inspections of aircraft, and that 84 discrepancies in 131390 had been recorded in pilots' and maintenance forms, even though no definite trends towards a possible cause or factor in the crash could

A US Navy WV-2 radar intelligence/early warning aircraft, similar to the one that crashed following catastrophic break-up over West Germany. (UPI/ Corbis-Bettmann)

be made from this information. It was further noted that while also not a precipitating element in its loss, the WV-2 had been some 2,300lb (1,050kg) overweight.

Date: 10 September 1962 (c.11:05)
Location: Near Milan, Washington, US
Operator: US Air Force
Aircraft type: Boeing KC-135A (60-352)

Operated by the Strategic Air Command, the jet tanker crashed in mountainous terrain about 30 miles (50km) north-east of Fairchild Air Force Base, located near Spokane, where it was to have landed. All 44 men aboard perished, including a crew of four; except for one civilian passenger, the victims were Air Force personnel. The accident occurred near the end of an internal US passenger flight from Ellsworth Air Force Base, in South Dakota. Its undercarriage down and flaps retracted, the aircraft was longitudinally level but banked slightly to the right when it slammed into a wooded slope at an approximate elevation of 4,400ft (1,350m), exploded and burned during the approach to Runway 23 utilising very-high-frequency omni-directional range (VOR) and instrument landing system (ILS) procedures. At the moment of impact, it was completing a right turn in order to effect alignment with the 20-degree radial

Date: 30 January 1963 (c.02:00)
Location: North Atlantic Ocean
Operator: US Navy
Aircraft type: Lockheed P-3A (149672)

One of the first of the then-new four-engine turboprop patrol aircraft to be delivered to the Navy, 149672 had been in service only about half-a-year and was participating in an anti-submarine warfare (ASW) training exercise when it crashed approximately 250 miles (400km) east-south-east of Atlantic City, New Jersey, US, in an area where the depth of the water was around 12,000ft (3,700m). Searchers recovered some wreckage and the body of the aircraft commander, but there were no survivors among the 14 crewmen assigned to 149672. As part of the exercise, the P-3 was to have conducted a mock search and attack on an American submarine, although the location of the crash indicated that the crew may have been pursuing a false contact. No distress message from 149672 was heard, and examination of recovered debris indicated a post-impact fire or explosion, but no such in-flight occurrence. Nor was there evidence that the survival equipment found floating in the ocean had been used. It was dark at the time, and the weather in the area consisted of scattered clouds, with bases of 2,500 to 3,000ft (750–1,000m) and a visibility of 10 miles (c.15km). The moon and stars could not be seen due to the overcast, and there was no visible horizon or any outside visual references. The aircraft had been engaged in low-altitude ASW tactics when it crashed, but neither the cause nor its final manoeuvres before impact could be determined. Though the pilot may have flown it into the water, when considering his experience and qualifications, a Navy board of inquiry considered it more likely that some extenuating circumstances came into play. Perhaps significant were a number of shortcomings identified in the aircraft type. Tests indicated performance limitations with respect to weak static longitudinal stability that resulted in poor trim characteristics during ASW operations, when accurate manoeuvering close to the water is required. Experience also showed that the altitude hold feature of the automatic flight control system had a tendency to disengage without apparent warning at low altitudes due to fluctuating signals in its APN-117 radar altimeter. And if electrical power were to be lost, the altimeter would continue to indicate the last reading without a system failure warning to the crew. Since standard operating procedures for most pilots was to fly with the autopilot on and the altitude hold engaged, such a situation could create a false sense of security in the event of such a power loss, a fact of which most P-3 crews were found to be unaware. Subsequent modifications were made in the type to correct oscillations of the altimeter, provide red flashing lights to warn of altimeter

A swath was cut in the forest by the KC-135 jet tanker, which crashed while approaching to land at Fairchild Air Force Base. (AP/Wide World Photos)

of the Mead VOR station, and proceeding on a magnetic heading of 195 degrees, having failed to level off at the proper altitude. The local weather at the time of the accident consisted of a scattered to broken overcast at around 1,000ft (300m) and another cloud layer at 8,000ft (c.2,500m), with a visibility of 25 miles (40km). Although specific details were not disclosed by the Air Force, the primary cause of the crash was believed to have been an error by the navigator of 60-352.

disengagement and of masking the drive pointer of the APN-117 when the altitude hold feature is engaged. Such changes were incorporated into aircraft in production, and retrofit kits used to modify those already in service. Until these corrective actions were completed, the type was restricted to a minimum height of 500ft (150m) at night or in instrument flight rules conditions during ASW missions.

Date: 26 June 1963 (c.12:00)
Location: Near Augustdorf, West Germany
Operator: Force Aérienne Belge (Royal Belgian Air Force)
Aircraft type: Fairchild C-119 (CP-45)

The twin-engine transport, its passengers all Belgian Army paratroopers, crashed in flames about 5 miles (10km) south-west of Detmold after a freak case of 'friendly fire', and 38 servicemen aboard were killed, including the crew of five Belgian Air Force personnel. Nine paratroopers jumped from the stricken aircraft and survived. Following a flight originating at Melsbroek Air Base, near Brussels, Belgium, the C-119 was to have landed at Gutersloh Air Base, but during a ground-controlled approach, it passed over the Sennelager military camp and firing range and was hit accidentally on one wing by a phosphorus mortar shell fired by a British Army unit. The splash of this incandescent agent immediately set the aircraft afire, both externally and internally, and the intensity of the blaze was increased by the fact that its fuel tanks and crew oxygen supply system were also hit. Rendered uncontrollable by the fire, CP-45 ultimately plummeted to the ground from an approximate height of 2,500ft (750m). At the time, the local weather was cloudy, with 4/8 coverage at 3,000ft (1,000m) and a visibility of about 15 miles (25km). According to a British military spokesman, aircraft flying over the firing range were to remain above an altitude of 10,000ft (3,000m) to ensure their safety.

Date: 28 August 1963 (c.12:30)
Location: North Atlantic Ocean

First aircraft
Operator: US Air Force
Type: Boeing KC-135A (61-0319)

Second aircraft
Operator: US Air Force
Type: Boeing KC-135A (61-0322)

The two Strategic Air Command jet tankers had just finished refuelling three B-47 jet bombers, whose crews reported that they had turned west before losing sight of them when their own aircraft entered a deck of cirrus clouds. Nothing further was heard from either KC-135, and the following day

The Lockheed P-3A Orion anti-submarine/patrol aircraft suffered its first major crash about half-a-year after the type became operational with the US Navy. (Lockheed Martin)

searchers sighted flier-type life jackets floating in the water some 700 miles (1,125km) north-east of Homestead Air Force Base, in Florida, US, itself located about 25 miles (40km) south-west of Miami and where both were stationed. Some debris identified as belonging to both tankers was subsequently recovered from the water, but no trace could be found of the 11 crewmen assigned to the two aircraft, six from 0319 and five from 0322. In an investigative report, the loss of the two tankers was ascribed to an 'apparent' mid-air collision, the exact circumstances of which were unknown.

Date: 18 October 1963 (time unknown)
Location: Near Aswan, Egypt
Operator: Soviet Air Force
Aircraft type: Antonov An-12

During an attempted landing at Aswan Airport, in evening darkness and conditions of reduced visibility due to blowing sand, the four-engine turboprop transport crashed and burned, killing all 31 military personnel aboard, including a Soviet crew. The passengers were all Egyptians. No additional information about the accident was disclosed.

Date: 8 May 1964 (c.20:20)
Location: Near Santa Rosa, Lima, Peru
Operator: Fuerza Aérea Argentina (Argentine Air Force)
Aircraft type: Douglas C-54 (T-47)

The four-engine transport, which was operated by the Correo Aereo Militar al Exterior courier branch, had been on a regular service originating at Buenos Aires, Argentina. The C-54 was carrying as passengers, both military personnel and civilians, when it crashed and burned 20 miles (30km) north of the city of Lima, where it was to have landed. All but three of the 49 persons aboard the aircraft lost their lives; the survivors, consisting of two children and a member of the crew of seven, suffered serious injuries. Its undercarriage extended, the C-54 slammed into a sand dune during the final phase of the approach to Lima-Callao International Airport, the crash occurring in darkness and instrument meteorological conditions, with heavy fog. The accident was attributed to improper instrument flight rules procedures on the part of the pilot.

Date: 11 May 1964 (c.19:20)
Location: Near Angeles, Papanga, the Philippines
Operator: US Air Force
Aircraft type: Boeing C-135B (61-0332)

Operated by the Military Air Transport Service and carrying mostly US Air Force and Navy enlisted men, the jet transport crashed and burned while attempting to land at Clark Air Base, located about 50 miles (80km) north-west of Manila, in the process hitting a taxi-cab that had been travelling along Mitchell Highway. Except for two Chinese Nationalist passengers, the 79 military personnel killed in the disaster were Americans, including five

of the aircraft's 10 crew members, and one riding in the vehicle. The five survivors from the C-135, including the pilot and co-pilot, and the other occupants of the taxi suffered serious injuries. Having completed a transpacific flight from the US, which had originated at Travis Air Force Base in California and stopped at Hickam Air Force Base in Hawaii, the aircraft began a precision radar (PAR) approach to Runway 02 in darkness and adverse meteorological conditions, with thunderstorm activity, heavy rain showers and an indefinite ceiling of 300ft (100m). Just before the accident the winds, which were blowing at around 20 knots, had shifted from a north-easterly direction to almost due north. At a point some 3 miles (5km) from the threshold, it first descended below the glide path, and this deviation continued despite three advisories from the PAR controller. About 2 miles (3km) out, it exceeded the PAR lower safety limit, whereupon the controller advised the crew to initiate a go-around. Almost immediately, however, the co-pilot reported the runway in sight. The transport was then given the radio frequency of the control tower, which in turn transmitted the latest wind information and gave it landing clearance. The extended undercarriage initially struck the top of a base perimeter fence approximately 7ft (2m) above the ground and some 3,500ft (1,050m) from the threshold of the runway but on its extended centreline, and the aircraft then clipped a tower with its left wing and finally slammed to earth. Crossing the highway, it broke apart, ultimately coming to rest around 2,000ft (600m) from the end of the runway and approximately 300ft (100m) to the left of the extended centreline. The factors leading to the unstabilised approach and the crash itself were not disclosed by the Air Force. It was noted in the investigative report, however, that just before the accident the visibility had improved slightly, to about 1.2 miles (2km).

A US Air Force Boeing C-135B Stratolifter jet transport, identical to the aircraft that crashed at Clark Air Base in the Philippines. (Boeing)

Date: 4 September 1964 (c.19:00)
Location: Near Vaong Nong, Thailand
Operator: Royal Thai Air Force
Aircraft type: Douglas C-47

The twin-engine transport, carrying Thai military personnel and their dependents, crashed and burst into flames 200 miles (320km) north-east of Bangkok and approximately 1.2 miles (2km) from the airport serving Ubol, where it was to have landed. Killed in the accident were 28 of the 34 persons aboard the aircraft; the survivors suffered various injuries. Having nearly completed an internal flight from Khoke Kathiam, the C-47 struck a tree and slammed to earth during its landing approach, the crash occurring in darkness and conditions of poor visibility. No information regarding the probable cause of the accident was disclosed.

Date: 19 October 1964 (c.11:35)
Location: Near Belgrade, Yugoslavia
Operator: Soviet Air Force
Aircraft type: Ilyushin Il-18

The four-engine turboprop transport crashed while attempting to land at Surcin Airport, located 10 miles (15km) west of Belgrade, following a flight from Moscow, USSR. All 33 persons aboard were killed, including a crew of 11; among the passengers were seven high-ranking Soviet military officers, one of them the nation's Army Chief of Staff, Marshal Sergei S. Biryuzov. Instructed by the control tower to approach from the west, the aircraft was reportedly 'too low and not on course' when it struck 1,700ft (520m) Avala Hill, approximately 120ft (35m) below its peak, exploding on impact. The weather at the time consisted of rain and fog, with winds of around 25 knots. This aircraft

may have been part of the fleet of the Soviet airline Aeroflot.

Date: 11 December 1964 (time unknown)
Location: Near Da Nang, South Vietnam
Operator: (South) Vietnamese Air Force
Aircraft type: Fairchild C-123

All 38 servicemen aboard lost their lives when the twin-engine transport slammed into a mountain north of Da Nang Air Base, from where it had taken off shortly before. Except for two American passengers, the victims were South Vietnamese military personnel, including the crew of six. The crash occurred in evening darkness and during what was described as a 'secret' mission, but no further details were made available.

Date: 16 January 1965 (c.09:30)
Location: Wichita, Kansas, US
Operator: US Air Force
Aircraft type: Boeing KC-135A (57-1442)

The Strategic Air Command jet tanker crashed and exploded in a residential section of the city approximately 5 miles (10km) north-north-west of McConnell Air Force Base, from where it had taken off about 3½ minutes earlier, on an aerial refuelling mission. All seven crewmen of the aircraft and 22 persons on the ground, the latter including a pregnant woman, perished in the disaster, while 17 others suffered injuries. In the impact and resulting fires, 14 houses were demolished. The scene of the tragedy was 10 blocks west of Wichita State University. Following its departure from Runway 36-Left, the aircraft had climbed to an approximate height of 500 to 700ft (150–200m) before it started to descend. A 'Mayday' distress message was transmitted from the tanker, and the crew escape hatch

A number of houses were levelled or set ablaze by the crash of the US Air Force KC-135 in a neighbourhood of Wichita, Kansas, US. (AP/Wide World Photos)

had been jettisoned prior to the crash, further indication of an in-flight emergency. According to witnesses, the KC-135 initiated a left bank while proceeding in a southerly direction, trying to return to the base, and completed a rotation of about 180 degrees as it plunged to earth in a steep nose-down attitude. The weather at the time was clear and cold, with high cirrus clouds and a north-north-easterly wind of 5 knots. Remains of a parachute were found in the No.1 engine of 57-1442, which could have resulted in an asymmetrical thrust condition. The control difficulties that may have factored in the crash would have been even worse had it also become entangled in one of the aircraft's ailerons.

Date: 15 June 1965 (c.09:50)
Location: Near Columbus, Georgia, US

First aircraft
Operator: US Army
Type: Bell UH-1D (63-8760)

Second aircraft
Operator: US Army
Type: Bell UH-1D (63-8840)

During a tactical troop lift operation, the two turbine-engine helicopters collided in mid-air and crashed at the Fort Benning military base about 5 miles north-north-west of the town of Cusseta, killing 18 American servicemen. There were no survivors among the occupants of either aircraft, 10 aboard 8760 and eight aboard 8840; the victims

One engine of the US Air Force C-135A jet transport lies on the ridge struck by the aircraft following take-off from the El Toro Marine Corps Air Station. (UPI/Corbis-Bettmann)

included a three-member crew assigned to each aircraft. The two involved in the accident were among eight UH-1D helicopters flying in two groups of four aircraft each. After the pilot of the lead helicopter of one approximately diamond-shaped formation decided to leave the flight for a weather check, he radioed his intentions to the No. 2 aircraft, 8760, in front of which he would make his turn, assuming that the No. 3, 8840, which was to his left rear, would remain in position. But when the flight leader accelerated and initiated a climbing right turn, the No. 3 inexplicably turned the same direction, as if to follow, while the No. 2 made a slight left turn. The resulting collision occurred at an above-ground height of approximately 300 to 350ft (100–105m), despite an evasive bank by 8840. Both helicopters lost their main rotor blades and plummeted to earth, and 8760 burned after its impact with the ground. The fourth UH-1D in the group banked to the right and managed to avoid the flying debris. Despite rain showers in the vicinity, the meteorological conditions were apparently good at the time and location of the accident.

Date: 25 June 1965 (01:46)
Location: Near Santa Ana, California, US
Operator: US Air Force
Aircraft type: Boeing C-135A (60-0373)

Operated by the Military Air Transport Service and bound for Okinawa, with a planned stop at Hickam Air Force Base, in Hawaii, US, the jet transport crashed 40 miles (65km) south-east of Los Angeles, about a minute after its departure from El Toro Marine Corps Air Station. All 85 American servicemen aboard perished, including a crew of 12 Air Force personnel; the passengers were members of the Marine Corps. After taking off from Runway 34R, the aircraft struck Loma Ridge at an approximate elevation of 1,000ft (300m), or only about 200ft (60m) below its crest, some 3 miles (5km) north-north-west of the base, exploding on impact. The crash occurred in darkness, and the meteorological conditions in the area at the time consisted of light drizzle, fog and a low overcast, with broken clouds at 500ft (150m) and solid coverage at 900ft (275m), and a visibility of 3 miles (5km). The wind was from due south at 4 knots. For undetermined reasons, 60-0373 had failed to make a left proce-dural turn following take-off, and as a result flew into the rising terrain.

Date: 6 July 1965 (c.16:00)
Location: Near Oxford, England
Operator: Royal Air Force
Aircraft type: Handley Page Hastings C Mark 1 (TG577)

The four-engine transport, which was on a paratroop dropping sortie, crashed 35 miles

(55km) north-west of London, and all 41 British servicemen aboard perished, including a crew of six. The passengers consisted of both Army and RAF personnel. Soon after it had taken off from Abingdon airfield, a member of the flight crew reported control difficulties and that the aircraft needed to return for an immediate landing. Granted such clearance, TG577 was south-east of the base when it abruptly climbed to an approximate height of 2,000ft (600m), then turned to the left, plummeted to earth and exploded. The accident was attributed to the fatigue fracture of the two upper bolts that attached the right outer elevator out-rigger to the drag member of the horizontal stabiliser. As a result, the outer portion of the elevator became uncontrollable. It was the opinion of a

Top *An RAF Transport Command Handley Page Hastings of the type that crashed near Oxford, England, on 6 July 1965.* (British Aerospace)

Bottom *A helicopter swoops low over the smouldering wreckage of the RAF transport after the accident that killed 41 servicemen.* (AP/Wide World Photos)

board of inquiry that abnormal friction in the bearings due to the distortion of the hinge line, coupled with the drooping of the outer half of the elevator, produced the abnormal pitch-up and subsequent stall. The weather at the time was good and did not factor in the crash. A temporary grounding of the entire RAF Hastings fleet was required in order to complete inspections and required modifications.

Date: 7 July 1965 (time unknown)
Location: Near Cairo, Egypt
Operator: Soviet Air Force
Aircraft type: Antonov An-12

The four-engine turboprop transport, its passengers all Egyptian Army soldiers, crashed and burned shortly after taking off from Almaza Airport, on a flight to Yemen. All but one of the 31 servicemen aboard the aircraft were killed, the sole survivor being one member of the crew of nine Soviet Air Force personnel.

Date: 25 July 1965 (c.07:40)
Location: Near Libacao, Aklan, the Philippines
Operator: Philippine Air Force
Aircraft type: Douglas C-47 (777)

All 37 persons aboard perished when the twin-engine transport, on a domestic flight to San Jose Buenavista, Antique, from Nichols Air Base, located near Manila, crashed and burned on Panay Island, 60 miles (100km) north-north-east of its destination. The victims included seven military crewmen, but more than half of the passengers were civilians. Last reported cruising at 7,000ft (2,000m), the southbound aircraft had struck a wooded, north-eastern slope of Mount Madiac, the accident occurring in adverse weather conditions consisting of low clouds and rain. Wreckage was located three days later at an approximate elevation of 6,000ft (1,800m), which was no less than 1,000ft (300m) from the top of the mountain. At the time of impact, it was slightly off course, and although this deviation may have resulted from the winds it encountered, estimated to have been as high as 30 to 40 knots, no official findings pertaining to the cause of the crash were released by the Philippine Air Force.

Date: 24 August 1965 (c.10:10)
Location: Hong Kong
Operator: US Marine Corps
Aircraft type: Lockheed KC-130F (149802)

The four-engine turboprop tanker/transport crashed in Kowloon Bay immediately after it had taken off from Hong Kong (Kai Tak) International Airport, bound for Da Nang and Saigon, South Vietnam. Killed in the accident were

One wing is raised from Kowloon Bay near Hong Kong's international airport, the scene of the US Marine Corps KC-130 crash that claimed 59 lives. (Associated Press)

59 American servicemen aboard the aircraft, including one passenger who succumbed to his injuries about a week later and two members of the crew of six. The 12 survivors, among them both the pilot and co-pilot, suffered various injuries. This was a disaster that had its origin in material failure, but which ultimately resulted from what a board of investigation report would later deem as 'the negligence, inefficiency and exercise of poor judgement' on the part of a Marine captain, who was the designated aircraft commander of this particular flight. Some two weeks before the crash, 149802 had been grounded due to a malfunction in its No. 1 power plant; two days later, that engine was changed, but not the corresponding propeller. Difficulties with it persisted, however, right up to the take-off that ended in tragedy. With the No. 1 developing only partial power, the commander, who was in the right seat on the flight deck, announced to the pilot, in the left seat, that they would proceed on three engines. He also instructed the pilot, who had limited experience in the type, to fly the aircraft. The crew neither feathered the propeller of the malfunctioning power plant, nor trimmed the KC-130 Hercules for a three-engine take-off. When all four power levers were advanced as the No. 1 remained under only partial power, it created an asymmetrical condition. Despite the use of nosewheel steering, the pilot could not maintain directional control, and the transport began to drift to the left of Runway 13, after reaching a speed of about 100mph (150kph). Just before it departed the pavement, the flight engineer called 'Abort', and the pilot tried to reduce power, but immediately the commander blocked the power levers and commenced rotation. Rolling across an area of grass in a nose-high attitude, the aircraft became airborne and flew in a semi-stalled condition at a height of around 100 to 200ft (30–60m), while banked to the left, until its port wing struck a sea-wall, which was 6ft (2m) high, some 500ft (150m) to the left of the runway. After traversing a distance of approximately 800ft (250m) in the air, the Hercules finally crashed and caught fire about 400ft (120m) beyond the sea-wall, its undercarriage and flaps still extended at the moment of impact. All of the victims' bodies were subsequently recovered, their deaths attributed to drowning and/or the effects of the fire. Some of the occupants who managed to escape from the wreckage could not be rescued. At the time of the accident, the local weather conditions were good, the wind calm. Procedures outlined in the KC-130 pilot's handbook dictated that in a three-engine take-off, wherein an outboard power plant is inoperative, the opposite outboard one be placed at the flight idle position, while both inboard engines be advanced to take-off power. The operating outboard engine is then to be given increased power during the ground roll as directional control becomes available. Three-engine

take-offs were prohibited on passenger flights, but as the No. 1 power plant of 149802 was not totally inoperative, neither this restriction nor the engine-out procedure would have been technically applicable. Compounding the error by the aircraft commander was the fact that he had not been seated in the pilot's position, ie to the left on the flight deck, which initially deprived him of recognising the difficulty in controlling the direction of the take-off roll through contact with the nose wheel steering; and in surrendering operation of the power levers, he made possible what may well have been a critical reduction in power when his subordinate crewmen decided to abandon the take-off. Prior to the attempted take-off, the aircraft's No. 1 engine was determined to have been overspeeding slightly, and not developing enough power to offset the drag produced by the corresponding propeller. After switching to mechanical governing and shifting several times had no corrective effect on this condition, the commander elected to proceed on three engines. The board considered it possible that the same propeller had gone into reverse at a critical point, but this could not be proven because neither it nor the power plant itself were recovered from the water, as was most of the wreckage. Among the recommendations made in the accident report was one that action be taken within the squadron to which 149802 had belonged to promulgate and require compliance with the Naval Air Training and Operating Procedures Standardization Program (NATOPS).

Date: 2 November 1965 (time unknown)
Location: Obock, French Somaliland (Djibouti)
Operator: L'Armée de l'Air (French Air Force)
Aircraft type: Douglas C-47A (316410)

Operated by the Commandement du Transport Aerien Militaire branch and having completed a short flight from the city of Djibouti, the aircraft crashed and exploded while attempting to land at the local airport. Including a crew of five, all 30 French servicemen aboard the twin-engine transport lost their lives in the afternoon accident; the passengers were members of a hand-ball team. No further details about the crash or suspected cause were released.

Date: 3 November 1965 (c.07:30)
Location: Off Northern Panama
Operator: Fuerza Aérea Argentina (Argentine Air Force)
Aircraft type: Douglas C-54 (TC-48)

The four-engine transport crashed in the Caribbean Sea with 68 persons aboard, including a military crew of nine. No survivors or bodies were found, and searchers recovered only personal effects – clothing and life vests – floating in the Gulf

A US Air Force Fairchild C-123 transport, two of which were involved in fatal crashes in South Vietnam during the winter of 1965–66. (Fairchild Aircraft)

of Mosquitos near the mouth of the Miguel River. Most of its passengers consisting of Argentine Air Force cadets, the aircraft had been en route from Howard Air Force Base, located in the Canal Zone, to San Salvador, El Salvador, its first refuelling stop during a flight with an ultimate destination of the United States, when the pilot sent a distress message, reporting a fire in the No. 3 power plant, and announced he was diverting to Limon, Costa Rica. No determination was made as to the cause of the reported blaze.

Date: 11 December 1965 (c.15:00)
Location: Near Tuy Hoa, South Vietnam
Operator: US Air Force
Aircraft type: Fairchild C-123B (56-4376)

All 85 servicemen aboard perished when the twin-engine transport, which was on a South Vietnamese internal flight from Pleiku to the Tuy Hoa airfield, crashed about 20 miles (30km) west of

its destination and some 250 miles (400km) north-east of Saigon. The victims included a crew of four US Air Force personnel; the passengers were all troops of the Army of South Vietnam. Apparently proceeding on a south-easterly heading and probably descending, the aircraft initially hit trees atop a mountain at an approximate elevation of 4,000ft (1,200m). After continuing airborne a short distance farther, it fell vertically some 1,000ft (300m), and appeared to have struck the ground in a flat spin, with no forward velocity, then disintegrated and burned. The weather in the area at the time was characterised by low ceilings, which could have varied from 50 to 1,000ft (15–300m), as well as rain showers and variable winds. These conditions hampered the search for 56-4376 for nearly two weeks, after which its positive identification was made. Due to the fact that the crash occurred in hostile territory, in which there were concentrations of Viet Cong troops, neither recovery nor a ground examination of the aircraft's wreckage was possible.

1966–1990

Introduced during the Second World War and refined in Korea, the helicopter would finally make its mark as a useful military tool during the conflict in South-East Asia. Used primarily by US and South Vietnamese military forces, rotary-wing aircraft would prove their value by transporting troops into and evacuating them out of battle areas and, coupled with improved medical techniques, saving the lives of countless wounded soldiers. But the aircraft and their crews also paid a heavy price, with the US alone losing nearly 5,000 helicopters during its long involvement in the conflict. Large turboprop and jet transports also saw extensive use in the war. The two worst US military aviation disasters in fact took place in South Vietnam, one a combat loss and the other resulting from accidental causes; the second of these was the tragic C-5A babylift crash occurring in the final days before the collapse of South Vietnam. The former Soviet Union experienced its own Vietnam-type debacle in Afghanistan, suffering its own share of aircraft losses due to accidents or hostile action. One such combat loss resulted in the highest death toll ever in a single military aircraft disaster. Other 'brush' wars flared up during this period in Africa and Central America. Due to their willingness to share information, the majority of the accounts covered in the 25-year span of this section involved US military forces.

Date: 25 January 1966 (c.10:15)
Location: Near Binh Khe, South Vietnam
Operator: US Air Force
Aircraft type: Fairchild C-123B (54-702)

The twin-engine transport crashed and burned 300 miles (480km) north-east of Saigon and approximately 5 miles (10km) east of the An Khe airfield, from where it had taken off less than 10 minutes earlier. All 46 American servicemen aboard, including a crew of four Air Force personnel, were killed. The accident occurred as the aircraft was on a South Vietnamese internal flight to Bong Son, its passengers comprising army troops. Banked slightly to the right, the C-123 initially struck trees atop a 2,000ft (600m) hill, which sheared off about 20ft (6m) of its starboard wing and half of its horizontal stabiliser/elevator assembly. It then rolled uncontrollably to the right and slammed to earth inverted. At the time of the crash, the weather in the area consisted of broken clouds at 1,000ft (300m) and an overcast of 2,500ft (750m). Operating under a visual flight rules (VFR) clearance, 54-702 had last been observed proceeding normally in an easterly direction and at a low altitude below a ragged layer of clouds prior to the crash. An examination of the No. 2 power plant revealed that an in-flight magnesium fire had consumed the carburettor, accessory and blower sections, and that at the moment of impact the corresponding propeller was windmilling under little or no power. Of unknown significance was that the same engine had stopped twice on the ground before the transport took off. The exact cause of the blaze could not be determined, but all the components from the firewall to the point that the fuel entered the blower case to the fuel feed valve were suspected. Whatever maintenance or operating factors may have led or contributed to the accident were not disclosed by Air Force authorities. Noted in the investigative report were the hazards faced by such Vietnam-era flights, including hostile action, inadequate navigational aids and the fact that they were often conducted under VFR in marginal meteorological conditions.

Date: 4 May 1966 (c.08:00)
Location: Near Di Linh, South Vietnam
Operator: US Army
Aircraft type: Boeing/Vertol CH-47A (64-13138)

All 21 American servicemen aboard (17 passengers and a crew of four) were killed when the twin-rotor, turbine-engine helicopter crashed around 15 miles (25km) north-west of Nhon Co, from where it had taken off earlier, on a re-supply mission. As the aircraft approached its intended landing site, located 110 miles (175km) north-east of Saigon, some US military personnel on the ground observed smoke and flames emanating from its aft portion. It then executed a series of turns to the left before plummeting vertically into a wooded area, while banked steeply to port, then exploded and burned. A portion of an aft main rotor blade measuring 12ft (3.5m) in length was found to have separated in flight. Blamed for the accident was the material failure of the aircraft's No. 2 pinion drive shaft thrust bearing. The weather was not considered a factor.

Date: 17 August 1966 (c.13:40)
Location: Near Da Nang, South Vietnam
Operator: US Marine Corps
Aircraft type: Chance Vought F-8E (150321)

Immediately after taking off from north/south runway at Da Nang Air Base, on a combat mission, the bomb-laden jet fighter crashed into a village, reportedly following engine failure. Although its pilot (and only occupant) ejected safely, 33 persons on the ground were killed and about 20 injured in the impact and ensuing explosions.

Date: 11 November 1966 (c.01:30)
Location: North Atlantic Ocean
Operator: US Air Force
Aircraft type: Lockheed EC-121H (55-5262)

The airborne early warning and control aircraft crashed 140 miles (225km) east-south-east of Chatham, located on the eastern tip of the Cape Cod peninsula, Massachusetts, US, in an area where the depth of the water was about 175 to 200ft (55–60m) deep. Among the 19 crewmen, searchers found no survivors nor any of the victims' bodies. None of the recovered wreckage showed evidence of in-flight fire, explosion or mechanical failure. However, shortly before the crash, 55-5262 was observed at a height of only about 200ft (60m), on a north-north-easterly heading and apparently in a level attitude while emitting smoke or vapor. After passing over a fishing vessel with at least one of its four engines back-firing, the aircraft struck the surface of the ocean, apparently extremely hard and in a nose-up, right-banking attitude, with its undercarriage retracted, exploding on impact and leaving flames burning atop the water. The crash occurred in early morning darkness, but the weather in the area at the time was clear, with a visibility of around 5 miles (10km) and winds out of the south ranging from approximately 10 to 20 knots.

Date: 26 November 1966 (c.19:20)
Location: Near Saigon, South Vietnam
Operator: US Air Force
Aircraft type: Douglas C-47D (44-76574)

The twin-engine transport crashed and burst into flames in a rice paddy, killing all 25 persons aboard. Except for one American civilian, the victims were all US servicemen, including the crew of six. Due to a malfunction in the left power plant, the aircraft was returning to Tan Son Nhut Airport, from where it had taken off shortly before, ultimately bound for Korat Air Base in Thailand. The first approach, to Runway 07, ended in a go-around manoeuvre because the undercarriage could not be extended. The crash occurred as the C-47 was proceeding on a north-easterly heading with its left propeller feathered, the pilot having radioed his intention to circle back and land on the same runway. It was dark at the time, but the meteorological conditions in the area were good, with a broken overcast and a visibility of around 10 miles (15km). No information was released pertaining to the cause of the engine trouble or the crash itself.

Date: 10 March 1967 (c.16:20)
Location: Near Phan Rang, South Vietnam
Operator: US Navy
Aircraft type: Douglas C-47J (99844)

All 25 American servicemen aboard were killed when the twin-engine transport, which had been on an internal South Vietnamese flight to Saigon from Cam Ranh Bay Air Base, crashed and exploded about 170 miles (275km) east-north-east of its intended destination. No further details, including the suspected cause of the crash, were released.

Date: 8 April 1967 (c.11:00)
Location: Seoul, South Korea
Operator: Republic of Korea Air Force
Aircraft type: Curtiss-Wright C-46

The twin-engine transport, which had been on an internal South Korean flight to Taegu, Kyongsang Pukto, crashed and burst into flames in a residential section in the Seoul suburb of Chonggu-dong. A total of 59 persons lost their lives in the disaster, all 15 South Korean service personnel aboard the aircraft (12 passengers and a crew of three) and the rest on the ground; 23 others suffered injuries. According to an official statement, the accident, which occurred minutes after the C-46 had taken off from Yoido Air Base, was precipitated by a malfunction in the left power plant, after which the pilot must have lost control in the inclement weather conditions, which consisted of fog and drizzling rain.

Date: 17 April 1967 (c.17:40)
Location: Near Mamuniyeh, Tehran, Iran
Operator: Imperial Iranian Air Force
Aircraft type: Lockheed C-130B (5-107)

During a domestic flight from Shiraz to the city of Tehran, the four-engine turboprop transport crashed and burned 50 miles (80km) south-west of its destination, and all 23 persons aboard were killed. Most of the victims were Iranian military personnel, including the crew of nine, but the passengers included some civilian dependents. The aircraft had been cruising in an area of thunderstorm activity and reportedly exploded in mid-air after being struck by lightning.

Date: 15 June 1967 (c.05:00)
Location: Near Coari, Amazonas, Brazil
Operator: Força Aérea Brasileira (Brazilian Air Force)
Aircraft type: Douglas C-47 (C-47.2068)

The twin-engine transport had been on an internal flight originating at Belem, bound for the military base at Cachimbo, when the pilot reported the failure of its radio compass. Turning back, in the darkness he was apparently unable to locate Jacareacanga, also in Para, where it had last stopped for refuelling. He then reported proceeding on towards Manaus. In his last radio transmission, the pilot said he would attempt a forced landing in the jungle. About 10 days later, the wreckage of 2068 was found submerged in a swamp, the aircraft having struck trees and lost a wing before plunging into the water. Of the 25 persons aboard the transport, all of whom were military personnel except two civilian passengers, five survivors were located, the latter including one member of the crew of five. It was believed that the C-47 had been forced down before dawn by fuel exhaustion.

Date: 17 June 1967 (c.19:30)
Location: An Khe, South Vietnam
Operator: US Air Force
Aircraft type: Lockheed C-130B (60-0293)

Operating on a scheduled South Vietnamese internal passenger service originating at and ultimately destined for Tan Son Nhut Airport, serving Saigon, the four-engine turboprop transport crashed after an aborted take-off at the An Khe Army airfield, one of seven en-route stops. Among the 56 persons aboard, 35 passengers lost their lives; the victims included US, South Vietnamese and South Korean service personnel and five civilians, one an American. The survivors, 10 of whom suffered injuries, included the seven-man US Air Force crew. The aircraft was bound for Qui Nhon, one segment of the flight, when it began its take-off on Runway 21, its elevator control being held back intentionally in order to aerodynamically lighten the load on the nose wheel strut due to the rough surface. Except for extremely hot air entering the cargo compartment of the aircraft, where the air-conditioning system was inoperative, indications were normal during the ground roll until the occurrence of a bright flash of light on the port side, whereupon the C-130 veered to the left and departed the runway at a point approximately 2,400ft (730m) from the point of brake release. Nosewheel steering was effective in returning it to the runway, at which time the crew applied reverse power. Crossing it diagonally, the transport went off the right side of the runway and down a 25ft (7.5m) embankment, coming to rest 400ft (120m) from the end of the hard surface. The impact was not severe, but fire that erupted on the right wing subsequently consumed much of 60-0293. The weather at the time was good and not considered a factor in the accident, which occurred at dusk. No information pertaining to the cause of the crash or the events leading up to it were released by the military authorities.

Date: 23 June 1967 (c.09:00)
Location: Near Jacksonville, North Carolina, US

First aircraft
Operator: US Marine Corps
Type: Bell UH-1B (638572)

Second aircraft
Operator: US Marine Corps
Type: Sikorsky CH-53A (153305)

The two turbine-engine helicopters collided in mid-air, and both then crashed and burned at

The path of the US Air Force C-130 that crashed after an aborted take-off from the An Khe airstrip on 17 June 1967. (US Air Force)

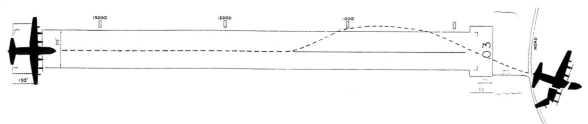

the New River Marine Corps Air Facility, located on the grounds of Camp LeJeune. Including both pilots (and the only occupants) of the smaller UH-1 and two members of the crew of four assigned to the twin-engine CH-53A Sea Stallion, 22 American servicemen were killed in the accident; with the exception of one victim who succumbed to the effects of the post-crash fire, the fatalities resulted from impact trauma. The 13 survivors from the CH-53, among them the pilot and co-pilot, suffered various injuries. At the time of the collision, 638572 was engaged in a syllabus instructional flight, and 153305 on a troop lift exercise. The crew of the former, planning a touch-and-go landing, received authorisation to turn down-wind and also acknowledged a traffic advisory from the control tower concerning the latter, which was preparing to land, but the pilot apparently took no action in response to this information. He evidently was not ready to make the turn at that point, however, and choose to continue straight ahead until a more advantageous position could be attained. The UH-1 was on or near the ground about two minutes before it proceeded in accordance with the original clearance, flying parallel to Runway 23, while starting to ascend. Meanwhile, the CH-53, which had been authorised for a straight-in landing approach, similarly flew parallel to the same runway and started to descend with its undercarriage extended. As indicated by an evasive roll to the right initiated by the aircraft, one or both pilots of 638572 probably saw 153305 at the last instant, but the helicopters nevertheless collided at an approximate height of 500ft (150m). Losing its tail rotor, the UH-1 fell to the ground immediately, while the CH-53 descended to about 100ft (30m) before plunging out of control after losing its tail boom and rotor. Considered the primary factor in the accident was the inexperience and lack of perception on the part of the tower controller, who, not fully aware of the inherent dangers associated in the controlling aircraft with a wide variation in speed, did not accurately perceive the impending conflict until it was too late. Aggravating this shortcoming was the fact that the pilots involved in the disaster had developed confidence in tower personnel to exert strict supervision of air traffic operating within the control zone. Additionally, tower personnel did not at first realise that the landing site the CH-53 pilot had intended to utilise was directly off the end of the runway, believing it to be some 1,000 to 1,500ft (300–500m) off to its right side, with the aircraft thus following a corresponding line of flight. Neither was the pilot of the UH-1 himself aware of the landing site to be used by the CH-53; such knowledge might have led to a different reaction on his part. The lack of available information on the zone was considered a contributing factor in the accident. The pilot of 153305 was aware of 638572, but he assumed the tower controller would maintain adequate clearance

through timely traffic advisories, since he had been cleared directly into the landing zone. Neither crew apparently had visual contact with each others' aircraft in the final seconds before the accident until it was too late. The weather was not a factor in the collision. Noted in the investigative report was that the delay between its clearance and the time 638572 proceeded on the originally-planned touch-and-go landing had been too long for such an authorisation to be considered still valid, and that a simple clearing turn on the spot from a hover would have been the minimum effort by its crew to maintain a safe level of flight. It was therefore recommended in the report on this accident that a definite regulation be established and published concerning the length of time a helicopter may remain on or near the ground when cleared for such a procedure. Another recommendation was to clearly describe and label in the Marine Corps' air operations manual the landing sites within the control zone of the New River facility.

Date: 29 July 1967 (c.11:00)
Location: Gulf of Tonkin (USS *Forrestal*)
Operator: US Navy
Aircraft type: McDonnell F-4B (153061)

This aviation/marine disaster occurred during the height of the American involvement in the war in South-east Asia. On this day, the naval aircraft carrier USS *Forrestal* (CVA-59) was operating off the coast of North Vietnam, preparing for an air strike against targets in that nation. Its location at the time was approximately 175 miles (280km) north of Dan Nang, South Vietnam. The vessel had turned into the wind on a launch course of almost due north when a Zuni rocket mounted on 153061 was accidentally fired from its launcher. Crossing the flight deck, the Zuni struck another combat jet, an A-4E, which was located on the port side of the carrier, some 100ft (30m) away, also being readied for launch. That aircraft's 400 gallon (1,500l) fuel tank was ruptured, touching off a fire and the beginning of a holocaust. The burning fuel was spread aft and fanned by a 32-knot wind as well as the exhausts of three other jets that had their engines running. The first of seven explosions that further spread the flames occurred about 90 seconds after the start of the blaze, when a bomb that had fallen from an aircraft detonated. The conflagration was fed by some 40,000 gallons (150,000l) of JP-5 jet fuel. The last of the flames on the deck were extinguished in less than an hour, but scattered fires continued to burn in other parts of the ship until early the following morning. The final toll in the disaster was 134 men killed, including the pilot of the aircraft hit by the rocket, and 161 injured. Miraculously, all but four of the 20 men who jumped, fell or got thrown overboard were rescued. Of the 21 jets destroyed – three RA-5Cs,

More than a score of aircraft were destroyed in explosions and fire on the flight deck of the US Navy carrier USS Forrestal *in a disaster off the Vietnamese coast.* (UPI/Corbis-Bettmann)

seven F-4Bs and 11 A-4Es – four had to be jettisoned over the side of the vessel because they were afire or leaking fuel. Another 40 aircraft sustained damage. Total costs exceeded $70 million. An investigation revealed that the initial firing of the Zuni rocket resulted from simultaneous material failures of aircraft and armament components of 153061 and its loaded ordnance stores, in conjunction with human error. Specifically, the pilot of the F-4B may have triggered the firing by superimposing enough transient voltage upon the existing stray voltage when he switched from external to internal electrical power preparatory to starting the aircraft's left engine, having already started the right one. Alternatively, two members of the weapons loading team could have been responsible for it by either arming the safety switch while checking whether the safety pin was securely in place or by mistakenly placing the three-point home/step toggle switch located at the rear of the triple ejector rack in the 'stepping' rather than 'homing' position after the rocket launchers had been plugged in and the shorting device on one of the other two launchers been faulty. Contributing to the unplanned rocket launch was the defective design of the pylon electrical disconnect, which proved to be susceptible to shorting by moisture, and the poor and outdated doctrinal and technical documentation of both ordnance and aircraft equipment and procedures, which were evident at all levels of command. One endorsement in the investigative report concluded that the Zuni

would probably not have fired had the rocket harness cable that made the electrical connection between it and the launcher not been plugged in until 153061 was on the catapult, in accordance with prescribed regulations, although this was considered a vague directive. Among the recommendations made in the report was the immediate discontinuation of use of the type launcher involved until modifications could be carried out and the issuance of directives outlining precise procedures for conducting rocket firing circuit stray voltage checks.

Date: 8 October 1967 (c.09:40)
Location: Near Huong Thuy, South Vietnam
Operator: US Air Force
Aircraft type: Lockheed C-130B (61-2649)

In what was classified as a scheduled tactical resupply mission, the four-engine turboprop transport had been on an internal South Vietnamese flight to Da Nang when it crashed 15 miles (25km) east-south-east of the Hue/Phu Bai airfield, from where it had taken off about 10 minutes earlier. All 23 American servicemen aboard (18 passengers and a crew of five) perished. Proceeding under visual flight rules procedures in meteorological conditions consisting of a low overcast, with a visibility of around 5 miles (10km) and ground fog in the area, the aircraft struck a mountain at an approximate elevation of 1,700ft (520m), or only about 150ft

(50m) below the summit, while on an east-north-easterly heading. Impact was determined to have been with the aircraft in a level attitude and at a speed of approximately 290mph (465kph), where-upon the C-130 exploded and disintegrated. The wreckage of 61-2649 was located two days later, but due to its location and the difficulty in maintaining security in an area of hostile action, no items could be removed from the site for further examination.

Date: 30 November 1967 (c.14:30)
Location: Near Qui Nhon, South Vietnam
Operator: US Air Force
Aircraft type: de Havilland C-7A Buffalo (62-4175)

All 26 persons aboard were killed, including four US Air Force crewmen, when the twin-engine turboprop transport crashed and burned on the eastern slope of a mountain. The passengers included two American civilians. The accident occurred at an approximate elevation of 1,850ft (565m) and 5 miles (10km) south of Qui Nhon Air Base, where the aircraft had been scheduled to land, after the pilot radioed that he was proceeding to Nha Trang Air Base, located 125 miles (200km) to the south, upon being advised that the weather at the former had fallen below the visual flight rules minimums. In the area at the time, the meteorological conditions consisted of a low overcast, with a visibility of 1½ to 2½ miles (2.5–4km) in drizzle or light rain. The wind was blowing from a north-easterly direction at 17 knots. As the crash occurred in hostile, inaccessible territory, no wreckage from 62-4175 was recovered.

Date: 8 January 1968 (c.17:00)
Location: Near Quang Tri, South Vietnam
Operator: US Marine Corps
Aircraft type: Sikorsky CH-53A (153710)

The turbine-engine helicopter was on an internal South Vietnamese flight originating at the Marble Mountain Air Facility when it slammed into a mountain and burned 20 miles (30km) south of Dong Ha airfield, where it had last stopped before proceeding on towards its intended destination of Hue. All 42 American servicemen aboard (37 passengers and a crew of five) perished. Having apparently lifted off under visual flight rules proce-dures on what was presumed to have been an instrument flight rules short-range clearance, with directions from the control tower to contact the Dong Ha ground-controlled approach (GCA) radar facility, the rotorcraft proceeded under the control of Dong Ha and later the Hue GCA without such a clearance ever being confirmed or its limits defined. Subsequently, 153710 was cleared to the 10 nautical mile fix on the 360-degree radial of the Hue tactical air navigation (TACAN) facility, via the 25 nautical mile fix on the 330-degree radial, and to maintain

an altitude of 3,000ft (1,000m). Just before these instructions were given to the helicopter, the Dong Ha GCA controller advised the pilot of a slight right drift in its course, but the reception was reported to have been garbled and thus not under-stood. As the helicopter continued to track south-ward, its target disappeared from the radarscope due to the 'shadow effect' of the surrounding terrain, and around this time radio contact was also lost. Wreckage was located two days later on the 186-degree radial of the Dong Ha TACAN, the CH-53 having crashed approximately at its assigned flight level and about 200ft (60m) below the peak of the mountain. At the time of its take-off, the weather at Dong Ha consisted of a low ceiling, with scattered clouds at 300ft (100m) and solid coverage at 1,000ft (300m), and a visibility of 3 miles (5km) in fog and light rain. It was ruled that the pilot had erred in judgement in accepting a clearance containing no limit and then proceeding towards the hazardous terrain with both inoperative distance-measuring equipment and poor radio communications. With regard to the primary cause, however, one endorsement of the investigative report noted that the control tower failed to provide a complete clearance even though one had been requested. Considered a factor in the deviation from established operating procedures that contributed to the disaster were the combat environment under which the aircraft and the controlling agencies had been operating. A possible contributing factor was the use of non-standard procedures by the Dong Ha agency due to its lack of communications with the Hue approach control facility. Other factors identified in the report were the instrument meteorological conditions encoun-tered by 153710 and the 'operationally deficient' ultra-high-frequency reception characteristics of the earlier model of the CH-53, with a significantly reduced range whenever the aircraft was flying away from the transmitting station. In order to ensure safety, the short-range clearance from Dong Ha began to share with the one used by Quang Tri Marine base, and improvements were also made in the land line communications between air-traffic control agencies in the region.

Date: 10 January 1968 (c.14:00)
Location: Near Copper Canyon, Nevada, US
Operator: US Marine Corps
Aircraft type: Douglas C-54P (50850)

The four-engine transport crashed and burned 30 miles (50km) south-west of Battle Mountain, and all 19 servicemen aboard were killed. Including the crew of seven, the victims were all US service personnel except for one passenger, a British Royal Marine who survived the impact but succumbed to the extremely cold temperature. The downed aircraft was located the following morning on the east side of Mount Tobin, which rises to nearly 10,000ft (3,000m). Impact had occurred about 300ft (100m) from its peak, after which the wreckage slid some 1,000ft (300m) down the mountain. En route from Buckley Air National Guard Base, near Denver, Colorado, to the Naval Air Station at Seattle, Washington, the final segment of a domestic transcontinental flight originating at the Marine Corps Air Station at Quantico, Virginia, the C-54 had been proceeding along a prescribed airway when a member of the flight crew reported difficulty maintaining a cruising height of 12,000ft (3,700m). A request was granted by the Salt Lake City Regional Air Traffic Control Centre to descend to 10,500ft (3,200m), but some time later, the aircraft reported being in icing conditions and requested vectoring around them. Turning down an offer from the control centre to ascend to a higher altitude, the crew then radioed that it was out of the icing conditions. Around 20 minutes later, in its final transmission, the transport reported losing altitude and requested clearance down to 10,000ft (3,000m), which was about 2,000ft (600m) below the minimum height for terrain clearance in this area. Although the possibility of moderate to heavy icing and snow showers over western Nevada had been included in a pilot briefing, the Salt Lake control centre had, in response to its vector request, informed 50850 that there were no storm cells and no reports of icing along the airway being used. As a result, the pilot of the aircraft involved in the accident was unaware that the turbulence actually encountered would be hazardous, worse than that predicted at the time of the take-off. These turbulent conditions apparently caused the uncontrolled descent of the C-54 into the ground. It was further noted in the investigative report on the crash that the pilot was not technically qualified in the type aircraft, and that had he been aware of the existing weather conditions, he should have discontinued the flight.

Date: 7 February 1968 (c.15:00)
Location: Northern India
Operator: Indian Air Force
Aircraft type: Antonov An-12

During an internal flight from Chandigarh, Punjab, to Leh, Kashmir, the Soviet-built four-engine turboprop transport vanished over the Himalayas with 98 persons aboard. Except for one civilian passenger, the occupants were Indian military personnel, including the crew of six. Unable to land due to bad weather conditions, the aircraft had reported turning back before it apparently encountered a severe snowstorm and was lost in the vicinity of the Rohtang Pass, the elevation of which is about 20,000ft (6,000m). The wreckage and victims would probably have been buried in deep snow.

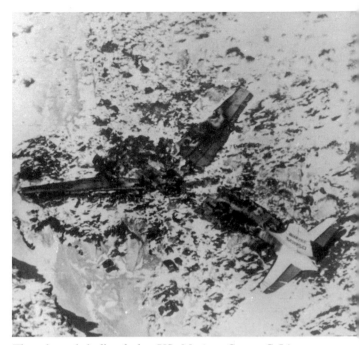

The charred hulk of the US Marine Corps C-54 transport where it came to rest after crashing into a mountain in turbulent conditions. (AP/Wide World Photos)

Date: 6 March 1968 (c.08:00)
Location: Near Khe Sanh, South Vietnam
Operator: US Air Force
Aircraft type: Fairchild C-123K (54-0590)

The transport, which had completed an internal South Vietnamese flight from the Hue/Phu Bai airfield was bringing in a load of US Marine Corps troops, was shot down by enemy forces as it prepared to land at the Khe Sanh garrison, located 400 miles (650km) north of Saigon. All 49 men aboard, one a civilian photographer riding as a passenger and the rest American service personnel, including a four-member Air Force crew, were killed. Forced to abandon its approach to the airstrip by a light military aeroplane landing in front of it, the C-123 was hit by ground fire during a go-around manoeuvre. Apparently struck in the right turbine, one of two auxiliary jet engines supplementing its two piston power plants, the transport then plummeted to earth in flames into enemy territory.

Date: 9 March 1968 (c.23:20)
Location: Near Saint-Denis, Reunion
Operator: L'Armée de l'Air (French Air Force)
Aircraft type: Douglas DC-6B (43748)

Operated by the Commandement du Transport Aerien Militaire branch and bound for Paris, the aircraft struck a hill and burst into flames soon after taking off from the airport on this Indian Ocean island, the crash occurring in darkness and during rain. Among the 19 persons killed were General Charles Aillerett, the chief of staff of the French military and its highest-ranking officer, his wife and daughter; the sole survivor, a hostess and member of the crew assigned to the DC-6B, was seriously injured. Though not officially reported, the cause of the crash was apparently operational in nature, with the four-engine transport having not followed the correct departure procedure of turning out towards the sea after take-off, instead turning right and proceeding inland.

Date: 19 April 1968 (c.10:45)
Location: Near Cheo Reo, South Vietnam

First aircraft
Operator: US Army
Type: Bell UH-1H (66-16441)

Second aircraft
Operator: US Army
Type: Bell UH-1H (67-17255)

The two turbine-engine helicopters, carrying as passengers South Vietnamese troops, collided in mid-air, then crashed and burned 60 miles (100km) south-west of Qui Nhon. Including a crew of four US Army personnel assigned to each one, all 26 servicemen aboard both aircraft were killed. Having taken off earlier from the Cheo Reo airfield, the two helicopters were flying on an approximate westerly heading when 16441, which was to the right rear of 17255, struck the lead

aircraft, only their main rotor blades making contact. The collision occurred at an altitude estimated at 1,000 to 1,500ft (300–500m). Five of the victims must have either jumped or fallen out before the impact with the ground. Examination of the victims and wreckage indicated that the mid-air crash probably did not result from hostile action.

Date: 30 April 1968 (time unknown)
Location: Near Chaklala, West Pakistan
Operator: Pakistan Air Force
Aircraft type: Lockheed L-100-10 (64145)

All 22 persons aboard were killed in the crash of the four-engine turboprop transport. The victims of the morning accident were both civilians and military personnel, the latter including the crew. Few other details were released, although a preliminary report indicated a possible in-flight break-up of the aircraft, which may have been turbulence-related.

Date: 12 May 1968 (c.07:20)
Location: Near An Hoa, South Vietnam
Operator: US Air Force
Aircraft type: Lockheed C-130B (60-0297)

The four-engine turboprop transport, carrying approximately 150 South Vietnamese military personnel and their dependents and five US Air Force crewmen, was shot down 350 miles (560km) north-east of Saigon. There were no survivors. Hit by unknown ground fire, the aircraft fell in flames about 2½ miles (4km) east of Kham Duc, from where it had taken off shortly before.

A US Army Bell UH-1H, the type of helicopter involved in two disastrous collisions over South Vietnam during a two-month period in 1968. (Bell Helicopter Textron)

Date: 25 June 1968 (c.07:30)
Location: Near Bearcat, South Vietnam

First aircraft
Operator: US Army
Type: Bell UH-1H (66-16206)

Second aircraft
Operator: US Army
Type: Bell UH-1H (66-16592)

Third aircraft
Operator: US Army
Type: Bell UH-1H (66-16601)

This triple crash occurred 15 miles (25km) south-east of Saigon and in conditions of restricted visibility, with clouds obscuring nearly half of the sky as well as fog and haze. Two of the three turbine-engine rotorcraft involved were among 10 helicopters engaged in a combat assault mission. A total of 29 service personnel lost their lives in the accident, including four US Army crewmen assigned to each aircraft; the passengers were troops belonging to the Royal Thai Volunteer Regiment. There were no survivors. With the group having descended to 900ft (275m), where the weather was better, and turned on to a heading of 60 degrees, the flight leader had just entered and then emerged from a cloud when he observed an unidentified helicopter approaching from his immediate right and at the same altitude. The latter was later identified as 16601, the command and control aircraft, which had gone ahead of the group for a weather check. The leader successfully initiated an evasive manoeuvre, breaking down and to the left, but in pulling up and to the left, 16601 collided with 16592, with the latter's main rotor blades severing the former's tail rotor/boom section. The other rotorcraft in the group avoided the resulting fireball except for 16206, which was directly behind 16592 and flew into the explosion and mass of debris. Two of them exploded on impact with the ground and burned, but not 16592, which fell into a swamp after losing its main rotor and transmission assemblies in the collision. The meteorological conditions were considered a contributing factor in the accident.

Date: 3 October 1968 (c.16:10)
Location: Near Camp Evans, South Vietnam

First aircraft
Operator: US Air Force
Type: de Havilland C-7A Buffalo (63-9753)

Second aircraft
Operator: US Army
Type: Boeing/Vertol CH-47A (66-19041)

This mid-air collision between the twin-engine turboprop, fixed-wing transport and the twin-rotor, turbine-engine helicopter, which occurred about 10 miles (15km) north of Hue, claimed the lives of 25 servicemen, all but one of them American. There were no survivors from either aircraft. Carrying 10 passengers and a crew of four and on an internal South Vietnamese flight to Hue, the C-7 had taken off from Runway 36 at Camp Evans airfield, then made a climbing right turn on to a heading of approximately 130 degrees. Meanwhile, the CH-47 had been on a heading of around 170 degrees and in a shallow descent as it prepared to land at the camp helipad, located east and 1,000ft (300m) south of the approach end of the same runway, which was an en-route stop during a scheduled passenger and mail service. Aboard were 11 men, including a crew of six. Converging at a shallow angle, with the speed of the aeroplane estimated at around 120mph (190kph) and that of the helicopter about 100mph (185kph), they collided at an altitude of approximately 1,100ft (335m). In an apparent evasive manoeuvre, 63-9753 had initiated a roll to the right before the rear rotor blades of 66-19041 sliced into its cockpit section, killing the former's two pilots. The C-7 then went into a steep descending turn to the right and plunged to earth; there was no post-impact fire. All three of the rear rotor blades having been severed in the collision and its rear rotor pylon separating thereafter, the CH-47 fell to the ground with virtually no forward speed and exploded. Two victims actually fell from the helicopter before it crashed. The local weather conditions at the time were good, with a visibility of more than 5 miles (10km), broken cumulus and alto-cumulus clouds above the collision altitude and high cirro-stratus, and a five-knot wind from a north-easterly direction. Though not officially reported by either military branch, there were indications that the Army rotorcraft did not conform to the prescribed airfield circuit procedures during its approach. Specifically, it did not follow the traffic pattern of fixed-wing aircraft and had remained above the maximum height of 600ft (180m) required for helicopters. Additionally, its crew had failed to radio the control tower for clearance to land.

Date: 21 October 1968 (c.06:00)
Location: Near Ban Me Thuot, South Vietnam
Operator: US Air Force
Aircraft type: Douglas C-47D (45-0934)

All 23 persons aboard were killed in the crash of the twin-engine transport, which occurred in mountainous terrain 110 miles (175km) north-east of Saigon. Except for two civilian passengers, both Americans, the victims were all US military personnel, including the the crew. Having taken off earlier from Saigon, the aircraft was to have stopped for refuelling at Da Nang, also in South Vietnam, during a flight with an ultimate destination of Hong

Kong. It was last reported at its assigned cruising altitude of 9,000ft (2,700m) before transmitting a 'Mayday' distress message, the pilot reporting the failure of its No. 2 power plant and that the corresponding propeller could not be feathered. Also stating that he could not maintain altitude, the pilot requested vectors to Ban Me Thuot airfield that would provide adequate terrain clearance. Radio and radar contact with 45-0934 was subsequently lost, the C-47 having crashed about 20 miles (30km) south of the airfield, at an approximate elevation of 2,300ft (700m) and in pre-dawn darkness and overcast weather conditions, with broken alto-cumulus clouds at 7,000ft (2,000m) and scattered stratus down to 1,000ft (300m). The visibility in the area was around 5 miles (10km). No further details pertaining to the cause of the the initial engine malfunction nor the subsequent accident were released.

Date: 14 January 1969 (c.08:20)
Location: North Pacific Ocean (USS *Enterprise*)
Operator: US Navy
Aircraft type: McDonnell F-4J (155804)

Started by the detonation of some Zuni rockets mounted on the jet fighter, a series of explosions rocked the flight deck of the nuclear-powered aircraft carrier USS *Enterprise* (CVAN-65), which at the time was proceeding on a true course of 90 degrees and at a position some 75 miles (120km) south-west of Honolulu, Hawaii, US. Killed in the disaster were a total of 27 servicemen, while nearly 350 others suffered varying degrees of injury. Damage exceeded $50 million, including the destruction of eight F-4J, six A-7B and one EKA-3B jet aircraft. Investigation revealed that as the ship was preparing to launch a group of aircraft, an MD-3A starting unit had been positioned adjacent to 155804, and jet exhaust gasses emanating from the unit were, or had been, impinging on the Zuni launcher, which was mounted on the aircraft's starboard wing and contained four rockets. The exhaust outlet of the MD-3A was found to have been within 2ft (600mm) of the launcher, and tests indicated that under similar circumstances, a Zuni warhead would deflagrate in only a little more than a minute. The shrapnel from the initial blast damaged the fuel tanks of the F-4J and four other aircraft, and the resulting fire rapidly spread across the carrier's flight deck, detonating other bombs. The fires were brought under control within 40 minutes, and completely extinguished about 2½ hours after the initial explosion. The primary cause of the accident was determined to have been in the design of the starting unit. It was noted in the investigative report that properly applied design and safety criteria would not have allowed the use of a piece of flight deck support equipment that was capable of detonating a weapon. A significant

contributing factor was considered to be the failure at many levels of responsbility to recognize the inherent hazards of the unit. The operating instructions for the MD-3A, for example, did not include specific reference to its potential threat to explosives. Other factors were related to the training, experience and knowledge of personnel and the environment in which they worked. The investigation revealed that at least four of the vessel's crewmen were apparently aware and concerned about the position of the unit relative to the aircraft, but the launcher exploded before any action could be taken. New operating procedures and safety precautions were implemented within a month of the disaster and were to remain in effect until replacement or modification of the MD-3A units could be completed.

Date: 5 February 1969 (c.11:45)
Location: (Western) Pacific Ocean
Operator: US Air Force
Aircraft type: Lockheed HC-130H (65-0990)

In searching for 17 crew members from a sunken Japanese ship, the aircraft itself met with disaster, crashing in Bashi Channel, north of the (Philippine) Batan Islands (21′39″N/22′08″E). Among its 14 crewmen, only one seriously injured survivor was found. Having arrived from Clark Air Force Base in the Philippines, 65-0990 was among three aircraft participating in the search and rescue operation. The four-engine turboprop had been flying in a wings-level attitude at a low altitude when it slammed into the surface and caught fire. The weather in the area at the time consisted of an overcast at 1,500ft (500m) and a visibility of 7 miles (11km). The wind was from a direction of 30 degrees at 30 to 35 knots, which contributed to ocean swells estimated at 20 to 30ft (6–10m). There was no evidence of severe turbulence or wind shear, or that down-draughts could have contributed to the crash. It was not raining in the area, but the crews of the other aircraft reported that salt spray was reducing visibility at low altitudes. It was also noted in the investigative report that as most of the aircraft operating in the area had been using a common altimeter setting, air pressure remained relatively constant. The type of accident was described as 'inadvertant contact with the water' during low-level flight over open sea.

Date: 2 April 1969 (c.12:40)
Location: Near Quang Tri, South Vietnam
Operator: US Army
Aircraft type: Boeing/Vertol CH-47C (67-18523)

Laden with South Vietnamese Army troops, the turbine-engine helicopter crashed about 110 miles (175km) north-west of Da Nang, and 24 of the 78 military personnel aboard were killed, including one of the aircraft's five US Army crewmen. Among the survivors, only one soldier escaped unscathed, the rest suffering varying degrees of injury. As the CH-47 was climbing out following a vertical take-off and after it had assumed forward flight, the pilots noted a loss in rotor speed. Its commander then took over the controls, bringing the aircraft into a hover and, by lowering the collective pitch, initiating a descent. Touching down almost vertically on the right side of a ravine 150ft (50m) from its take-off point, the helicopter then slid down the embankment and rolled to the left, at which time its rotor blades hit the ground. Fire erupted seconds after it had come to a rest, and explosions occurred 3 to 5 minutes later, ultimately resulting in the destruction of 67-18523. Being no safety belts or other restraints in the cabin, occupants had been thrown atop each other when the aircraft rolled over. The cause of the power loss was not disclosed by Army authorities.

Date: 15 April 1969 (c.13:50)
Location: Off Chongjin, North Korea
Operator: US Navy
Aircraft type: Lockheed EC-121M (135749)

The four-engine radar intelligence aircraft, with a crew of 31 men aboard, was shot down over the Sea of Japan by two North Korean MiG jet fighters. Searchers recovered the bodies of only two of the victims; there were no survivors. At the time of the attack, 135749 was believed to have been approximately 90 miles (145km) off the North Korean coast, over international waters. American President Richard Nixon announced three days later that the reconnaissance flights would continue, with fighter escorts.

Date: 25 April 1969 (c.16:00)
Location: Near Nakhon Ratchasima, Thailand
Operator: US Air Force
Aircraft type: Lockheed EC-121R (67-21493)

Ten days after hostile action claimed the US Navy EC-121, this aircraft was lost accidentally to adverse meteorological conditions. All 18 crewmen were killed, and a girl on the ground was slightly injured, when 67-21493 crashed in flat terrain some 150 miles (250km) north-east of Bangkok and around 4 miles (6.5km) west-south-west of the Korat Air Base, from where it had taken off about a minute earlier, on a combat tactical mission. Lifting off from Runway 24, the four-engine aircraft had climbed to an approximate height of 500ft (150m) above the ground before it plunged to earth, exploded and burned. The accident took place in an area of thunderstorm activity, with an overcast of 3,000ft (1,000m) and a visibility that had been reduced to 2 miles (3km) by rain showers and blowing dust. The EC-121 was believed to have entered an area of severe wind

Two separate crashes in South Vietnam of US Army Boeing/Vertol CH-47 Chinook helicopters, such as this one, claimed more than 50 lives in the spring of 1969. (Boeing Helicopters Division)

shear, flying into a head wind of 20 knots and then a tail wind reaching near-hurricane velocity, leading to the uncontrolled descent, with full recovery not being begun in time to prevent the crash.

Date: 6 May 1969 (c.13:20)
Location: Near Chon Thanh, South Vietnam
Operator: US Army
Aircraft type: Boeing/Vertol CH-47A (66-19029)

The turbine-engine helicopter, its passengers mostly South Vietnamese Army troops, crashed and burned about 75 miles (120km) north-east of Saigon. Including one member of the aircraft's crew of five US Army personnel, 39 servicemen aboard lost their lives in the accident; all but two of the 44 survivors were injured. As it lifted off from Song Be airfield, on an approximate heading of 96 degrees, the helicopter experienced a loss of rotor speed. As the aircraft approached a precipice, the commander elected against aborting the take-off, but its rear undercarriage became entangled in a strand of copper wire and the CH-47 was dragged down, then skidded along the ground and finally tumbled over the cliff. Although the cause was not given, the investigative report noted that due to the intensity of the post-crash fire, physical examination of the wreckage could not be considered reliable in attempting to determine what led to the accident. A fluctuating tachometer was apparently not a factor, and both combat damage and maintenance error were ruled out.

Date: 5 June 1969 (time unknown)
Location: Bering Sea
Operator: US Air Force
Aircraft type: Boeing RC-135E (62-4137)

Operated by the Strategic Air Command and flying between two Alaskan air bases, from Shemya, in the Aleutian Islands, to Eielson, located near Fairbanks, the four-engine reconnaissance jet vanished with 19 crewmen aboard. A search that began within hours after it was reported missing ended nine days later, with no trace of the aircraft or its occupants having been found. Cleared to a cruising altitude of 25,000ft (7,500m), the RC-135 had last reported being at a position about 200 miles (320km) north of the Amchitka Pass, a passageway between the Rat and Andreanof Islands, before a member of the crew radioed, at 07:36 local time, that they were experiencing vibration. Though uncertain of the emergency, he stated that the aircraft was under control. In response to the ground controller's query, 'You say you're not declaring an emergency', the crewman responded 'Roger'. After a long pause, he was heard to say, 'Crew go to oxygen'. There were no further verbal communications from 62-4137, but there was evidence, through the keying of its transmitter, of continued attempts to send a message, which were heard until 08:42. Communications were probably stifled by a malfunction in the aircraft's transmitter. At the time and place of the disappearance, the weather was cloudy, with tops at 7,000 to 8,000ft (2,000–2,500m). The visibility was otherwise good, with no reported turbulence and a 20-knot north-north-easterly wind.

Date: 2 September 1969 (c.11:15)
Location: Near Pakse, Laos
Operator: Royal Lao Air Force
Aircraft type: Douglas C-47

The twin-engine transport crashed in the vicinity of the Meking River, and all 35 persons aboard were killed. The passengers included some civilians. Having nearly completed a domestic flight from Savannakhet to Pakse, the aircraft was apparently unable to land due to an obscuring of the airport and surrounding terrain by low clouds, and it must have run out of fuel.

Date: 8 September 1969 (c.14:00)
Location: Near Medina, Cundinamarca, Colombia
Operator: Fuerza Aérea Colombiana (Colombian Air Force)
Aircraft type: Douglas DC-3 (FAC-685)

All 33 persons aboard were killed when the twin-engine transport crashed some 30 miles (50km) north-east of Villavicencio, Meta, where it was to have landed. The victims included a pregnant woman passenger and three military crewmen. Operated by the military airline, Servicio de Aeronavegación a Territorios Nacionales (SATENA), and on a scheduled domestic service that had originated at Bogotá and last stopped at Monterrey, the aircraft may have been diverted from its intended destination by strong winds and rain associated with a severe storm before it clipped a mountain peak, crashing on a ranch. The weather was believed to have been the primary factor in the accident.

Date: 2 October 1969 (c.07:10)
Location: Gulf of Tonkin
Operator: US Navy
Aircraft type: Grumman C-2A (152796)

The twin-engine turboprop transport, which was bound for an aircraft carrier on station in the Tonkin Gulf from Subi Point, in the Philippines, went down less than 30 miles (50km) from the ship. Except for one passenger, who was an American civilian, the 26 men killed in the crash were US Navy personnel, including the crew. There were no survivors. Salvage operations went on for more than a month, but proved unsuccessful in locating the main wreckage due to the adverse and frequently hazardous environmental and weather conditions, and so the cause of the tragedy remained unknown. Of the possible causes, the one considered the most probable was a sudden and catastrophic power plant failure involving a reduction gear, a propeller or the engine truss (support). (Subsequent instrumented flight tests confirmed the truss and gearbox assemblies as primary failure suspects in the loss of 152796 and a previous, though far less serious, C-2 accident that occurred three months earlier.) Steps taken to prevent a recurrence of the suspected failure were the imposition of interim time limits on power plant components; certain operating restrictions; increasing the frequency of oil sample analyses; the establishment of balancing and post-flight propeller inspection criteria; a requirement for the identification of any existing weaknesses,

A US Navy Grumman C-2A Greyhound carrier-based transport, the type lost over the Tonkin Gulf after suspected catastrophic mechanical failure. (Northrop Grumman)

evaluation of material conditions and corrections of all deficiencies noted, and re-design of the engine gearbox and mounting structure of the aircraft type to increase its strength as required to meet design limit sink rates and abnormal landing conditions. The US Navy grounded its C-2 fleet pending these corrective actions.

Date: 22 December 1969 (c.10:30)
Location: Near San Diego, California, US
Operator: US Navy
Aircraft type: LTV F-8J (150879)

Following engine failure and the successful ejection of its pilot (and sole occupant), the jet fighter crashed at the Miramar Naval Air Station. The accident claimed the lives of 14 men on the ground, one of them a civilian worker and the rest US Navy personnel. Numerous others were injured, nine seriously. Having taken off earlier from the base, the aircraft was on a combat manoeuvring practice flight over the Pacific Ocean when the pilot noted an instrument indication of zero engine oil pressure and turned back. Cleared to land at the base, it was at a position of approximately 1 mile (1.5km) from the threshold of Runway 24-Right and a height of about 500ft (150m) above the ground when it experienced a complete flame-out, prompting the pilot to eject. He landed by parachute without injury, but after

Little damage is visible outside but much was done inside the hangar struck by the crashing F-8 jet fighter at Miramar Naval Air Station. (AP/Wide World Photos)

his abandoning of it, the F-8 veered from the approach heading of 240 degrees and into a descending right turn. Its undercarriage extended and tail hook raised, the fighter then struck an aircraft hangar and burst into flames. Besides 150879, three Navy F-4J jet fighters parked in the building were destroyed and four other aircraft of the same type substantially damaged. Investigation revealed that due to an oil pressure discrepancy occurring 2½ weeks before the accident, the oil pressure relief valve on 150879 had been replaced. The very next day, the new valve was removed by someone else, but not properly re-installed; specifically, it had not been safety-wired in accordance with existing directives. This maintenance error resulted in the separation of the upper support housing of the valve from its lower support housing, causing oil starvation in the bearings and, in turn, the power plant seizure that led to the crash. The proper functioning of the emergency ram-air turbine prevented a complete control systems failure. However, a loss of electrical power occurring concurrent with the engine seizure returned the roll and yaw stabilisation system actuators to a neutral position, resulting in a rather abrupt control shift that the pilot interpreted as a loss of control. His decision to bail out was possibly influenced by his lack of knowledge as to the position of the ram-air unit. It was noted in the investigative report that in ejecting, the pilot had been following prescribed procedures. Nevertheless, in the wake of this accident, all Naval Air Training and Operating Procedures Standardization Program (NATOPs) flight manuals were expanded with respect to flight crews faced with emergencies involving unusual circumstances. These now stated that the decision to abandon an aircraft must be influenced by the concern for the safety of persons on the ground. With regard to the underlying cause of the accident, the report noted that the maintenance personnel were not familiar with the proper installation procedures, and neither did they consult the appropriate publications prior to doing the work. Furthermore, the individual who inspected it was not familiar with the configuration of a properly-installed relief valve. A revision in the procedure for changing such valves on F-8 engines was one of the recommendations made in the report. The weather was not a factor in the crash.

Date: 12 January 1970 (c.12:00)
Location: Near Villia, Attiki, Greece
Operator: Royal Hellenic Air Force
Aircraft type: Douglas C-47

The twin-engine transport, its passengers consisting of paratroopers, crashed and burned on a mountain 50 miles (80km) west-north-west of Athens, the accident occurring in foggy weather

conditions. Twenty-three Greek servicemen aboard were killed but three paratroopers and one of the aircraft's five crewmen survived with injuries. No details regarding the suspected cause of the crash were disclosed.

Date: 16 March 1970 (c.11:30)
Location: Near Da Nang, South Vietnam
Operator: US Navy
Aircraft type: Lockheed EC-121M (145927)

Its No. 4 power plant having been shut down and the corresponding propeller feathered due to generator over-temperature, the reconnaissance aircraft crashed at Da Nang Air Base, where it was to have landed at the end of a flight from Taiwan. Killed in the accident were 23 of the 31 crewmen, one of whom succumbed to cardiac arrest; six of the survivors and two other US military personnel on the ground suffered injuries. During the otherwise normal three-engine, visual landing approach to Runway 35L, the first 1,000ft (300m) of which, significantly, had been closed, the pilots apparently tried to 'stretch' their approach to avoid the overrun area where workers and equipment were present. In the process, however, the aircraft commander allowed 145927 to descend to about 50ft (15m) above the ground, which was half the minimum height prescribed for the initiation of a missed approach procedure, and its air speed dropped too low. A go-around was nevertheless begun, but the aircraft assumed a slight nose-high, banking attitude, with the latter increasing to about 90 degrees, never gained altitude and ultimately struck a concrete revetment, broke into three major sections and burst into flames, its undercarriage down and flaps extended on impact. Several structures, two trucks and a US Navy F-4D jet fighter were also destroyed. The accident was attributed not only to the error by the aircraft commander, but also to the actions of the co-pilot, who had been at the controls of 145927 and, according to the investigative report, placed it in 'an inherently hazardous position'. The meteorological conditions at the time were comparatively good, with a visibility of 7 miles (11km), scattered clouds at 1,500ft (500m) and a broken overcast at 3,000ft (1,000m), but the winds, blowing from the north at 16 knots and gusting to 22, were considered a minor contributing factor. In view of the fact that seven of the occupants who suffered fatal head injuries might have survived had they been wearing helmets, one of the recommendations made in the investigative report was for all EC-121 flight personnel to use such protective headgear during take-offs and landings. Another recommendation was for the re-design and/or reinforcement of seats and stations to provide adequate crash protection for crews flying this type of aircraft.

Date: 18 July 1970 (time unknown)
Location: North Atlantic Ocean
Operator: Soviet Air Force
Aircraft type: Antonov An-22 (SSSR-09303)

The four-engine turboprop transport, which belonged to the fleet of the Soviet airline Aeroflot and was carrying a field hospital to earthquake-ravaged Peru, vanished with 23 persons aboard. Having last stopped at Keflavik, Iceland, the aircraft was to have landed at Halifax, Nova Scotia, Canada, one segment of a flight originating at Moscow. It was officially reported missing at 17:00 Halifax time. Search for the aircraft was finally abandoned about a month later, and the Soviet relief mission, which had been suspended for a week after the loss of the An-22, subsequently ended completely after only nine more flights.

Date: 26 August 1970 (time unknown)
Location: Near Tam Ky, South Vietnam
Operator: US Army
Aircraft type: Boeing/Vertol CH-47B (67-18445)

The turbine-engine helicopter was shot down during the afternoon by enemy ground forces about 300 miles (480km) north-north-east of Saigon. All but two of the 32 American servicemen aboard the aircraft, which had been struck by a rocket grenade, and two others on the ground in the area where it crashed were killed. The pilot, who was a member of the aircraft's crew of five, the sole surviving passenger and five men on the ground suffered injuries.

Date: 2 October 1970 (14:07)
Location: Northern Taiwan
Operator: US Air Force
Aircraft type: Lockheed C-130E (64-0536)

All 43 American servicemen aboard (37 passengers and a crew of six) perished when the four-engine turboprop transport crashed 20 miles (30km) south-south-west of T'ai-pei, about 6 minutes after its departure from the city's international airport, on an internal Taiwanese flight to Ching Chuan Kang. The aircraft, which was operating under instrument flight rules procedures, made a right turn after taking off and entered a low overcast during its climb-out. Subsequently, it was instructed to ascend to 6,000ft (1,800m) and report when over the second radio fix, but it did not acknowledge this transmission. Wreckage was located nearly a week later, the C-130 having struck a mountain ridge only about 30ft (10m) below its crest, at an approximate elevation of 6,150ft (1,875m) and while on a heading of around 210 degrees, exploded and burned. At the time and location of the accident, the visibility was believed to have been zero, with the cloud tops extending to

The versatile Lockheed C-130 Hercules turboprop transport, one of which, similar to this earlier model, crashed on Taiwan. (Lockheed Martin)

at least 20,000ft (6,000m). Had 64-0536 assumed its planned course, ie, to a heading of 252 degrees, it would have cleared the terrain along the route by no less than 3,000ft (1,000m). The reason for its deviation to the south, if known, was not disclosed by Air Force authorities.

Date: 24 November 1970 (c.09:30)
Location: Near Can Tho, South Vietnam

First aircraft
Operator: (South) Vietnamese Air Force
Type: Bell UH-1H (560)

Second aircraft
Operator: US Army
Type: de Havilland RU-6A Beaver (53-7324)

A mid-air collision and resulting crash of the two aircraft, which occurred about 5 miles (10km) south-east of Can Tho Army airfield and 80 miles (130km) south of Saigon, claimed the lives of 18 persons. The victims included a Vietnamese infant who had been a passenger on the turbine-engine helicopter and the three occupants, all US servicemen, of the single-engine aeroplane; there were no survivors. Having taken off shortly before on an avionics test flight, the RU-6 was apparently in a right-hand turn and on a heading of between 240 and 260 degrees, while the UH-1, on an internal re-supply mission from Soc Trang to Binh Thuy, flying in a north-north-westerly direction and probably in a straight climb, when they collided at an approximate height of 1,200ft (350m) above the ground. The impact with the helicopter's main rotor blades sheared off the aeroplane's empennage and left wing, close to the fuselage. At the time, the local weather consisted of a layer of scattered clouds at 1,500ft (500m). Except that the US Army pilot would have been operating under the 'see-and-be-seen' rules associated with visual flight rules, an investigation revealed no factors that could have contributed to the collision.

Date: 27 November 1970 (c.13:30)
Location: Near Nha Trang, South Vietnam
Operator: US Air Force
Aircraft type: Fairchild C-123K (55-4574)

The transport, which was on an internal South Vietnamese flight from Saigon to Nha Trang Air Base, crashed into a mountain 15 miles (25km) south-west of its destination. Including a crew of six US Air Force personnel, all 79 servicemen aboard perished; the passengers were troops belonging to the Army of South Vietnam. Airborne for around 10 minutes, the aircraft, which had two auxiliary jet engines to supplement its twin piston power plants, was on a heading of 220 degrees and in a wings-level attitude when it struck some trees that were about 80ft (25m) tall at an approximate elevation of 4,600ft (1,400m), or some 500ft (150m) below the crest of the ridge. Its burned wreckage was found nine days later. At the time and location of the disaster, the meteorological conditions consisted of an overcast, which was variable at 1,000ft (300m) and broken at 2,000ft (600m), with a visibility of 1 mile (1.5km). The wind was from a direction of 30 degrees at 10–15 knots. No distress message had been received from 55-4574, and no proven or suspected causative factors were disclosed in this apparent controlled-flight-into-terrain accident.

Date: 29 November 1970 (c.07:35)
Location: Near Cam Ranh, South Vietnam
Operator: US Air Force
Aircraft type: Fairchild C-123K (54-0649)

The transport, with 44 US and South Vietnamese servicemen aboard, slammed into a dense jungle area and burned some 165 miles (265km) north-east of Saigon and about 15 miles (25km) south-west of Cam Ranh Bay Air Base, where it was to have landed. Wreckage was located five days later with only two of the occupants alive, both of them American passengers who had suffered injuries in the crash. Among those killed were the five members of the crew, all US Air Force personnel. Less than 10 minutes before the accident, the twin piston-engine aircraft, which was also fitted with two auxiliary jets, had taken off from Phan Rang, along the coast of South Vietnam. It was last observed heading for the North Pass, a valley about 2 miles (3km) wide and 10 miles (15km) long, with high terrain on both sides. The pilot had reported proceeding along a prescribed airway that extended on a heading of 30 degrees before requesting a precision radar approach. In its last message, 54-0649 acknowledged instructions to a change of course to 100 degrees and an ascent to 2,700ft (820m), and the C-123 was on that heading, at that approximate height and in level flight at the time of impact. The weather at the scene of the crash was poor, with a ceiling estimated at only 300ft (100m), light rain and zero visibility. The wind was from an east-north-easterly direction at 30 knots. No information regarding possible or probable causative factors in this accident were released by Air Force authorities.

Date: 20 January 1971 (c.14:30)
Location: Near Pacae, Junin, Peru
Operator: Fureza Aérea del Peru (Peruvian Air Force)
Aircraft type: Curtiss-Wright C-46 (FAP-381)

All 35 persons aboard perished when the twin-engine transport, on an internal Peruvian flight from Mazamari to Lima, crashed and burned on a mountain in the Andes range 35 miles (55km) north-west of Tarma. Most of the victims were Peruvian military personnel, including the crew of five, but some had been accompanied by their dependents. Though not officially reported, mechanical failure was believed to have been a factor in the accident, as the aircraft appeared to be experiencing power plant difficulties just before-hand, according to witnesses on the ground.

The flight path of the US Air Force C-123 that crashed in South Vietnam indicates collision with trees prior to impact on the mountainside. (US Air Force)

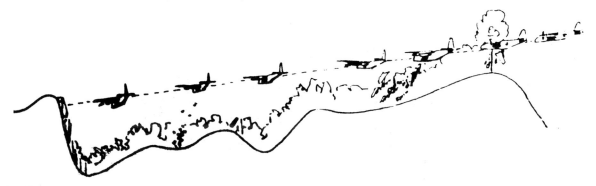

Date: 21 January 1971 (c.10:00)
Location: Near Privas, Ardeche, France
Operator: L'Armée de l'Air (French Air Force)
Aircraft type: Nord 262A (44)

The twin-engine turboprop transport slammed into a mountain at an approximate elevation of 3,600ft (1,100m), or only about 700ft (200m) from its peak, west of the Rhône River. Including a crew of four military personnel, all 21 persons aboard were killed; the passengers included seven top French civilian nuclear research experts. The crash occurred during a snowstorm as the aircraft was preparing to land following an internal flight from Paris to the Pierrelatte nuclear facility. When considering the adverse weather conditions, there was speculation that the pilots became disorientated, resulting in a controlled-flight-into-terrain accident. There was no evidence of instrument failure, and the absence of a distress message seemed to rule out icing or some other in-flight emergency. The official cause was not released however.

Date: 15 April 1971 (c.07:00)
Location: Near San Jose, Pampanga, the
   Philippines
Operator: Philippine Air Force
Aircraft type: Douglas C-47A (293246)

The twin-engine transport crashed in a rice field about half-a-mile (0.8km) from Basa Air Base, located near Floridablanca, from where it had taken off moments earlier. Most of the 40 persons killed in the accident were Philippine military personnel, including the aircraft's four crewmen; one of the passengers, a 3-year-old boy, succumbed to his injuries three days later, leaving no survivors. Bound for Nichols Air Base, located near the Philippine capital of Manila, the C-47 reportedly climbed to a height of approximately 200ft (60m) above the ground before it banked to the left, stalled and plummeted to earth. Although no official report was released, there were indications that the crash had been precipitated by the failure of the aircraft's right power plant, after which the crew apparently tried to return to the base.

Date: 26 May 1971 (c.15:00)
Location: Near Capetown, South Africa
Operator: South African Air Force (3 aircraft)
Aircraft types: Hawker Siddeley HS 125-400B (01)
   Hawker Siddeley HS 125-400B (02)
   Hawker Siddeley HS 125-400B (03)

As they were practicing for an upcoming exhibition, the three twin-engine jets struck Devil's Peak and exploded, and all 11 men aboard them perished. The victims included the flight crews and ground personnel. According to eye-witnesses, the

aircraft were flying in a V-formation through a thick mist when they slammed into the mountain. No additional information was released regarding the probable cause of the apparent controlled-flight-into-terrain accident.

Date: 13 June 1971 (c.13:30)
Location: North Pacific Ocean
Operator: US Air Force
Aircraft type: Boeing C-135B (61-0331)

Assigned to the classified Project III, with the intention of monitoring French above-ground nuclear testing in the South Pacific, the modified jet transport had, the previous day, successfully completed a test mission from Hickam Air Force Base, in Hawaii, US, to Pago Pago, American Samoa. On the return flight, however, it met with what was described as a 'catastrophic event', leading to an uncontrolled plunge into the sea about 700 miles (1,100km) south-south-west of its destination. By the time search operations were terminated four days later, only pieces of secondary aircraft structure and the undamaged crash position indicator had been recovered; no trace of the 24 crewmen, who comprised both military personnel and civilians, was found. Last reported at an altitude of 33,000ft (10,050m), while on a probable true

The spots on the aircraft diagram illustrate the small amount of aircraft structure that was recovered from the downed C-135B. (US Air Force)

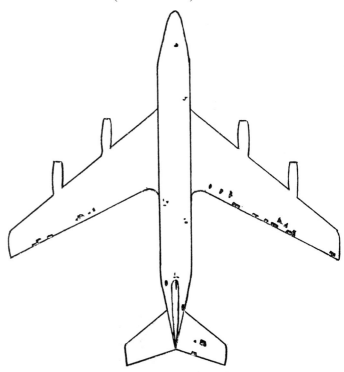

heading of 20 degrees and flying at an estimated air speed of around 540mph (870kph), 61-331 had apparently begun a radio transmission that could not be deciphered and which ended abruptly at approximately 13:25 local time. The C-135 was believed to have subsequently struck the surface of the ocean at a high speed and a steep angle of descent, and the absence in the water of helmets, clothing and other personal effects indicated that it had been intact until the moment of impact, whereupon it must have disintegrated. There was no evidence of either in-flight or post-crash fire or explosion. The weather in the area at the time was generally clear, with scattered cumulus clouds well below the flight level of the aircraft and a south-south-westerly wind of 25 knots. There was no evidence that the modifications in 61-331, which included 11 additional windows and, significantly, a canoe-shaped fairing with radome atop its fuselage, had in any way affected the structural integrity of the aircraft. Nevertheless, nine years later a US federal court ruled that the 12 civilian victims of the tragedy were entitled to wrongful death damages from LTV, which had attached the radome.

Date: 30 July 1971 (c.15:00)
Location: Near Pau, Pyrenees-Atlantiques, France
Operator: L'Armée de l'Air (French Air Force)
Aircraft type: Nord 2501 Noratlas (49)

Operated by the Commandement du Transport Aerien Militaire and carrying as passengers army paratroopers and three jump masters, the twin-engine aircraft crashed in flat terrain along the base of the Pyrenees. All 37 French servicemen aboard, including a crew of three Air Force personnel, were killed. After fire had erupted in one power plant, the pilot requested clearance to land immediately at Pau-Uzein Air Base, but as it was turning on to the final approach leg the transport plummeted to earth and exploded. Two paratroopers managed to jump safely from the aircraft before the start of the in-flight emergency.

Date: 18 August 1971 (c.09:40)
Location: Near Pegnitz, West Germany
Operator: US Army
Aircraft type: Boeing/Vertol CH-47A (66-19023)

All 37 American servicemen aboard perished, including a crew of five, when the turbine-engine helicopter, which was flying between two military installations, from Dolan Barracks, near Ludwigsburg, to the training area near Grafenwohr, crashed and burned 20 miles (30km) north-west of its intended destination, and about 25 miles (40km) north-east of Nurnberg. The aircraft had been cruising under visual flight rules procedures at an estimated air speed of around 115mph (185kph) and on a north-easterly heading when an aft main rotor blade separated at the root, the structural failure occurring at an altitude of 2,700ft (820m), or approximately 1,000ft (300m) above the ground. It then plunged into the rolling terrain in a nose-first, inverted attitude, with its fuselage at an angle of around 45 degrees. The rotor failure was attributed

A French Air Force Nord Noratlas transport, the type that crashed near Pau-Uzein Air Base, killing all 37 military personnel aboard. (Philip Jarrett)

A front main gear assembly is the only easily recognisable part of the US Army CH-47A helicopter that crashed in West Germany after in-flight rotor failure. (UPI/Corbis-Bettmann)

to a fatigue fracture of the subject blade root, which originated on the bottom side and extended in a chordwise direction for about 7 inches (3cm). Although its age was unknown, the crack must have existed for a sufficient period of time to allow a considerable amount of corrosion to accumulate in about half the area of the fracture face.

Date: 23 October 1971 (time unknown)
Location: Near Qui Nhon, South Vietnam
Operator: (South) Vietnamese Air Force
Aircraft type: Douglas C-47

The crash of the twin-engine transport, which occurred in adverse weather conditions associated with a typhoon, claimed the lives of 22 persons aboard the aircraft. There was only one survivor from the accident, further details about which were not made available.

Date: 9 November 1971 (c.05:40)
Location: Off Livorno, Toscana, Italy
Operator: Royal Air Force
Aircraft type: Lockheed C-130K (XV216)

In the worst peacetime accident in the history of the RAF, all 52 servicemen aboard were killed when the four-engine turboprop transport plunged into the Ligurian Sea about 20 miles (30km) west of Pisa. The accident occurred in predawn darkness shortly after the aircraft, carrying 46 Italian Army paratroopers and six British military personnel, including a parachute instructor, had taken off from San Giusto Airport, near Pisa, bound for Sardinia. The wreckage was located and the bodies of the victims recovered after an extensive search. Despite a report of a possible in-flight structural failure, no investigation findings on this crash have been released by RAF officials.

Date: 28 November 1971 (c.13:30)
Location: Near Hue, South Vietnam
Operator: US Army
Aircraft type: Boeing/Vertol CH-47C (68-15866)

During a South Vietnamese internal flight from Da Nang to Camp Eagle, the turbine-engine helicopter crashed and burned 12 miles (20km) north-west of the Hue/Phu Bai airfield. Wreckage was located a few days later on a jungled mountainside, with no survivors among the 34 American servicemen aboard, including a crew of five. Operating under visual flight rules procedures, the aircraft had proceeded up the coastline before turning inland, in an apparent attempt to fly through a lowland region, probably due to deteriorating weather along the regular route. It then assumed an approximately due westerly course to avoid mountainous terrain, which would have been at its 2 o'clock position. During this time, however, it inadvertently entered instrument meteorological conditions, with a ceiling of 1,000ft (300m), a broken overcast at 600ft (180m) and scattered clouds down to only 300ft (100m), and a visibility of 1 mile (1.5km) or less. Declaring an emergency to Hue approach control, the crew started a left turn away from the mountains. During this 180-degree turn, however, a north-westerly wind apparently caused the helicopter to drift southward and into the another area where the terrain was higher. At the moment of impact, 68-15866 may have been in a slight descent as the crew tried to break through the lowest layer of clouds.

Date: 21 January 1972 (c.10:30)
Location: Near Betania, Choco, Colombia
Operator: Fuerza Aérea Colombiana (Colombian Air Force)
Aircraft type: Douglas C-47 (FAC-661)

All 39 persons aboard were killed, including a crew of four military personnel, when the twin-engine transport slammed into a mountain and exploded. The accident occurred during a thunderstorm and rain, about 60 miles (100km) from Medellin, Antioquia, from where the aircraft, which was operated by the military airline Servicio de Aeronavegación a Territorios Nacionales (SATENA), had taken off earlier, on a non-scheduled domestic passenger flight to Quibdo, Choco. No details as to the suspected cause were released, although the weather may have played a significant role in the crash.

Date: 10 May 1972 (c.10:25)
Location: Near Gia Dinh, South Vietnam
Operator: US Army
Aircraft type: Boeing/Vertol CH-47A (64-13157)

The turbine-engine helicopter crashed and exploded in a jungle area some 20 miles (30km) north-east of Saigon while on a South Vietnamese internal flight from Bien Hoa to Vung Tau. All 34 American servicemen aboard the aircraft, including its two-member flight crew, perished. Proceeding on a compass heading of 190 degrees at an indicated air speed of approximately 90mph (145kph), the CH-47 had been at a height of 2,000ft (600m) when a main blade was slung from the aft rotor head. The aft pylon was then torn from the airframe, landing some 300ft (100m) from the main wreckage. The accident was attributed to metal fatigue of the spar in the blade that failed.

Date: 13 June 1972 (time unknown)
Location: Near An Loc, South Vietnam
Operator: (South) Vietnamese Air Force
Aircraft type: Boeing/Vertol CH-47

All 47 persons aboard were killed, including a military crew, when the turbine-engine helicopter was shot down 60 miles (100km) north of Saigon, shortly after it had taken off. The aircraft was brought down by ground fire while transporting refugees out of the besieged area.

Date: 11 July 1972 (time unknown)
Location: Near Quang Tri, South Vietnam
Operator: US Marine Corps
Aircraft type: Sikorsky CH-53D (156658)

Approximately 50 South Vietnamese Army troops and two US Marine Corps crewmen lost their lives when the turbine-engine helicopter was reportedly shot down. Five other members of the aircraft's crew and 10 troops survived.

Date: 11 July 1972 (c.16:00)
Location: Near Grytoya, Norway
Operator: Kongelige Norske Luftforsvaret (Royal Norwegian Air Force)
Aircraft type: de Havilland DHC-6 Twin Otter Series 100 (67-056)

The twin-engine turboprop crashed into a mountain and burned on the island of Hinno, 50 miles (80km) north-west of Narvik, while preparing to land at Skagon Airport, which was an intermediate stop during an internal service from Bardufoss to Bodoe. Including a two-man military flight crew, all 17 persons aboard the aircraft lost their lives. A number of civilians, four of them children, were among the passengers. The accident occurred in conditions of poor visibility due to rain and fog. According to a military summary report, the crash was attributed to 'navigational errors and miscalculations'. About a month later, however, it was revealed that the pilot of the Twin Otter, a Norwegian Air Force major, had at the time been under the influence of alcohol, which undoubtedly led to these mistakes. An autopsy performed on his body found his blood level to be more than twice that allowed under Norwegian law. He had apparently consumed alcoholic beverages the night before, though no other pilots reported any indication he was drunk on the day of the accident. Also, there was no evidence of recent alcohol consumption on the part of the co-pilot. This disturbing finding led to the creation of a military committee to study the issue of alcohol regulations and rest periods for pilots, as fatigue may have been an additional contributing factor in this particular crash.

Date: 12 August 1972 (c.04:00)
Location: Near Soc Trang (Khanh Hung), South
  Vietnam
Operator: US Air Force
Aircraft type: Lockheed C-130E (62-1853)

The four-engine turboprop transport was shot
down in predawn darkness over the Mekong
Delta region about 100 miles (150km) south-west of
Saigon. Killed were 30 of the 44 American and
South Vietnamese military personnel aboard,
including all but one of the aircraft's eight US Air
Force crewmen. The aircraft had been hit in a
power plant by small arms ground fire shortly after
it had taken off from Soc Trang Air Base, on a
support mission.

Date: 28 August 1972 (c.14:30)
Location: Papua New Guinea
Operator: Royal Australian Air Force (RAAF)
Aircraft type: de Havilland Canada DHC-4
  Caribou (A4-233)

The passengers comprising mostly Papua New
Guinea Army cadets, the twin-engine transport
was on an intra-island flight from Lae to Port
Moresby. Twenty-five minutes after it had taken off,
the aircraft was reported at 6,500ft (1,980m) over
town of Wau, but no further radio transmissions
were heard. Three days later, the five injured cadets
who had survived the crash of the Caribou were
found, one at the accident site, but the latter
succumbed in hospital after his rescue. The final toll
in the accident was 25 persons killed, including the
aircraft's crew of three RAAF personnel. Evidence
indicated that the southbound transport had
entered a region known as the Kudjeru Gap at its
reported altitude. At the location where the valley
narrows, however, the weather deteriorated down
to 6/8 stratus clouds with a base of only 600ft
(180m) above the ground and isolated areas of
precipitation. The cloud tops were at 10,500ft
(3,200m). Confronted with the lowering overcast,
which prevented him from maintaining visual flight
within the mountainous terrain, the pilot reversed
his direction and initiated a climb. During this sharp
right turn, at which time A4-233 may have entered
the clouds, the starboard wing clipped trees at an
approximate elevation of 5,000ft (1,500m), or only
about 50ft (15m) below the crest of the ridge,
resulting in a loss of control. The Caribou then
slammed into the woods, broke apart and burned.
The scene of the crash was 20 miles (30km) south of
Wau. The accident was attributed to 'error of skill'
on the part of the pilot-in-command. Although he
had flown between Lae and Port Moresby a total of
20 times, twice earlier on the day of the crash, there
was strong evidence to suggest that on none of
these occasions had he attempted to negotiate the
Kudjeru Gap below a low overcast. His decision to

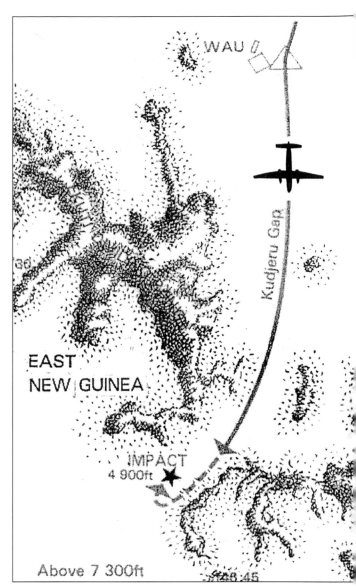

*The flight path in the final moments of the RAAF
Caribou, including the sudden reverse of direction that
preceded impact with high terrain.* (RAAF
Directorate of Flying Safety)

enter the valley was probably influenced by the
clear weather in the Wau area. It was noted in the
investigative report, however, that a pilot with more
experience in Papua New Guinea operations would
have, under the prevailing conditions, expected
clouds in the valley and elected to fly above them.
Likewise, one with more experience who had
planned to fly below the cloud level would have
probably turned back earlier. However, the report
labelled as 'speculative' the suggestion that a pilot
with more knowledge of the local area would not
have made the same error.

Date: 13 September 1972 (c.12:00)
Location: Near Dhulikhel, Nepal
Operator: Royal Nepalese Air Force
Aircraft type: Douglas C-47 (9N-RF10)

The twin-engine transport was on a paratroop training mission, flying internally from Panchkhal to Tribuvan Airport, serving Kathmandu, when it crashed after reportedly striking an electric power pole. All 31 Nepalese servicemen aboard were killed, including a crew of four.

Date: 13 October 1972 (c.15:30)
Location: Near El Sosneado, Mendoza, Argentina
Operator: Fuerza Aérea Uruguaya (Uruguayan Air Force)
Aircraft type: Fairchild Hiller FH-227D (T-571)

The twin-engine turboprop operated by the Transporte Aéreo Militar Uruguaya (TAMU) branch had taken off the previous day from Montevideo, Uruguay, on a non-scheduled international service to Santiago, Chile. The passengers included 16 members of the 'Old Christian Brothers', an amateur Uruguayan rugby team, five of who would live through what would become an epic story of survival. The aircraft landed at Malargue, Mendoza, Argentina, due to adverse meteorological conditions, before proceeding over the highest part of the Andes Mountains on this Friday the 13th with 45 persons aboard.

A photograph taken by one of the survivors of the others huddled around the wreckage of the Uruguayan Air Force FH-227 that crashed in the Andes. (Sygma)

During the second leg of the flight, T-571 had encountered a strong head-wind after turning from a south-westerly on to a north-westerly direction, which reduced its ground speed by about 35mph (55kph). Over the Andean Cordillera, and in accordance with their planned route, the crew turned back on to a north-north-easterly heading. But although the pilot had reported reaching Curico, where the turn was supposed to have been made, the FH-227 had in fact still been some 50 miles (80km) from that point. After giving his position, he was cleared to begin a slow descent. Minutes later, the aircraft entered a cloud bank, then encountered down-draughts, and after emerging from the overcast it clipped a mountain, the impact shearing off most of the right wing, which in turn struck and severed the tail assembly. Some of the occupants were at this point tossed out at the point of the fuselage break. Miraculously, the main fuselage section landed and slid to a stop on a snowy down-slope, coming to rest at an approximate elevation of 12,000ft (3,700m) near the Tinguiririca Volcano. The scene of the crash was about 120 miles (190km) south-east of its destination. The transport was still missing when two of the passengers who had hiked out were found four days before Christmas, and one of them helped guide helicopters to the crash site, locating 14 other survivors, who had sustained themselves during their two-month ordeal by eating the flesh of the dead. Among the 29 persons who lost their lives were the five members of the aircraft's crew, all military personnel, and eight killed in an avalanche at the crash site on 30 October.

Date: 31 October 1972 (c.18:00)
Location: Near My Tho, South Vietnam
Operator: US Army
Aircraft type: Boeing/Vertol CH-47

The turbine-engine helicopter was apparently shot down around nightfall over the Mekong Delta region about 35 miles (55km) south-west of Saigon, and all 22 military personnel aboard, mostly Americans but also including several South Vietnamese, were killed.

Date: 28 February 1973 (c.23:50)
Location: Near Szczecin, Poland
Operator: Polska Wojska Lotnicze (Polish Air Force)
Aircraft type: Antonov An-24B (012)

The twin-engine turboprop transport crashed and burned while attempting to land, killing all 15 persons aboard, including a military crew. During its landing approach to a combined military/civil airport, which was being conducted in darkness and conditions of poor visibility, the aircraft had apparently encountered a severe down-draught.

Date: 12 April 1973 (c.15:00)
Location: Near Sunnyvale, California, US

First aircraft
Operator: (US) National Aeronautics and Space
  Administration (NASA)
Type: Convair 990A (N711NA)

Second aircraft
Operator: US Navy
Type: Lockheed P-3C (157332)

As they were approaching to land at Moffett
Field Naval Air Station, the NASA research jet,
a modified airliner known as the 'flying laboratory',
and the turboprop patrol aircraft collided in mid-air
about 10 miles (15km) north-west of San Jose, and
both then crashed and burned on a golf course.
Among the 16 persons killed were eight scientists
and technicians plus the three-member flight crew
aboard the NASA jet, and five Naval personnel
from the patrol aircraft. A sixth Navy crewman, the
sole survivor of the accident, was seriously injured.
A Moffett Field ground controller had mistakenly
cleared both aircraft to land on the same runway.
The Convair 990, which was supposed to use
Runway 32-Right, had been given the wrong
instructions, and as a result settled atop the P-3, the
collision occurring at an approximate height of
300ft (100m) above the ground.

Date: 28 August 1973 (c.21:45)
Location: Near Huete, Cuenca, Spain
Operator: US Air Force
Aircraft type: Lockheed C-141A (63-8077)

Operated by the Military Airlift Command, the
jet transport crashed and burned 40 miles
(65km) east of Madrid, about 25 miles (40km) east
of Torrejon de Ardoz Air Base, where it was to have
landed, killing 24 persons aboard. Only the navigator, one of the eight Air Force crewmen assigned to
the aircraft and who was seriously injured in the
accident, survived. The passengers included some
civilian dependents, but most were also American
military personnel. Having nearly completed a flight
from Athens, Greece, 63-8077 was cleared by
Madrid approach control to proceed to the Torrejon
non-directional beacon and for descent to 5,000ft
(1,500m). The return transmission from the C-141,
'Understand ... clear to descend to three thousand
and Castejon radio beacon', which contained two
significant errors, was, however, blocked out by
another aircraft calling the same ground facility.
The transport then received authorisation for a
ground-controlled radar-monitored instrument
landing system approach to Runway 23, but simultaneous with its radio message '... passing five for
three thousand', the controller was issuing instructions to another military aircraft, an F-4 jet fighter,

*The main wreckage area of the US Air Force C-141 that crashed near Madrid, Spain, with the arrow pointing to
the inverted tail assembly.* (US Air Force)

and hearing from the former only 'MAC-38077', requested the crew to 'Stand by'. Following a 30 second delay, radio transmissions to the C-141 resumed, but it failed to respond, and its target was no longer observed on radar. Cleanly-configured, the aircraft had slammed into a mesa at an approximate elevation of 3,000ft (1,000m), while on a heading of 292 degrees and at a ground speed of around 250mph (400kph), according its flight data recorder read-out. It then became airborne, and after passing over a ravine it rolled over and crashed inverted. The accident occurred on a moonless night, but the weather was clear, with a visibility of at least 10 miles (15km). The wind was from a north-easterly direction at 11 knots. Evidence indicated that the aircraft's radar altimeter was functioning, but no conclusions could be made in its barometic altimeter readings. Though the interrupted radio communications undoubtedly factored in the crash, the cause was not disclosed by Air Force authorities.

Date: 21 December 1973 (time unknown)
Location: Near Saigon, South Vietnam
Operator: (South) Vietnamese Air Force
Aircraft type: Boeing/Vertol CH-47

The turbine-engine helicopter, which was loaded with ammunition, exploded while apparently on the ground in the Mekong Delta region. Most or all of the 20 persons killed and 17 injured were believed to have been South Vietnamese military personnel.

Date: 9 January 1974 (16:36)
Location: Near Neiva, Huila, Colombia
Operator: Fuerza Aérea Colombiana (Colombian Air Force)
Aircraft type: Hawker Siddeley HS 748-2A (FAC-1103)

All 31 persons aboard perished, including a crew of three military personnel, when the twin-engine turboprop, which was operated by the military airline Servicio de Aeronavegación a Territorios Nacionales (SATENA) and on a scheduled domestic service to Bogotá, crashed and burned on a mountain 15 miles (25km) north of Florencia, from where it had taken off shortly before. The late afternoon accident was attributed to a sudden change in the weather, but Colombian aviation authorities provided no further details.

Date: 10 January 1974 (time unknown)
Location: Northern Bolivia
Operator: Fuerza Aérea Boliviana (Bolivian Air Force)
Aircraft type: Douglas C-54 (TAM-52)

Operated by Transportes Aereos Militares and on a non-scheduled domestic service of the Bolivian military-operated airline to La Paz, the four-engine aircraft vanished with 24 persons aboard (21 passengers and a crew of three). Having departed shortly before 16:00 local time from Santa Rosa, Beni, the aircraft was to have arrived at the capital city about an hour later.

Date: 18 August 1974 (time unknown)
Location: Near Kisangani, Haut-Zaire, Zaire
Operator: Force Aérienne Zairoise (Zairean Air Force)
Aircraft type: Lockheed C-130H (9T-TCD)

The crash of the four-engine turboprop transport claimed the lives of all 31 persons aboard the aircraft (24 passengers and a crew of seven). No further details about the accident were known.

Date: 12 December 1974 (time unknown)
Location: Near Moc Hoa, South Vietnam
Operator: (South) Vietnamese Air Force
Aircraft type: Boeing/Vertol CH-47

All 54 South Vietnamese military personnel aboard were killed when the turbine-engine

Hawker Siddeley 748-2A (FAC-1103) of the military airline SATENA, the actual aircraft that crashed during an internal Colombian flight. (Philip Jarrett)

helicopter was shot down 50 miles (80km) west of Saigon. The aircraft was engaged in a troop movement when hit by a surface-to-air missile.

Date: 8 January 1975 (c.08:30)
Location: Near Doncello, Caqueta, Colombia
Operator: Fuerza Aérea Colombiana (Colombian Air Force)
Aircraft type: Douglas DC-3 (FAC-688)

The vintage transport, which was operated by the Colombian military airline Servicio de Aeronavegación a Territorios Nacionales (SATENA), crashed and burned in a mountainous region while en route from San Vicente del Caguan to Florencia, one segment of a domestic passenger service that had originated at Neiva, Huila. Including a crew of four military personnel, all 21 persons aboard were killed. Using an inadequate flight plan, the pilot-in-command of FAC-668 had proceeded over the mountains in adverse meteorological conditions, which had reduced visibility along the route.

Date: 9 February 1975 (c.17:30)
Location: Near Souda, Crete
Operator: Luftwaffe (West German Air Force)
Aircraft type: Transall C-160D (50+63)

In the worst peacetime aviation disaster in the history of German military forces, all 40 servicemen aboard were killed, including a crew of five, when the twin-engine turboprop transport crashed about 5 miles (10km) south-east of Canea, where it was to have landed. The aircraft slammed into a mountain at an approximate height of 5,000ft (1,500m) during an instrument approach that was being conducted around dusk and in the midst of a snow shower. No information regarding the probable cause of the accident was disclosed by German military authorities.

Date: 16 March 1975 (13:40)
Location: Near Barito, Rio Negro, Argentina
Operator: Fuerza Aérea Argentina (Argentine Air Force)
Aircraft type: Fokker F.27 Mark 400M (TC-72)

Operated by the military airline Lineas Aéreas del Estado (LADE), the twin-engine turboprop transport crashed and burned 25 miles (40km) west of San Carlos de Bariloche, where it was to have landed. All 55 persons aboard were killed, including the five Air Force crewmen. The accident occurred near the end of a domestic flight that had originated at El Palomar Air Base, located near Buenos Aires, its passengers, except for two Uruguayans, consisting of Argentine military personnel and their dependents. During the final phase of the instrument landing system approach, which was being conducted in adverse meteorological conditions, the aircraft struck a mountain after the pilots had apparently descended below the minimum safe altitude before obtaining reliable navigational signals. A possible contributing factor was the crew's lack of knowledge of the winds at their flight altitude.

The worst German peacetime military air disaster involved a Luftwaffe-operated Transall C-160 turboprop transport, identical to this one. (Philip Jarrett)

This is the Argentine Air Force Fokker F.27 Mark 400M (TC-72), operated by the military airline LADE, involved in the accident on 16 March 1975. (Philip Jarrett)

Date: 20 March 1975 (c.23:00)
Location: Near Quilcene, Washington, US
Operator: US Air Force
Aircraft type: Lockheed C-141A (64-641)

Flown by the Military Airlift Command, the jet transport crashed, exploded and burned in Olympic National Park around 25 miles (40km) south-south-east of Port Angeles, and all 16 American servicemen aboard perished. Among the victims were six navy personnel riding as passengers. The aircraft had been on its assigned heading of 150 degrees when it struck a ridge of Mount Constance at an approximate elevation of 7,000ft (2,000m), or only about 150ft (50m) below the terrain level, some 60 miles (100km) north-west of McChord Air Force Base, where it was to have landed at the end of a transpacific cargo flight. This had originated at Clark Air Base, in the Philippines, with an en-route stop in Japan. The impact triggered an avalanche that buried much of the wreckage in the valley below. It was dark at the time, and the weather in the area consisted of clouds that extended from the ground to 15,000ft (5,000m), with a visibility of only about a quarter of a mile (500m). The wind was blowing from due south at 25 knots. In its last recorded radio transmission, 64-641 had acknowledged authorisation by the Seattle air-traffic control centre for descent from 10,000ft (3,000m), actually the minimum altitude at the scene of the accident, to 5,000ft (1,500m). This faulty clearance resulted from the controller's mis-identification of the C-141 with another aircraft, a US Navy A-6 jet, which had been at the same height but flying in a northerly direction. It was noted in the investigative report that pilots deviating from the airway structure usually have no

way of verifying their altitudes for the basis of challenging ATC height assignments.

Date: 4 April 1975 (c.16:30)
Location: Near Saigon, South Vietnam
Operator: US Air Force
Aircraft type: Lockheed C-5A (68-218)

During the final days before the collapse of South Vietnam, the United States was engaged in a frantic effort to evacuate civilians and military personnel from the war-torn nation it had supported for more than a decade. One series of missions, dubbed Operation *Babylift*, involved the transport of hundreds of Vietnamese orphans, many the children of American service personnel, for re-location in the US. This particular flight would be conducted by the largest fixed-wing aircraft in use by the American forces, and would end in the worst single non-combat US military aviation disaster. Flown by the Military Airlift Command, the C-5A had taken off from Saigon's Tan Son Nhut Airport, bound for the Philippines. Besides the children, the passengers included nurses and a number of other American civilians serving as escorts. Less than a quarter-of-an-hour into the flight, at 16:15 local time, while flying over the South China Sea on a heading of 136 degrees and at a position of 25 miles (40km) south-east of Vung Tau, South Vietnam, the rear cargo door and loading ramp blew off. This resulted in a rapid decompression that in turn ejected several victims out of the fuselage. In the process, the aircraft's torque deck was ruptured, its rudder and elevators cables severed and two of its hydraulic systems rendered inoperative, resulting in a loss of pitch

A Lockheed C-5A Galaxy wide-bodied jet transport, the largest fixed-wing aircraft in the US Air Force fleet and the type involved in the Vietnamese 'Babylift' disaster. (Lockheed Martin)

control. The crew was only able to maintain control using their flight spoilers, starboard aileron and engine thrust. Having turned back toward its point of departure, 68-218 began an approach to Runway 25L. In order to effect alignment with the runway, a left turn was initiated, but at this time the nose of the aircraft dropped. At that point, the pilot levelled out and set down in a rice paddy about 2½ miles (4km) short of the runway. Touching down at an approximate speed of 310mph (500kph) with its undercarriage extended and left wing slightly low,

the wide-bodied jet transport became airborne briefly, and after the second impact with a dike on the western bank of the Saigon River, broke apart and burst into flames. Killed in the tragedy were 155 of the 330 persons aboard, including about 100 children and five members of the aircraft's crew of 16 Air Force personnel; most of the survivors suffered injuries, some of them related to the in-flight decompression. The flight crew, who escaped serious injury, were later commended for displaying 'great ingenuity and professionalism' in coping with

Despite the almost complete break-up of the C-5A following a crash landing in a rice paddy, more than half of the 330 persons aboard survived. (US Air Force)

a critical situation which, as noted in the investigative report, was not covered in any flight manual. Two significant actions of the pilot were the increase of power after the initial loss of pitch control to arrest the descent of the aircraft and the levelling of the aircraft during the turn on to the final approach course, which probably prevented a complete loss of control. It was determined that the first three latches on the right side of the ramp became unlocked, resulting in the structural failure after the C-5A had ascended to just above 23,000ft (7,000m). An investigative board was unable to conclusively determine the specific reason for this, however, because a significant number of parts were not recovered. The ramp and part of the cargo door were later found by the US Navy, and a sequence of events was established leading up to their loss. Following the loss of support provided by the first three locks, the load was dynamically transferred through the ramp structure to the fuselage hinges and the four remaining locks of the right side, leading to a partial or complete failure of the tie rod between locks 3 and 4. Ultimately, the ramp was torn from right to left and both it and the pressure door separated from the aircraft. The entire failure sequence was believed to have occurred in less than a second. The weather conditions at the scene of the accident, with scattered clouds at 4,000ft (1,200m) and broken layers at higher altitudes, a visibility of 7 miles (c.11km) and a 15-knot wind from a direction of 120 degrees, were not considered a contributing factor. Prior to recommended changes in its locking system, the rear cargo door on all aircraft in the C-5A fleet would not be used for loading or unloading, and never again would one of the giant Lockheed transports be used to carry a large load of passengers.

Date: 13 May 1975 (c.21:15)
Location: Near Sakon Nakhon, Thailand
Operator: US Air Force
Aircraft type: Sikorsky CH-53C (68-10933)

Participating in a special operations mission to rescue the crew of the *Mayaguez*, an American cargo ship captured by Cambodian military forces, the turbine-engine helicopter crashed about 40 miles (65km) west of Nakhom Phanom Air Base, from where it had taken off earlier. All 23 American servicemen aboard the aircraft (19 passengers and a crew of four) perished. Bound for Utapao Air Base, also in Thailand, the CH-53 had been cruising in darkness on almost due westerly heading and at an approximate height of 9,000ft (2,700m) when it was observed by eye-witnesses to go into a descending, uncontrollable spiral before it slammed to earth in an inverted attitude, exploded and burned. Found a considerable distance from the crash site were the aircraft's main rotor head assembly and main gearbox, indicating the mid-air

separation of them. The tail rotor and tail gearbox then separated as part of the break-up sequence. The suspected cause of the accident was the failure due to cracking of a rotor sleeve/spindle assembly, which on a helicopter mates the main blade with the rotor head. The fracture in the threaded area of the sleeve started internally and propagated to its surface. Though its age could not be determined, the crack had undoubtedly existed prior to the fatal flight. The separation of the corresponding blade created an imbalance in the main rotor assembly, which in turn tore off the main gearbox and the five other blades. The local meteorological conditions at the time, with a visibility of 7 miles (11km) and a 15-knot wind from a direction of 150 degrees, were not considered as contributory to the accident.

Date: 3 August 1975 (c.19:30)
Location: Near Amapala, Valle, Honduras
Operator: Fuerza Aérea de Nicaragua (Nicaraguan Air Force)
Aircraft type: Douglas C-47 (412)

The twin-engine transport, its passengers comprising a group of Mexican performers, plunged into the Pacific Ocean about 1,000ft (300m) from shore and 150 miles (250km) south of San Salvador. There were no survivors among the 20 persons aboard the aircraft, including a crew of three Nicaraguan military personnel. Subsequently, all of the victims' bodies were recovered from the water. During a flight originating at Veracruz, Mexico, with an ultimate destination of Managua, Nicaragua, the aircraft had encountered adverse weather conditions and as a result was unable to land for refuelling at Ilopango, El Salvador. It was last seen flying over the water at a low altitude, apparently trying to land, before it crashed around sunset and in conditions of bad visibility due to the storm. Though not officially reported, fuel exhaustion and/or a loss of air speed may have factored in the accident.

Date: 27 October 1975 (c.06:45)
Location: Near Caranavi, La Paz, Bolivia
Operator: Fuerza Aérea Boliviana (Bolivian Air Force)
Aircraft type: Convair 440 (TAM-44)

Operated by the military airline Transportes Aereos Militares (TAM) and carrying as passengers mostly military personnel but also some civilians, the twin-engine aircraft crashed in the Cerro Colorado region of the Andes Mountains 50 miles (80km) north-east of the capital city of La Paz, which was the destination of this internal flight that had departed minutes earlier from Tomonoco. All 67 persons aboard, including a crew of four servicemen, were killed. Following its take-off on the north/south runway, the transport had reached a height of only about 300ft (100m) above the ground, which was insufficient to clear the high terrain surrounding the airport. The weather at the time was neither bad nor 'optimal', according to a military official. Having seats for less than 50 passengers, TAM-44 was apparently overloaded at the time of the accident, and this could have been a significant factor in its crash. However, no official findings were released.

Date: 25 November 1975 (c.18:50)
Location: Near Bir Lahfan, Egypt
Operator: Israel Defence Force Air Force
Aircraft type: Lockheed C-130H (011)

The four-engine turboprop transport crashed on the Israeli-occupied Sinai Peninsula, 25 miles (40km) south of El 'Arish, and all 20 military personnel aboard (nine passengers and a crew of 11) perished. Flying in darkness, the aircraft struck cloud-obscured Jebel Halal, which rises to nearly 3,000ft (1,000m), only about 15ft (5m) below the summit of the mountain. Apparently due to a navigational error, the pilot had assumed a course that took it directly into, instead of around, the high terrain.

Date: 20 January 1976 (c.07:15)
Location: Near Loja, Azuay, Ecuador
Operator: Fuerza Aérea Ecuatoriana (Ecuadorean Air Force)
Aircraft type: Hawker Siddeley 748 Series 2A-246 (FAE-683)

Operated by the military airline Transportes Aereos Militares Ecuatorianos (TAME) on a scheduled domestic service to Guayaquil, the twin-engine turboprop crashed at an approximate elevation of 9,000ft (2,700m) in the Chillacocha mountain range. Including the crew of six military personnel, 34 persons aboard were killed; the seven surviving passengers suffered various injuries. For reasons that were not determined, the aircraft lost height and slammed into a wooded area 10 minutes after it had taken off from Loja's La Toma Airport. The meteorological conditions were reportedly good and apparently not a factor in the accident.

Date: 9 May 1976 (c.16:30)
Location: Near Carrascosa del Campo, Cuenca, Spain
Operator: Imperial Iranian Air Force
Aircraft type: Boeing 747-131F (5-283)

All 17 persons aboard, including a crew of 10 Iranian and US service personnel, perished in the fiery crash of the wide-bodied jet transport, which took place about 60 miles (100km) east-south-east of Madrid. Some of its seven passengers were American civilians. The 747 had been on a military logistics flight originating at Tehran, Iran, with an ultimate destination of McGuire Air Force Base, in New Jersey, US, when it plummeted into farmland after an explosion shattered its left wing, the accident occurring during a landing approach to Barajas Airport, located near the Spanish capital and an intermediate stop. The last radio transmission from 5-283 was the acknowledgement of clearance, which the crew had requested, to proceed on a heading of 260 degrees, or to the left of the direct course, to avoid adverse weather conditions, and for descent from 10,000 to 5,000ft (3,000–1,500m). As confirmed by the pattern of wreckage, which was scattered along a south-westerly heading over an

The world-famous Boeing 747 wide-bodied jetliner, one of which, flown by the Imperial Iranian Air Force and virtually identical to this aircraft, crashed in Spain. (Boeing)

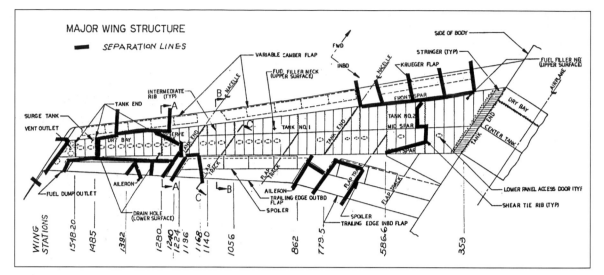

A diagram of the wing section indicating the pattern of break-up of the Iranian military Boeing 747 apparently struck by lightning. (National Transportation Safety Board)

area some 5 miles (10km) long and approximately 2½ miles (4km) wide, and by the reading of an electric altimeter, which remained fixed to the moment of power cessation, the break-up had occurred shortly after that message, when the cleanly-configured aircraft was at an altitude of around 6,000ft (1,800m) above the ground. Due to the circumstances of the accident and because it involved an American-built jet transport used widely in commercial airline operations throughout the world, the US National Transportation Safety Board (NTSB) requested and was granted permission to assist in the investigation, and its findings were published in a report released some two years later. Since the aircraft's flight data recorder had been inoperative at the time of the crash, the probe concentrated on information obtained from the cockpit voice recorder (CVR) and through examination of the wing itself, which was found to have broken into 15 major pieces in the air. The remains of the wing were re-assembled in a mock-up at the National Aviation Facilities Experimental Centre of the US Federal Aviation Administration, in Atlantic City, New Jersey. Comments of the crew transcribed by the CVR and eye-witness reports confirmed the presence of severe thunderstorm activity at the time and location of the accident. An electrical transient heard on the voice recorder tape was interpreted as an indication that the 747 had been struck by lightning in flight. An explosion took place a fraction of a second afterwards; shortly thereafter, the pilot-in-command was heard to say, 'The flight control is not working', and the gear warning horn started to sound. Nearly a minute elapsed between the transient and the end of the recording. As further indication of such a strike, pitting and localised burning areas typical of lightning attachment

damage were found on the left wing tip and on the vertical stabiliser, at the location of the very-high-frequency antenna. Following an analysis of the available evidence, it was concluded that the most probable sequence of events culminating in the multiple structural failures that ended with the separation of the wing, began with the lightning-induced ignition of vapours, produced by the mixture of JP-4 and kerosene with which 5-283 had been fuelled, and which were present in the No. 1 wing tank. The damage to the structure in the area of the tank provided positive indications of an explosion. The most convincing evidence of such 'over-pressure' was the symmetry of damage and the direction of the forces applied to closure ribs, spars and skin, as indicated by the directions of the fractures, bends and fastener-hole deformation; the collapse of the fuel jettison tube located within the tank, and the pattern of heat damage and soot on the structure adjacent to the tank. In line with this theory, the explosion would have caused the failure of the fasteners that held the stringers to the ribs and the skin to the spars, resulting in a loss in the integrity of the aft wing box, which greatly reduced the torsional strength of the wing itself; support of the No. 1 power plant in the pitch plane was also lost. The outer wing then began to oscillate, with lateral loads being generated by the vibrating engine, ultimately leading to the failure of the outer wing section. Evidence indicated that lightning first entered a forward part of the aircraft, perhaps on top of the flight deck section, and exited from a static discharger on the left wing tip. The flash 'hung on' to the initial attachment point as the 747 progressed forward until its vertical stabiliser reached that location, whereupon it re-attached to the fin and continued to exit from the left wing tip.

The conductive path of the lightning current to the static discharger at the tip was through a bond strap along the trailing edge. Concentration of current at the riveted joint between this strap and a wing rib caused melting and the release of molten metal and gasses, which were sufficiently conductive to cause the flash to re-attach to this rivet and to leave the discharger. Carefully examined were how and where fuel vapour ignition might have occurred, with an electrical spark at one of the fuel line couplings considered one possibility. Most likely, however, was that the point of ignition centred in the immediate area of a motor-driven fuel valve, whose connecting drive shaft may have provided a path for an electric current to enter the tank and cause a spark. It was noted in the investigative report that lightning-induced ignition of fuel vapours had occurred in a few previous aircraft accidents, but only under a rare combination of circumstances, in accordance with the following scenario: an intermittently conductive path was available that closed and opened an electrical 'loop'; a lightning-induced current of sufficient intensity flowed in this path and formed a spark, and a flammable vapour surrounded this spark. Specialists from the US National Aeronautics and Space Administration, which participated in the inquiry, concluded that the wing failure resulted simply from the imposition of loads produced by the turbulence within the thunderstorm that exceeded the designed strength of the structure. According to the NTSB, however, this theory was not supported by the physical evidence, ie, the condition and dispersal of the wreckage, the comments of the crew transcribed by the CVR and eye-witness accounts.

Date: 28 August 1976 (c.12:40)
Location: Near Peterborough, Cambridge, England
Operator: US Air Force
Aircraft type: Lockheed C-141A (67-0006)

Operated by the Military Airlift Command (MAC), the jet transport crashed and burned in a field while preparing to land at Royal Air Force Mildenhall, located near Bury St Edmunds. All 18 American service personnel aboard, who included four passengers in addition to the crew of 14, perished. The C-141 had been on an airlift training mission from McGuire Air Force Base, New Jersey, US, to Torrejon de Ardoz Air Base, in Spain, when it broke up in flight and plummeted to earth about 25 miles (40km) north-west of the RAF facility, which was an en-route stop. Prior to the accident, 67-0006 had requested radar vectors around an area of severe thunderstorm activity, to which the ground controller replied, 'There's no way I can get you around it'. Subsequently, the crew attempted to navigate visually between storm cells, and in their last radio transmission, they reported turning back towards the base, on to a heading of 140 degrees, and requested a precision radar (PAR) approach to Runway 11. At the moment it suffered structural failure, the cleanly-configured transport was at an approximate height of 9,000ft (2,700m) and flying in a south-south-easterly direction, with all four

A US Air Force Lockheed C-141A Starlifter jet transport, two of which crashed fatally during a single day in August 1976. (Lockheed Martin)

Emergency personnel converge on the scene where the C-141 plummeted into the British countryside after breaking up during a thunderstorm. (AP/Wide World Photos)

engines, its starboard wing, horizontal stabiliser and upper half of its vertical tail fin separating from the aircraft. Some 15 miles (25km) south-south-west of the crash site, it was raining, with a broken overcast at 4,000ft (1,200m), scattered stratus clouds down to about 1,000ft (300m) and maximum cloud tops at 26,000ft (8,000m). The thunderstorm itself was capable of extreme turbulence. Its radar track indicated that the C-141 had intercepted the leading edge of the storm, actually the inflow or up-draught area, which would create the greatest turbulence potential. Whether this condition led directly to the destruction of the aircraft was not revealed in the investigative report. However, it was noted that due to the lack of evidence, a lightning strike apparently did not precipitate the break-up sequence.

Date: 28 August 1976 (c.12:40)
Location: Near Holsteinborg, Greenland
Operator: US Air Force
Aircraft type: Lockheed C-141A (67-0008)

The second fatal MAC C-141 crash within about three hours occurred as the jet transport was landing at Sondrestrom Air Base, following an airlift mission from Thule Air Base, also located on Greenland. Killed in this second accident were 23 persons aboard the aircraft, including eight Danish civilians; two of the victims succumbed within a three-day period about two weeks later. Three passengers and one of the eight crewmen assigned

to 67-0008, all US Air Force personnel, survived with various injuries. After a PAR approach, the aircraft touched down on Runway 11 on its extended undercarriage and with flaps fully deployed, but at approximately the mid-field position, the left wing tip contacted the pavement. As it proceeded, the C-141 drifted first to the left before departing the runway off its right side and some 2,400ft (730m) short of the departure end. The aircraft was destroyed by impact forces and by fire, which had erupted when the wing first scraped the ground. At the time, the weather consisted of a high, broken overcast, with a visibility of 10 miles (15km) and a light, north-westerly wind. The type of accident was described in the investigative report as a 'hard landing', in which the aircraft's nose gear collapsed rearward. Although no conclusions were given, the absence of evidence of material failure in the engines, flight controls or flight instruments pointed to some operational factor as causing the crash.

Date: 3 September 1976 (c.21:45)
Location: Azores Islands, Portugal
Operator: Fuerza Aérea Venezolana (Venezuelan Air Force)
Aircraft type: Lockheed C-130H (7772)

All 68 persons aboard were killed, including a crew of 10 military personnel, when the four-engine turboprop transport crashed and burned on Terceira Island, as it was attempting to land at the

Lajes Air Base, located near Praira da Vitoria. Most of the passengers of the aircraft, which was on a transatlantic flight originating at Simon Bolivar Airport, serving Caracas, belonged to a Venezuelan college choir slated to perform in Barcelona, Spain. During its approach to Runway 16, in darkness and adverse meteorological conditions consisting of little or no visibility, heavy rain and winds of up to around 30 knots, the C-130 slammed into a hill approximately a mile (1.5km) from its threshold. Reportedly, it had not been properly aligned with the runway at the time of impact, with the bad weather, which was associated with the passage of hurricane *Emmy*, being considered as the primary causative factor. The control tower had reportedly tried unsuccessfully to correct the erroneous flight path of the aircraft in the final seconds before the crash.

Date: 3 March 1977 (c.15:00)
Location: Near Cascina, Toscana, Italy
Operator: Aeronautica Militare Italiano (Italian Air Force)
Aircraft type: Lockheed C-130H (MM61995)

The four-engine turboprop transport, carrying 38 naval cadets on an 'orientation flight' with an officer accompanying them, plus a crew of five Air Force personnel, crashed on Mount Serra 10 miles (15km) north-east of Pisa. All 44 Italian servicemen aboard perished. Having taken off about five minutes earlier from Runway 04 at San Giusto Airport, serving Pisa, the aircraft was observed by eye-witnesses to initiate an evasive manoeuvre, pulling up and banking to the right, just before it slammed into the wooded terrain at an approximate elevation of 2,600ft (800m), or about 600ft (180m) below the top of the mountain, bursting into flames on impact. The local meteorological conditions around the time of the accident consisted of a low overcast that obscured the terrain surrounding the airport, with 5/8 strato-cumulus at around 2,500ft (750m) and 4/8 alto-cumulus down to 800ft (250m), and a visibility of about 3½ miles (6km) in haze. The wind was calm. Although no official cause was given, released information indicated that the highly-experienced pilot at the controls of the C-130 had deviated from the assigned flight path. There had been no distress message from MM61995, and sabotage or any other type of in-flight explosion was definitely ruled out by military authorities after an initial examination of the wreckage.

Date: 10 May 1977 (c.20:30)
Location: Near Jericho, Jordan
Operator: Israel Defence Force Air Force
Aircraft type: Sikorsky CH-53D (360)

All 54 Israeli servicemen aboard were killed when the turbine-engine helicopter crashed

The aftermath of the Venezuelan Air Force C-130 crash on Terceira Island, in the Azores, which wiped out a college choir on their way to Spain. (UPI/Corbis-Bettmann)

and exploded in a sandy desert region of the occupied West Bank, 5 miles (10km) west of the Jordan River. The victims included a crew of four; most of the passengers were army paratroopers participating in a joint exercise with the Air Force. Occurring a few minutes after the aircraft had taken off, the accident was attributed to pilot error, specifically, flight in darkness below a safe altitude.

Date: 21 June 1977 (c.22:30)
Location: Off Wake Island
Operator: US Navy
Aircraft type: Lockheed EC-130Q (156176)

The airborne command and control aircraft, with a crew of 16 military personnel aboard, crashed in the Pacific Ocean moments after taking off from Wake Island Naval Air Station, on an operational mission. Searchers found only one body; there were no survivors. Also recovered were two power plants, a portion of one wing and some other debris, but the main wreckage of 156176 was lost at sea. Climbing to no higher than 400ft (120m), the four-engine turboprop slammed into the water approximately one mile (1.5km) from the end of Runway 10, which it had used, exploding on impact and creating a fire that burned for a while on the surface of the ocean. The accident occurred in moonlit darkness and weather conditions consisting of a

2,000ft (600m) ceiling and winds out of the east at 17 knots, gusting to 22. For unknown reasons, the EC-130 had failed to follow the normal climb-out profile. One possible explanation for the crash was that the pilots had lost their visual and peripheral references immediately after passing over the departure end of the runway. One endorsement in the Navy investigative report expressed the opinion that the absence of control tower personnel on duty at the time of the take-off, who could have monitored the climb-out of the aircraft, deprived the crew of an additional safeguard.

Date: 14 July 1977 (c.12:30)
Location: Near Cuangar, Cuando Cubango, Angola
Operator: Força Aérea Populare de Angola (Angolan Air Force)
Aircraft type: Antonov An-26

The Soviet-built twin-engine turboprop transport was reportedly shot down by rebels near the border of Namibia, and all 30 persons aboard were killed. According to witnesses, the aircraft appeared to have been hit at an approximate height of 150ft (50m) above the ground immediately after it had taken off from an airstrip.

The remains of the US Air Force EC-135K that ploughed into the rising terrain shortly after taking off from Kirtland Air Force Base. (US Air Force)

Date: 24 July 1977 (c.19:00)
Location: Near Puerto Montt, Los Lagos, Chile
Operator: Fuerza Aérea de Chile (Chilean Air Force)
Aircraft type: Douglas DC-6B (FAC-989)

As it was attempting to land in darkness and during a heavy rain, the four-engine transport slammed into a swamp and burst into flames. Killed in the accident were 38 of the 82 persons aboard the aircraft, including its entire crew of seven military personnel; many of the surviving passengers suffered injuries. The crash occurred approximately 3 miles (5km) east of the runway during an instrument approach to El Tepual Air Base, an en-route stop during a domestic service originating at Punta Arenas, with an ultimate destination of Santiago. Offering no specific details, military authorities attributed the accident to the adverse weather conditions.

Date: 25 July 1977 (c.08:00)
Location: Near Yoro, Honduras
Operator: Fuerza Aérea Hondurena (Honduran Air Force)
Aircraft type: Douglas C-47 (301)

Apparently overloaded with public employees and their families, the twin-engine transport crashed and burned in a mountainous region shortly after taking off from the Yoro airport, bound for the Honduran capital of Tegucigalpa, 80 miles (130km) to the south. The accident claimed the lives of 25 persons aboard the aircraft, while the 15 survivors suffered various injuries. According to unofficial reports, the left power plant of the C-47 had 'exploded' in flight.

Date: 14 September 1977 (23:48)
Location: Near Albuquerque, New Mexico, US
Operator: US Air Force
Aircraft type: Boeing EC-135K (62-3536)

Operated by the Tactical Air Command as an airborne command and control platform, the modified jet tanker crashed about 2½ minutes after taking off from Kirtland Air Force Base, and its entire crew of 20 perished. The scene of the accident was in the Manzano Mountains, 5 miles (10km) beyond the departure end of Runway 08, which the aircraft had used, and at an approximate elevation of 6,500ft (1,980m). Climbing on a heading of 125 degrees, the cleanly-configured EC-135 was in a right bank of approximately 30 degrees when it struck a peak just 30ft (10m) below its summit. Examination of a recovered air speed indicator revealed a reading that correlated to around 185mph (300kph) at the moment of the crash. Initial contact was with its right wing and No. 4 power plant, and in the subsequent impact the aircraft exploded and disintegrated. It was dark at the time, but the meteorological conditions were otherwise good, with a broken overcast at 11,000ft (3,400m), a visibility of 15 miles (25km) and a south-easterly wind of 4 knots. The investigation found no evidence of in-flight fire, explosion or structural, electrical, instrument, engine or flight control failure prior to impact. It was reported that before the crash, 62-3536 had been observed on radar to be flying too low, and that a ground controller unsuccessfully instructed it to turn right and climb. Fatigue may have contributed to the crew's failure to follow the proper departure flight profile.

Date: 21 October 1977 (c.10:30)
Location: Mindoro, the Philippines
Operator: US Marine Corps
Aircraft type: Sikorsky CH-53D (157139)

The turbine-engine helicopter, carrying a load of troops and also lifting with an external sling an empty water container, or 'bull', crashed and burned in mountainous terrain 80 miles (130km) south-west of Manila. Killed in the accident were 24 of the 37 American servicemen aboard the aircraft, including the entire crew of four, while the 13 surviving passengers and a US Navy corpsman who came to the scene to help suffered injuries. After it began to lift the water trailer off the ground, the rotorcraft yawed to the right, whereupon the crew released the container. At that point, the CH-53 appeared to stabilise momentarily, but then continued with increasing speed in its clock-wise rotation, while in a nose-high attitude. During this time, a number of occupants were ejected from the rear cargo door. Still spinning, the aircraft descended until it struck the terrain 300ft (100m) below the saddle from which it had picked up the water trailer, the impact shearing off its tail rotor and a large portion of the tail assembly. It finally nosed down and slammed to earth, rolling over at least twice before coming to rest generally up-right. Around the time of the accident, the local weather consisted of scattered cumulus and strato-cumulus at 2,000ft (600m) and greater cloud coverage at higher altitudes, and a visibility of 15 miles (25km) in light haze. The wind was out of the north at 8 knots, gusting to almost twice that velocity. It was the opinion of the officer in charge of the investigation that the high gross weight of the aircraft and the density altitude conditions in which it had been operating, requiring high power while both hovering and lifting an external load, exceeded the authority of the tail rotor to counter the torque effect of the main rotor and thus maintain directionally-controlled flight. The external load was jettisoned in an unsuccessful attempt to regain control, and it appeared that the crew then lowered the collective pitch, reducing the power applied to the rotor system, and further tried to fly down the slope of the hill in order to effect recovery, without success. There was no evidence of any mechanical failure factoring in the accident. The investigating officer further expressed the opinion that with proper restraint, all of those killed except the two pilots would have survived the crash, and a number of serious injuries would have been prevented. Though highly experienced, the flight crew was considered negligent in trying to lift a load under the prevailing conditions, and the crew chief for not requiring the passengers to use the seat belts that were available; the pilots apparently also failed to supervise him in this respect. With regard to the latter factor, one of the recommendations made in the accident report was that Marine personnel wear helmets and use seat belts when riding as passengers aboard rotary-wing aircraft.

Date: 26 November 1977 (c.02:30)
Location: Near Beziers, Herault, France
Operator: L'Armée de l'Air (French Air Force)
Aircraft type: Nord Noratlas (182)

The twin-engine transport, which was carrying as passengers members of a military band, crashed on a mountain slope and exploded north of the city. Including a crew of three, all 34 French military personnel aboard were killed in the accident, which occurred in early morning darkness and adverse weather conditions, with fog and gusty winds. No distress message was transmitted prior to impact, casting doubt on some eye-witness accounts of an in-flight fire. However, no official findings pertaining to the cause of the crash were disclosed by the military authorities.

Date: 10 February 1978 (c.11:20)
Location: Near Artigas, Uruguay
Operator: Fuerza Aérea Uruguaya (Uruguayan Air Force)
Aircraft type: Douglas C-47A (T511)

Operated by TAMU on a domestic passenger service originating at and ultimately bound for Montevideo, the vintage twin-engine transport crashed in a field while attempting an emergency landing at Artigas Airport, from where it had taken off moments earlier. All 44 persons aboard, including a crew of four military personnel, were killed. The aircraft had just become airborne when one power plant apparently malfunctioned, and its pilot then requested clearance to return to the airport, but following a steep turn it plummeted to the ground on a ranch and burst into flames approximately one mile (1.5km) from the end of the runway. The weather at the time was clear, with little or no wind, and was not considered to be a factor in the accident.

Date: 14 September 1978 (c.14:50)
Location: Paranaque, the Philippines
Operator: Philippine Air Force
Aircraft type: Fokker F.27 Friendship Mark 200 (10328)

The twin-engine turboprop transport crashed in a residential section near Manila International Airport, where it was to have landed. Killed in the accident were 21 of the 28 persons aboard the aircraft, including the entire crew of four military personnel, as well as 12 others on the ground. The seven surviving passengers and 20 persons on the ground suffered injuries. Following a domestic flight from Laoag, the F.27 had begun its approach to Runway 06 in the midst of a thunderstorm, with heavy rain, wind gusts of around 35 knots and a visibility of 1/2 to 2 miles (0.8km–3km). Its undercarriage extended, the transport slammed to earth to the left of the runway centreline, exploded and burned, destroying 10 houses. Reports of a pre-impact lightning strike were never confirmed officially as a factor in the crash; other possible causes were the low visibility at the time and adverse affects on the aircraft's flight instruments by the poor atmospheric conditions.

Date: 19 November 1978 (c.11:00)
Location: Near Leh, Kashmir, India
Operator: Indian Air Force
Aircraft type: Antonov An-12

The four-engine turboprop transport crashed and burned while attempting to land at the city's airport, the elevation of which is about 10,000ft (3,000m). Killed in the accident were all 77 Indian military personnel aboard the aircraft, including a crew of seven, and a woman on the ground. The passengers were all Army Jawans. Having completed an internal flight from Chandigarh, Punjab, the aircraft spiralled to the ground approximately 1.2 miles (2km) short of the runway after reportedly experiencing a power plant malfunction during the approach.

Date: 7 June 1979 (c.11:00)
Location: Near Leh, Kashmir, India
Operator: Indian Air Force
Aircraft type: Hindustan HAL 748-2M (H2178)

All 27 Indian military personnel aboard lost their lives, including seven Air Force personnel, when the twin-engine turboprop transport crashed about 10 minutes after it had taken off from the city's airport, bound for a forward area. The passengers of the aircraft were Army Jawans. No further details are known about the accident or its possible cause.

Date: 22 December 1979 (c.14:00)
Location: Near Puerto Esperanza, Ucayali, Peru
Operator: Fuerza Aérea del Peru (Peruvian Air Force)
Aircraft type: de Havilland DHC-5 Buffalo (348)

During a domestic service from Pucallpa to Puerto Esperanza, the twin-engine turboprop transport crashed in a jungle region 20 miles

The crash of the Philippine Air Force Fokker F.27 wreaked havoc in a residential area near Manila International Airport. (UPI/Corbis-Bettmann)

A Soviet-built and operated Antonov An-12, similar to the Indian Air Force transport involved in the disastrous crash in November 1978. (Martin Bowman)

(30km) from its destination, and all 29 persons aboard were killed. The victims included the five-member crew of the aircraft, all of whom were military personnel. A severe thunderstorm associated with a hurricane and containing strong down-draughts was believed responsible for the crash.

Date: 24 January 1980 (c.06:20)
Location: Near Mandalay, Burma
Operator: Union of Burma Air Force
Aircraft type: Fokker FH-227B (5003)

The twin-engine turboprop transport crashed, and burned killing all but one of the 44 persons aboard. Due to a reported mechanical failure, the pilot had requested clearance to the air base from where it had taken off shortly before, but the aircraft struck the top of a building during the attempted emergency landing.

Date: 22 February 1980 (time unknown)
Location: Near Agra, Uttar Pradesh, India
Operator: Indian Air Force
Aircraft type: Fairchild C-119G

Loaded with paratroopers who were to have made a training jump, the twin-engine transport crashed and burned as it was taking off from a military base located 120 miles (190km) south-east of New Delhi. Killed were all but one of the 47 Indian servicemen aboard the aircraft, and one person on the ground; the latter victim was a bicyclist riding on the runway, who in trying to avoid

may have led the pilot to initiate a premature lift-off, possibly resulting in a stall.

Date: 28 February 1980 (time unknown)
Location: Northern Guatemala
Operator: Fuerza Aérea Guatemalteca
  (Guatemalan Air Force)
Aircraft type: Douglas C-47

The twin-engine transport, carrying as passengers Guatemalan servicemen and their dependents on a tour of Mayan ruins, crashed in a mountainous area in the vicinity of Sabanetas of Peten, and all 21 persons aboard were killed.

Date: 14 March 1980 (c.15:00)
Location: Near Yenice, Cilicia, Turkey
Operator: US Air Force
Aircraft type: Lockheed C-130H (74-2064)

The four-engine turboprop transport plummeted into hilly terrain 25 miles (40km) south-west of Adana and about 15 miles (25km) due west of Incirlik Air Base, which was the point of origin and ultimate destination of a logistics mission in which the aircraft had been engaged in support of US military installations throughout Turkey. Including a crew of six US Air Force personnel, all 18 persons aboard perished. Last observed on radar at a height of around 5,000ft (1,500m), the C-130 had been descending, as cleared, to 3,000ft (1,000m) and on a south-south-easterly heading when an explosion occurred in its left wing. The weather in the area at

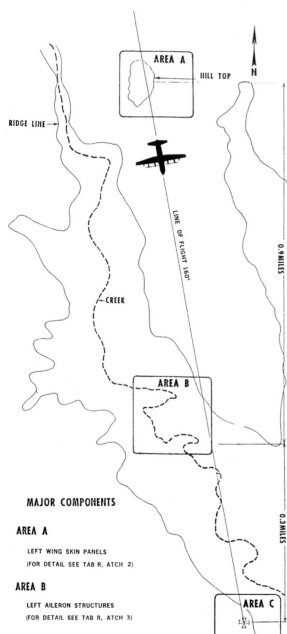

MAJOR COMPONENTS

AREA A

LEFT WING SKIN PANELS
(FOR DETAIL SEE TAB R, ATCH 2)

AREA B

LEFT AILERON STRUCTURES
(FOR DETAIL SEE TAB R, ATCH 3)

AREA C

MAIN CRASH SITE
(FOR DETAIL SEE TAB R, ATCH 4)

INCIRLIK TACAN
090° BEARING
14.5NM

Wreckage distribution chart showing the wide dispersal of debris following the in-flight explosion of a US Air Force C-130H. (US Air Force)

the time of the crash consisted of light rain, with a broken layer of cumulus clouds at 4,000ft (1,200m) and solid alto-stratus at 10,000ft (3,000m), with a visibility of around 5 miles (10km). The wind was calm. Although the combustible material was identified as fuel, the source of its ignition and the underlying material failure that led to the explosion remain a mystery.

Date: 15 September 1980 (c.00:00)
Location: Near Medina, Saudi Arabia
Operator: Royal Saudi Air Force
Aircraft type: Lockheed C-130E (453)

All 89 Saudi military personnel aboard (81 passengers and a crew of eight) perished in the flaming crash of the four-engine turboprop transport. The aircraft plummeted into the desert in early morning darkness, shortly after midnight, reportedly after a fire had erupted and then spread from the cockpit area.

Date: 17 September 1980 (time unknown)
Location: Near Kindu, Kivu, Zaire
Operator: Force Aérienne Zairoise (Zairean Air Force)
Aircraft type: de Havilland DHC-5 Buffalo (9T-CBA)

The twin-engine turboprop transport crashed immediately after it had taken off, killing all 36 persons aboard the aircraft. No specific details about the accident, including the possible cause, were made available.

Date: 30 September 1980 (time unknown)
Location: Badakshan, Afghanistan
Operator: Soviet Air Force
Aircraft type: Antonov An-12V (SSSR-11104)

The four-engine turboprop transport, which belonged to the Soviet airline Aeroflot, was apparently shot down by Afghan guerrilla forces while approaching to land at an unknown airfield, and all 45 persons aboard the aircraft were reportedly killed.

Date: 12 November 1980 (23:53)
Location: Near Cairo, Egypt
Operator: US Air Force
Aircraft type: Lockheed C-141A (67-0030)

Operated by the Military Airlift Command and completing a cargo flight from Ramstein Air Base, in West Germany, the jet transport crashed, disintegrated and burned in the desert as it was attempting to land at Cairo West Airport. All 13 American service personnel aboard (seven passengers and six crewmen) perished. Cleared for a visual approach to Runway 34, 67-0030 flew over the airport and then initiated a left turn near the mid-field point at an approximate height of 2,000ft (600m) and while descending. According to its

Little remains of the US Air Force C-141A jet transport that crashed in the desert during an attempted landing at Cairo West Airport. (AP/Wide World Photos)

flight data recorder read-out, the C-141 continued down with its left-banking attitude, speed and descent rate increasing dramatically until it struck the ground about a minute after initiating the left turn. Impact occurred 2 miles (3km) north-west of the assigned runway at an indicated air speed of around 290mph (465kph), with the cleanly-configured aircraft on a west-south-westerly heading. It was dark at the time of the accident, with no moon and little ground illumination, but the meteorological conditions were good, with a broken overcast at about 20,000ft (6,000m), a visibility of more than 5 miles (10km) and a north-easterly wind of 8 knots. The cause of the crash was not disclosed, but releasable findings revealed that the engines of the C-141 had been operating properly and also no evidence of flight control system failure prior to impact. Considered a contributing factor were the British Calvert System approach lights used at the airport. It was further noted in the investigative report that 67-0030 had been equipped, as are airliners, with a ground-proximity warning system, but because of its dependence on the aircraft's radar altimeter, it would not have provided timely warnings at extreme bank angles.

Date: 7 February 1981 (time unknown)
Location: Near Pargolovo, Russian Soviet
    Federated Socialist Republic, USSR
Operator: Soviet Navy
Aircraft type: Tupolev Tu-104A

Three high-ranking officers were among the 73 Soviet military personnel reportedly killed in the crash of the twin-jet transport, which occurred approximately 10 miles (15km) north of Leningrad shortly after it had taken off from that city's Pulkovo Airport. There were no survivors. The aircraft may have been part of the fleet of the Soviet airline Aeroflot.

Date: 26 February 1981 (c.05:25)
Location: South China Sea
Operator: US Air Force
Aircraft type: Lockheed MC-130E-1 (64-0564)

The four-engine turboprop aircraft crashed around 15 miles (25km) west-north-west of Subi Point Naval Air Station, from where it had taken off about an hour earlier, on a tactical exercise. Among the 24 servicemen aboard, all but one member of the crew of nine assigned to 64-0564 lost their lives. The seriously injured survivor was rescued by local fishermen, and the bodies of six victims were also recovered. The passengers consisted of American, Australian, Filipino and New Zealand military personnel. Local fishermen reported seeing the C-130, which had been flying at a low altitude in pre-dawn darkness and visual meteorological conditions, strike the surface of the water in a shallow descent, explode, burn and sink. No further information about the crash was, however, released by the US Air Force.

Date: 10 March 1981 (c.05:00)
Location: Comoro Islands
Operator: Aeronavale (French Naval Aviation)
Aircraft type: Dassault-Breguet Atlantique (29)

Shortly after it had taken off from the airport at Moroni, on Grande Comoro, the twin-engine turboprop patrol aircraft crashed into a hillside and exploded, killing all 18 French military personnel aboard. The victims included four maintenance workers riding as passengers in addition to the regular crew. Climbing to an approximate height of 500ft (150m), the Atlantique suddenly plummeted to earth after fire, which according to unofficial sources, had erupted in one power plant, the accident occurring in pre-dawn darkness at the beginning of an aerial surveillance mission.

Date: 6 May 1981 (c.10:50)
Location: Near Frederick, Maryland, US
Operator: US Air Force
Aircraft type: Boeing EC-135N (61-0328)

Originally designed as an astronaut relay and satellite tracking station, the modified jet transport, which was on a navigational training flight out of Wright-Patterson Air Force Base, in Ohio, crashed approximately 2 miles (3km) north-north-east of the town of Walkersville, located some 40 miles (65km) north-west of Baltimore. All 21 persons aboard perished; except for two dependents and one other civilian, the victims were all American military personnel, including the 17 designated crew members. One of the dependents, the wife of the aircraft's commander, had apparently been seated in the pilot's position at the start of the accident sequence. The EC-135 had been cruising at an altitude of 29,000ft (9,000m) and an indicated air speed of around 550mph (885kph) when, for undetermined reasons, its pitch trim moved to the full nose-down position, which was evident from post-impact examination of the cockpit indicator and the horizontal stabiliser mechanism itself. As a result, 61-0328 rapidly pitched down, most likely upon the release of the autopilot, which should have been able to overcome its trim except when near the full nose-down

position. This attitude would have induced sufficient negative gravitational forces to trip off line the generators, causing a total loss of electrical power and, in turn, preventing the pitch trim from being moved electrically. While unusual, this condition can easily be controlled with prompt corrective action, within 8 seconds, according to simulator tests, but in this case recovery was delayed, for reasons that could not be determined. (The pilot had apparently activated the stabiliser cut-out switch in an attempt to stop the trim from going into a more extreme position.) Under the circumstances, the pitch angle and the air speed of the aircraft would increase until the pitch trim is moved to the neutral position. Without electrical power, this must be accomplished manually with the control wheel on the console between the pilots' seats, which, in this situation, would have required about 35 revolutions to return the trim to zero. The four-engine jet was seen to emerge from a low overcast in a nose-down attitude of 20 to 30 degrees and at an air speed in excess of 460mph (740kph). It was around that time, and while at an approximate height of 1,500ft (500m) above the ground, that an explosion occurred in the pressurised compartment of the aircraft, resulting in the break-up of its fuselage and the separation of the wings. Around 90 seconds elapsed from the beginning of the descent until the final impact. Wreckage was strewn in an

A chart indicating the numerous break-up points of the US Air Force EC-135 that disintegrated during an uncontrolled dive. (US Air Force)

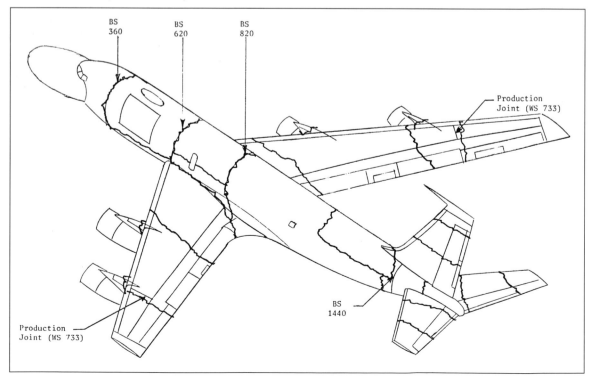

elliptical shape some 2,400ft (730m) long by about 1,800ft (550m) wide, with all debris being found within approximately 2½ miles (4km) of the main crash site. The surface weather in the area at the time was characterised by light rain, a slight breeze from a south-south-westerly direction, and a visibility of around 2½ miles (4km), but had been clear at the cruising altitude, with cloud tops at about 20,000ft (6,000m). The investigation found no evidence that the presence of passengers on the flight deck caused or contributed to the disaster, or of any explosion or structural failure prior to the uncontrolled descent. No previous problems had been reported with 61-0328, and although the cause of the pre-impact explosion could not be determined, the accident report concluded that by that time recovery from the dive would not have been possible and the crash was thus inevitable.

Date: 24 May 1981(c.15:00)
Location: Near Guachala, Zamora Chinchipe, Ecuador

First aircraft
Operator: Fuerza Aérea Ecuatoriana (Ecuadorean Air Force)
Type: Beechcraft Super King Air 200 (FAE-723)

Second aircraft
Operator: Fuerza Aérea Ecuatoriana (Ecuadorean Air Force)
Type: de Havilland DHC-6 Twin Otter Series 300 (FAE-457)

Both operated by the military airline Transportes Aereos Militares Ecuatorianos, the two twin-engine turboprop executive/transport aircraft, on internal flights from Quito to Macara, crashed and burned in mountainous terrain about 10 miles (15km) from the Peruvian border. A total of 27 persons were killed in the separate accidents, with no survivors from either aircraft; the nine aboard the Super King Air included Ecuadorean President Jaime Roldos and his wife, plus a crew of three. The separate accidents occurred as they were flying in formation in instrument meteorological conditions, with rain and fog.

Date: 26/27 May 1981 (c.00:00)
Location: North Atlantic Ocean (USS *Nimitz*)
Operator: US Marine Corps
Aircraft type: Grumman EA-6B (159910)

This crash and resulting explosions and fire wreaked havoc aboard the American nuclear-powered aircraft carrier USS *Nimitz* (CVN-68), which at the time was operating off the coast of Florida, US, 80 miles (130km) east of Jacksonville. Launched earlier in the evening from the Navy ship, on an electronic counter-measures training flight, the twin-jet aircraft involved in the accident

Heavy casualties and damage resulted from the crash of the US Marine Corps EA-6B atop the flight deck of the aircraft carrier USS Nimitz. (UPI/Corbis-Bettmann)

had been waved off in one unsuccessful landing attempt and as a result, was designated 'fuel critical'. Following a fuel-consuming interval, 159910 began a second approach, using the carrier's automatic landing system for guidance. After it crossed the centreline with a continuing right drift, power was applied at the order of the landing signal officer (LSO), but the EA-6B nevertheless crashed atop the vessel, careering across the flight deck and ploughing into aircraft parked toward its forward part. The initial accident, at approximately 23:50 local time, was followed about half-an-hour later by the detonation of a Sparrow air-to-air missile that had been knocked off an F-14 jet fighter. Killed in the aviation/marine disaster were a total of 14 Navy personnel, including the three crewmen of 159910, one of whom was lost at sea. Among the flight deck crew member casualties, two of those killed and more than half of the 42 injured were victims of the missile explosion. Eleven other aircraft were destroyed or damaged, with monetary costs exceeding $50 million. It was dark at the time of the crash, with scattered clouds at 3,500ft (1,050m) and broken layers estimated at 10,000ft (3,000m) and 25,000ft (7,500m), respectively, a visibility of around 5 miles (10km), and a relative wind (due to the 165-degree true heading of the ship) of 16 knots from a north-north-westerly direction. The horizon was not visible. There was also thunderstorm activity and rain in the area, which the carrier began to encounter within an hour of the crash. The accident was primarily attributed to the failure of the EA-6B to

666

maintain proper alignment during the landing. The primary contributing factor was the failure of the LSO to make a 'line-up' call and his faulty instructions to the pilot, 'Nice and easy, fly it down'. Also contributing to the error by the pilot were several psycho-physiological factors, most significantly, his use of a decongestant medication and of aspirin for treatment of a head cold from which he had been suffering. These were coupled with the stress associated with a night carrier landing, with which his experience was limited, in conditions of poor visibility that were conducive to vertigo and while facing a low-fuel situation due to the earlier 'boltered', or missed, pass. With regard to the first issue, the pilot had removed himself from the flight schedule on the morning of the accident, but in the afternoon reported feeling better. Although there was no record of him being prescribed a drug containing brompheniramine, an unusually high concentration of this element and also salicylates, found in aspirin, were found in his body in the subsequent autopsy. The side effects of the former include dizziness, lethargy and vision problems. A bottle of nasal spray was also found in a pocket of his flight suit. Additionally, the position of 159910 above the glide slope and viewed against a featureless background significantly impaired the ability of the LSO to see its starboard wing drop and increasing drift to the right of the centreline. There was no indication of a flight control system malfunction in the aircraft prior to impact. Revelation that six of the flight deck personnel killed were found to have used marijuana was considered more of a public relations dilemma for the Navy than a factor in their deaths, though the possible use of illegal drugs by emergency crews raised questions as to how it could have affected the post-crash fire-fighting efforts. As it was, their actions were considered 'commendable'. Among the recommendations made in the investigative report were to return to operational status on the *Nimitz* a centreline flasher system, which might have averted the crash, and for a review of procedures to insure aircraft fuel conservation in flight operations. With regard to the latter, it was noted that the EA-6B involved in the accident had apparently flown in a highly fuel-consuming configuration, ie, with its undercarriage and flaps extended, following the boltered pass.

Date: 22 September 1981 (c.12:00)
Location: Near Babaeski, Turkey
Operator: Turkish Air Force
Aircraft type: Northrop F-5A

The jet fighter crashed into a bivouac area 100 miles (150km) west of Istanbul, killing 40 military personnel on the ground. Among the 72 others injured was the pilot of the aircraft, who had ejected after an in-flight emergency.

Date: 29 September 1981 (c.19:00)
Location: Kahrizak, Tehran, Iran
Operator: Islamic Republic of Iran Air Force
Aircraft type: Lockheed C-130H (5-8552)

Four of the nation's top military leaders were among the estimated 80 persons killed when the four-engine turboprop transport crashed in Tir Square approximately 15 miles (25km) south of the city of Tehran, where it was to have landed. Some of the victims may have been on the ground. The aircraft was reportedly carrying dead and wounded service personnel from Ahvaz when the disaster occurred, in darkness.

Date: 14 January 1982 (time unknown)
Location: Near Addis Ababa, Ethiopia
Operator: Ethiopian Air Force
Aircraft type: Antonov An-12

All 73 persons were killed when the four-engine turboprop transport was shot down by rebel forces.

Date: 3 February 1982 (c.07:30)
Location: Djibouti
Operator: L'Armée de l'Air (French Air Force)
Aircraft type: Nord 2501 Noratlas (140/88-JA)

The twin-engine transport, carrying as passengers 29 members of the Foreign Legion plus a naval officer, crashed on a desert mountain before a planned paratroop drop. All 35 French military personnel aboard, including a crew of five, lost their lives in the accident, the cause of which was not disclosed.

Date: 5 February 1982 (c.15:00)
Location: Island of Cheju, South Korea
Operator: Republic of Korea Air Force
Aircraft type: Fairchild C-123

The twin-engine transport, carrying as passengers army troops participating in a training exercise, crashed into Mount Halla while it was approaching to land. All 53 South Korean servicemen aboard, including a crew of six, were killed. The accident occurred in adverse weather conditions, and may have resulted from an encounter with severe downdraughts.

Date: 7 February 1982 (time unknown)
Location: Near Srinagar, Jammu and Kashmir, India
Operator: Indian Air Force
Aircraft type: Fairchild C-119G

The crash of the twin-engine transport, which occurred in drizzle and falling snow, claimed the lives of all 23 persons aboard the aircraft.

Date: 19 March 1982 (c.21:10)
Location: Near Woodstock, Illinois, US
Operator: US Air Force
Aircraft type: Boeing KC-135A (58-0031)

Operated by the Strategic Air Command, the jet tanker crashed, exploded and burned 40 miles (65km) north-west of Chicago's O'Hare International Airport, where it was to have landed. All 27 American military personnel aboard perished, including four crewmen. The aircraft had earlier in the evening been on a training mission and making practice landing approaches to K.I. Sawyer Air Force Base, in Upper Michigan, then landed there to pick up a load of passengers, all of whom were stranded by the grounding of a C-130 transport due to mechanical trouble. After being cleared for descent from 22,000 to 8,000ft (6,700–2,500m), and seconds after acknowledging a request for a speed reduction, the KC-135 disintegrated, its fuselage breaking apart and vertical and horizontal stabilisers and all four engines separating. At the moment of its structural failure, the cleanly-configured aircraft had been descending on an almost due southerly heading at a true air speed of around 360mph (580kph) and was at an approximate height of 13,700ft (4,200m), and it then plummeted almost vertically into the wooded, marshy terrain. Wreckage was scattered over an area about 5 miles (10km) long and 2 miles (3km) wide. It was dark at the time of the accident, and the weather conditions in the area consisted of light to moderate rain showers, a ceiling of around 500ft (150m) and a surface visibility of 1 to 3 miles (1.5–5km). Winds at the approximate height of the break-up were about 30 knots from a south-westerly direction. According to the investigative report, the probability of thunderstorm activity being in the vicinity of the crash site at the time appeared 'extremely low'. Following a thorough examination of the wreckage, no conclusive evidence was found pinpointing what caused the disintegration of the aircraft. Considered as 'most probable', according to the investigative report, was an over-pressurisation under the cargo floor, an area that houses fuel and other potential sources of ignition. An explosion caused by the ignition of accumulated combustible vapours occurring in that area could, in fact, rapidly propagate to adjacent areas where fuel is present. There was also 'strong evidence' of explosive over-pressures in the forward, aft and upper fuel tank areas. Significantly, investigation showed that were the walls or fittings of the rubber bladder cells containing the volatile liquid to fail, fuel or vapour could be released into the tank cavity and in turn migrate to other parts of the aircraft. Although there was no evidence of a lightning strike, and no definite factor could be identified, the report noted that there would have been many potential sources of ignition throughout the KC-135. Among these were hot surfaces, such as

A muddy crater marks the impact site of the KC-135 that crashed following an unexplained mid-air explosion near Chicago. (AP/Wide World Photos)

boost pumps or bleed air lines; electrical arcing or chafing of electrical power lines. One recommendation was for the thorough examination of electrical wiring and antenna routeing to assure proper clearance in order to prevent chafing, especially in areas where fuel vapors are present. Subsequent testing, however, showed that the ignition of fuel vapours through chafing of the very-high-frequency antenna lead, one early concern, was 'not probable'.

Date: 13 April 1982 (c.14:40)
Location: Near Erzincan, Turkey
Operator: US Air Force
Aircraft type: Lockheed C-130H (74-01678)

All 27 persons aboard perished in the flaming crash of the four-engine turboprop transport, which occurred about 100 miles (150km) east of Sivas. Four of the victims were American civilians riding as passengers, the rest US service personnel, including the eight crewmen assigned to the aircraft. Operated by the Military Airlift Command, the C-130 was on an internal Turkish flight from Erzurum to Incirlik Air Base, located near Adana, where the mission had originated earlier in the day, when it suffered catastrophic structural failure. Last reported cruising at a height of 20,000ft (6,000m), 74-01678

A wide view of the US Air Force C-130 crash site following the in-flight break-up of the transport over Turkey. (US Air Force)

A Royal Navy Westland Sea King helicopter, the type involved in a fatal crash at sea during the Falklands War in the South Atlantic. (Westland Helicopters)

transmitted a 'Mayday' distress message before it fell in flames into mountainous terrain. Visual meteorological conditions prevailed in the area at the time of the accident. When considering their rotational markings and the fact that portions of their blades were found a distance from the main crash site, it was concluded that the two right propellers had come in contact with other parts of the aircraft and possibly each other. The break-up sequence apparently began with the failure of the No. 4 engine support structure. The No. 3 propeller and gear assembly also separated from the corresponding power plant and sliced into the wing structure, the first strike being against the nose of the starboard external fuel tank. Ultimately, the right outer wing experienced an 'over-pressure' and its outer portion was blown forward, resulting in an in-flight fire. The aerodynamic forces produced by this condition led to the failure of the left outer wing through overloading. According to the investigative report, there were indications that one of the two primary attachment bolts in the No. 4 power plant support had not been installed at the time of the crash, and that the left quick engine change (QEC) longerons, or longitudinal supports, had failed in tension and inboard bending. The QEC right upper attachment bolt had also failed, and the diagonal brace aft attachment fitting was sheared. The underlying reasons for these conditions were not disclosed.

Date: 19 May 1982 (c.19:15)
Location: South Atlantic Ocean
Operator: Royal Navy
Aircraft type: Westland Sea King HC. Mark 4 (ZA294)

During the war between England and Argentina over the Falkland Islands, the turbine-engine helicopter crashed while transporting members of the elite Special Air Service (SAS) fighting unit between ships, from HMS *Hermes* to HMS *Intrepid*. Killed in the accident, which occurred in darkness north of East Falkland, were 21 of the 30 British servicemen aboard the aircraft; the rescued survivors included both pilots. Following a loss of power, the Sea King plummeted into the water, rolled over and sank. Searchers recovered none of the victims' bodies or the main wreckage of ZA294, preventing a determination of the cause of the crash. Possible causes were a bird strike or major systems failure.

Date: 1 June 1982 (c.14:40)
Location: Near Songnam-si, Kyonggi-do, South Korea
Operator: Republic of Korea Air Force
Aircraft type: Fairchild C-123 (56-4391)

The second major South Korean C-123 disaster in less than four months, which resulted in the same number of fatalities as the February crash, occurred about 10 miles (15km) south-east of Seoul, shortly after the twin-engine transport, carrying as passengers army paratroopers, had taken off. All 53 South Korean servicemen aboard, including a crew of four, were killed. The accident took place in adverse meteorological conditions, which were probably a primary or contributing factor.

Date: 14 August 1982 (c.09:00)
Location: Near Managua, Nicaragua
Operator: Fuerza Aérea Sandinista (Nicaraguan Air Force)
Aircraft type: Israeli Aircraft Industries Arava 201 (223)

The twin-engine turboprop transport crashed and burned on take-off from the city's Augusto Cesar Sandino International Airport, and all 20 Nicaraguan servicemen aboard were killed outright or died later of their injuries. Carrying a load of medicine and bound for the town of El Rodeo, located on the nation's Atlantic coast, the aircraft rolled to the left and plummeted to earth about 500ft (150m) from the airport immediately after becoming airborne. Although no causative factors were given, the aircraft may have been overloaded.

Date: 11 September 1982 (c.12:50)
Location: Near Mannheim, West Germany
Operator: US Army
Aircraft type: Boeing/Vertol CH-47C (74-22292)

Loaded with mostly French but also German and British civilian sky-divers, who were to have jumped over Neuostheim Airport as part of the city of Mannheim's 375th birthday celebration, the turbine-engine helicopter crashed after experienc-

ing catastrophic mechanical and ensuing rotor failure. All 46 persons aboard perished in the disaster, including the four members of the aircraft's crew and four other US military personnel. The rotorcraft had ascended to an altitude of about 10,000ft (3,000m) before it began to descend without dropping the parachutists. Asked the reason for this, the pilot announced to another pilot who was on the ground, 'We had some noise in the aft and got a flicker on the master caution panel'. In preparation for landing at the airport, 74-22292 continued in a circling descent and appeared to enter the traffic pattern, turning right and proceeding approximately due south at an estimated air speed of 80 to 90mph (130–145kph). After it had reached an approximate height of 500ft (150m) above the ground and while completing a right turn on to the down-wind leg of the circuit for Runway 09, the aft rotor unit, transmission and pylon were seen to separate from the aircraft. The CH-47 then rotated about 180 degrees to the right and fell first in a tail-down attitude, levelling off in an uncontrolled, vertical descent before finally hitting the ground on its belly and lower starboard side, with its

The in-flight break-up of the US Army CH-47C is captured on film, preceding the crash that killed all 46 persons aboard the helicopter. (UPI/Corbis-Bettmann)

nose slightly low and in an estimated right bank of 45 degrees. Impact was on the median of a four-lane autobahn 1,500ft (500m) south of the airport, whereupon the aircraft exploded and burned. At the time, the local weather was hazy but otherwise good, the crew of 74-22292 having taken off under visual flight rules procedures. The crash was blamed on bearing failure in the forward transmission pack, which had caused the No. 1 synchronizing drive shaft to rotate in an eccentric manner and come in contact with the forward pylon structure. As a result, the forward and aft rotor systems lost synchronization and meshed, leading to the afore-mentioned blade and structural failures. Investigation revealed the pinion pack lubricator jets to be clogged with a combination of grease and walnut shell particles, leading to the bearing failure through lack of lubrication, with faulty design the underlying factor. The US Army's entire fleet of CH-47 helicopters was temporaily grounded for inspection in the wake of the disaster, and a modifi-cation of the lubrication system ordered.

Date: 9 December 1982 (c.14:30)
Location: Near San Andres de Bocay, Nueva Segovia, Nicaragua
Operator: Fuerza Aérea Sandinista (Nicaraguan Air Force)
Aircraft type: Mil Mi-8 (265)

In history's worst helicopter disaster, 84 persons aboard lost their lives when the turbine-engine rotorcraft crashed and burned in mountainous terrain 110 miles (175km) north of Managua. The victims included 75 children; the rest were the mothers of some of them. The eight survivors included the pilot and co-pilot, and the aircraft's other two military crew members. Nicaragua claimed that the Mi-8 had been shot down by anti-Sandinistan rebels.

Date: 19 April 1983 (c.07:20)
Location: Near Toba, Mie, Japan

First aircraft
Operator: Japan Air Self-Defence Force (JASDF)
Type: Kawasaki C-1 (58-1009)

Second aircraft
Operator: Japan Air Self-Defence Force (JASDF)
Type: Kawasaki C-1 (68-1015)

The two twin-jet transports, which were members of a six-aircraft formation flying between two Japanese air bases, from Komaki, in Aichi, to Iruma, in Saitama, crashed on the island of Suga. All 14 Japanese servicemen aboard the two aircraft lost their lives, eight on 58-1009 and six on 68-1015. According to unofficial reports, the group had been proceeding in instrument meteorological conditions consisting of rain and fog at a very low altitude, ie around 700ft (200m), when the lead pilot instructed the group to initiate an immediate 90-degree right turn. The two aircraft involved in the accident, which had been flying in tandem, subsequently slammed

The scene of the worst helicopter disaster in history, the crash of a Nicaraguan Mil Mi-8, which claimed the lives of 84 persons, nearly all of whom were children. (UPI/Corbis-Bettmann)

A Kawasaki C-1 jet transport, two of which, flown by the Japan Air Self-Defence Force, crashed simultaneously on Suga Island. (Martin Bowman)

into the north side of a hill, while a third C-1 brushed the treetops but managed to remain airborne.

Date: 5 May 1983 (c.10:20)
Location: Near Ban Ta Khli, Thailand
Operator: Royal Thai Air Force
Aircraft type: Fairchild C-123K

All 30 Thai servicemen aboard (24 passengers and a crew of six) were killed when the transport crashed and exploded in a rice field some 70 miles (115km) north of Bangkok. The aircraft had been approaching to land at the Ban Ta Khli Air Base when instructed by the control tower to execute a missed approach because the runway was not clear. Subsequently, the C-123 plummeted to earth approximately 700ft (200m) from the runway. According to a military source, a power plant malfunction was suspected as the cause of the accident.

Date: 6 June 1983 (c.12:40)
Location: Off Quemoy, Taiwan
Operator: Republic of China Air Force
Aircraft type: Fairchild C-119G

The twin-engine transport, which was carrying civilian passengers, crashed in the Formosa Strait, reportedly after its starboard power plant had caught fire. Of the 47 persons aboard the aircraft, including a crew of eight military personnel, nine survivors were rescued. The C-119 had taken off from the island about two minutes before it plummeted into the water.

Date: 16 February 1984 (time unknown)
Location: Near Debre Zelt, Shewa, Ethiopia
Operator: Ethiopian Air Force
Aircraft type: Unknown

During an attempted hijacking, the transport crashed some 25 miles (40km) south-east of Addis Ababa after the air pirate detonated a hand grenade when it tried to land at an the Debre Zelt air base. Killed in the explosion or subsequent crash, which occurred some 25 miles (40km) south-east of Addis Ababa, were 26 of the 38 persons aboard the aircraft, possibly an An-12 turboprop.

Date: 19 February 1984 (time unknown)
Location: Near San Gerardo, San Miguel, El Salvador

First aircraft
Operator: Fureza Aérea Salvadoreña (Salvadoran Air Force)
Type: Bell UH-1H

Second aircraft
Operator: Fuerza Aérea Salvadoreña (Salvadoran Air Force)
Type: Bell UH-1H

The two turbine-engine helicopters, carrying soldiers as passengers, collided in mid-air and crashed about 75 miles (120km) north-east of San Salvador, apparently after one of them was hit by guerrilla mortar fire and went out of control. All 28 military personnel aboard the two aircraft, including two pilots assigned to each one, were killed in the combat-related incident.

Date: 28 February 1984 (c.19:30)
Location: Near Borja, Aragon, Spain
Operator: US Air Force
Aircraft type: Lockheed C-130E (68-10944)

Operated by the Military Airlift Command, the four-engine turboprop transport was on an aerial delivery training mission and had been cleared for a low-level supply drop before it crashed and burned 30 miles (50km) north-west of Zaragoza Air Base. All 18 servicemen aboard lost their lives; except for a Spanish officer, the victims were American personnel, including the aircraft's nine-member crew. The C-130 had struck the south

A later model Sikorsky CH-53 Sea Stalion, similar to the US Marine Corps helicopter that crashed in South Korea. (Sikorsky)

face of a mesa at an approximate elevation of 2,200ft (670m), or less than 200ft (60m) from the top, at a comparatively low air speed of around 150mph (250kph), while on a north-north-westerly heading, with its wings level, nose slightly raised and flaps extended to 50 degrees. The crash occurred in darkness, and the local weather was overcast, with a ceiling of 1,200ft (350m) and a visibility of approximately 3½ miles (6km). There was little or no wind. Although the causative factors were omitted in the investigative report on the accident, releasable findings did not reveal any evidence of pre-impact structural, instrument or electrical failure, or propeller/power plant malfunction in the aircraft.

Date: 24 March 1984 (c.04:00)
Location: Near Hunghae, Kyongsang-Pukdo, South Korea
Operator: US Marine Corps
Aircraft type: Sikorsky CH-53D (157132)

All 29 servicemen aboard were killed in the crash of the turbine-engine helicopter, which occurred

200 miles (320km) south-east of Seoul. The majority of the victims were Americans, including the crew of four, but the passengers also included 11 South Korean personnel. The aircraft involved in the accident was one of eight helicopters engaged in a night assault mission between two air bases, from Pohang to Kannung. It was assigned to the number three position in the second of three groups. As the aircraft were proceeding in the pre-dawn darkness, operating under visual flight rules procedures, 157132 slammed into a wooded mountainside at an approximate elevation of 1,300ft (400m) and about 30 miles (50km) north-north-west of its departure point, bursting into flames on impact and sending wreckage tumbling down the steep terrain. The crash occurred 50ft (15m) below the ridgeline and while the CH-53 was banked approximately 45 to 60 degrees to the left, longitudinally level or in a slight nose-down attitude and on a heading of between 210 and 240 degrees, with its undercarriage retracted and rear loading ramp closed. Investigation revealed no evidence of mechanical failure or maintenance error as causing or contributing to the accident. One possible factor was the presence in the second division's lead aircraft of a Marine air wing division commanding general, which could have influenced the decisions of both its pilot and the mission commander, flying the lead aircraft in the first division, increasing their desire to complete the mission successfully. Primarily, the crash was believed to have resulted from pilot error attributable to one of three possible causes: a) Following a left turn by the lead aircraft, 157132 responded similarly, leading to the impact with the unseen high terrain; b) In attempting to catch up with the group, using a higher rate of speed, the CH-53 initiated a turn to port to avoid over-running them, or c) The aircraft involved in the accident lost sight of the leader, and in an attempt to re-establish visual contact, a 360-degree turn to the left was begun. Contributing to the crash was the failure of the second division's lead pilot to take off without wearing night-vision goggles and having to order a control change when he put them on, his continuation into the deteriorating weather and ambient light conditions, deviation from the proper course, and ultimate disorientation with regard to his position. As the use of night-vision goggles apparently factored in the accident, it was recommended that there be greater emphasis in training on the use of the vision-enhancement devices, as well as on flight in such conditions and in cockpit co-ordination.

Date: 8 May 1984 (time unknown)
Location: Elbet Beni Salama, Egypt
Operator: Egyptian Air Force
Aircraft type: McDonnell F-4E Phantom II

Both crewmen and 19 persons on the ground lost their lives when the jet fighter crashed into the village located about 80 miles (130km) from Cairo.

Date: 11 July 1984 (time unknown)
Location: Near Buenavista, Marinduque, the Philippines
Operator: Philippine Air Force
Aircraft type: Bell UH-1H

The turbine-engine helicopter crashed at sea 2 miles (3km) off shore from the island of Marinduque, and all 30 persons aboard were killed.

Date: 21 September 1984 (time unknown)
Location: Near Sarakchar, Lowgar, Afghanistan
Operator: Soviet Air Force
Aircraft type: Antonov An-12

An estimated 50 military personnel aboard were killed when the four-engine turboprop transport was shot down by Afghan rebels about 30 miles (50km) south of Kabul.

Date: 28 October 1984 (time unknown)
Location: Near Kabul, Afghanistan
Operator: Soviet Air Force
Aircraft type: Antonov An-22 (SSSR-08837)

In history's worst single-aircraft military aviation disaster, all 240 Soviet service personnel aboard were killed when the four-engine turboprop transport was shot down by Afghan guerrillas approximately 5 miles (10km) north of the capital city, from where the aircraft had taken off shortly before. The An-22 was believed to have been part of the fleet of the Soviet airline Aeroflot.

Date: 18 December 1984 (c.14:00)
Location: Near Denomindao El Valor, Amazonas, Peru
Operator: Fuerza Aérea del Peru (Peruvian Air Force)
Aircraft type: de Havilland Twin Otter Series 300 (307)

The twin-engine turboprop transport, which was flying between two stations of the Peruvian oil duct, crashed in flames approximately 2 minutes after taking off from a military air base. Including a crew of three military personnel, all 21 persons aboard the aircraft lost their lives; the passengers were all civilians. According to unofficial reports, the aircraft 'exploded' in the air.

Date: 22 January 1985 (c.09:35)
Location: Near Puerto Castilla, Colon, Honduras
Operator: US Air Force
Aircraft type: Lockheed C-130A (56-0501)

Flown by an Air Force reserve unit, the four-engine turboprop transport crashed in the Caribbean Sea approximately 8 miles (13km) north-west of Trujillo airport, where it was to have landed, an en-route stop during a scheduled re-supply mission originating at Howard Air Force Base, in the Panama Canal Zone, and ultimately bound for Comayagua, also in Honduras. Including a crew of five, all 21 American military personnel aboard were killed. The bodies of about half of the victims were found. During the initial phase of the

An Antonov An-22, shown here in the colour scheme of the Soviet airline Aeroflot, one of which was involved in history's worst single-aircraft military aviation disaster. (Philip Jarrett)

approach, the C-130 was observed to turn right towards the open sea, and examination of recovered debris indicated that it struck the surface of the ocean in a left wing-low attitude, with its undercarriage and flaps still retracted. Despite the retrieval of a considerable amount of wreckage, its prolonged immersion in the salt water, which was some 100ft (30m) deep at the site of the accident, had corrosive effects that greatly hindered its evaluation. No evidence could be found, however, of in-flight fire, explosion, or of any deficiencies in the aircraft's flight controls, instruments or power plants. There was an indication of a structural failure in the starboard wing and horizontal stabiliser, but if this occurred, it must have been almost simultaneous with, or resulted from, impact. At the time, the local weather was overcast, with a ceiling of 1,500ft (500m), and a visibility of 1½ miles (2.5km). The wind was estimated at 20 to 25 knots from a north-north-westerly direction.

Date: 28 March 1985 (c.09:50)
Location: Near Maracaibo, Caqueta, Colombia
Operator: Fuerza Aérea Colombiana (Colombian Air Force)
Aircraft type: Fokker F.28 Fellowship Mark 3000 (FAC-1140)

Operated by the military airline Servicio de Aeronavegación a Territorios Nacionales (SATENA) and on a scheduled domestic passenger service that had originated at Bogotá, with en-route stops at Neiva and San Vicente del Caguan, the twin-jet transport crashed 10 miles (15km) north of Florencia, while attempting to land at that city's airport. All 46 persons aboard, including a crew of six military personnel, were killed. In its last radio message, the aircraft was reported to be at 3,600ft (1,100m); less than 10 minutes later it struck a mountain and exploded, the accident occurring in rain and fog accompanied by a low overcast, meteorological conditions that were, according to press accounts, below the airport minima.

Date: 24 July 1985 (c.17:00)
Location: Near Leticia, Amazonas, Colombia
Operator: Fuerza Aérea Colombiana (Colombian Air Force)
Aircraft type: Douglas DC-6B (FAC-902)

The four-engine transport, which was providing a scheduled domestic passenger service owing to a strike by airline pilots in Colombia, crashed and burned in the Amazonian jungle. All 80 persons aboard, including a crew of four, were killed in the accident. About five minutes after the aircraft had taken off from Leticia Airport, bound for the capital city of Bogotá, the pilot reported a fire in the No. 3 power plant and that he was returning to land. The crash occurred moments later, after he radioed, 'We're falling'.

Date: 22 September 1985 (time unknown)
Location: Afghanistan
Operator: Soviet Air Force
Aircraft type: Antonov An-12

All 26 Soviet military personnel aboard lost their lives when the four-engine turboprop transport was shot down by Afghan rebels.

A Colombian Air Force Fokker F.28 jet transport, essentially the same as the aircraft operated by the military airline SATENA that crashed during a passenger flight. (Philip Jarrett)

Date: 25 November 1985 (time unknown)
Location: Near Luassingua, Kundo Kubango, Angola
Operator: Force Aérea Populaire de Angola (Angolan Air Force)
Aircraft type: Antonov An-26

The twin-engine turboprop transport was reportedly shot down by South African anti-aircraft fire, and all 22 Angolan and Soviet military personnel aboard were killed.

Date: 27 March 1986 (time unknown)
Location: Bangui, Ombella-Mpoko, Central African Republic
Operator: L'Armée de l'Air (French Air Force)
Aircraft type: Sepecat Jaguar A

Apparently developing mechanical trouble immediately after it had taken off, the jet fighter crashed into a school and nearby residential area. Many of the 35 persons killed were children, while about 40 others suffered injuries, including the pilot (and sole occupant) of the Jaguar, who had ejected from the stricken aircraft.

Date: 30 March 1986 (time unknown)
Location: Pemba, Cabo Delgado, Mozambique
Operator: Força Popular Aérea de Moçambique (Mozambique Air Force)
Aircraft type: Antonov An-26 (042)

The crash of the twin-engine turboprop transport killed 49 persons aboard, including the aircraft's three Soviet crewmen. Five others survived the morning accident with serious injuries. A member of the crew reported power plant trouble just after the aircraft had taken off, but as it was attempting to return for an emergency landing it slammed to earth near the airport runway, bounced, cartwheeled and burst into flames.

Date: 1 May 1986 (c.04:30)
Location: Near Planes del Pino, El Salvador
Operator: Fuerza Aérea Salvadoreña (Salvadoran Air Force)
Aircraft type: Douglas DC-6B (FAS302)

Bound for Panama City, Panama, the four-engine transport struck a hill and burst into flames 10 miles (15km) north of San Salvador about two minutes after taking off from Ilopango Air Base. All 37 Salvadoran military personnel aboard (33 passengers and a crew of four) perished in the crash, which occurred in pre-dawn darkness. According to official sources, the accident resulted from 'mechanical failure'.

Date: 3 May 1986 (time unknown)
Location: Northern Taiwan

First aircraft
Operator: Republic of China Air Force
Type: Bell UH-1H

Second aircraft
Operator: Republic of China Air Force
Type: Bell UH-1H

The two turbine-engine helicopters collided in mid-air and crashed in a rice paddy 20 miles

A Sepecat Jaguar A jet fighter, identical to the French Air Force aircraft that crashed in Africa, resulting in heavy loss of life on the ground. (E. Moreau)

(30km) south-west of Taipei, killing 22 Taiwanese military personnel aboard both aircraft and injuring both survivors of the accident.

Date: 18 May 1986 (c.08:30)
Location: Djibouti
Operator: Aeronavale (French Naval Aviation)
Aircraft type: Dassault Breguet Atlantique (19)

All 19 French servicemen aboard were killed, five of them passengers, when the twin-engine turboprop patrol aircraft crashed 25 miles (40km) north of the city of Djiboubti. The accident occurred

in adverse weather conditions, with heavy rain and low clouds that obscured the surrounding mountainous terrain, but no further details were disclosed.

Date: 19 July 1986 (c.16:00)
Location: Near La Cruz, Zelaya, Nicaragua
Operator: Fuerza Aérea Sandinista (Nicaraguan Air Force)
Aircraft type: Mil Mi-8 (269)

Shortly after taking off on an internal flood relief flight to Bluefields, the turbine-engine helicopter plunged into the Matagalpa River, 80

Below A Dassault-Breguet Atlantique, similar to the French Naval Aviation aircraft involved in a 19-fatality accident in Djibouti. (Dassault-Breguet)

Bottom A Soviet-built Mil Mi-8 helicopter, extensively used by Nicaraguan military forces and the type that crashed during a flood relief flight. (Philip Jarrett)

miles (130km) north-west of its destination. Among the 23 persons aboard, only the co-pilot, one member of the aircraft's crew of eight military personnel, survived the crash.

Date: 14 August 1986 (c.11:30)
Location: Near Wampusirpi, Gracias a Dios, Honduras
Operator: Fuerza Aérea Hondurena (Honduran Air Force)
Aircraft type: Lockheed C-130D (556)

The four-engine turboprop transport, on an internal flight from Tegucigalpa to Durzana Air Base, crashed in a jungle area near its destination. All 59 persons aboard perished, including 11 civilian passengers and the aircraft's crew of six. The accident occurred in adverse weather conditions, which may have been a primary or contributing factor.

Date: 19 October 1986 (c.21:00)
Location: Near Nelspruit, Transvaal, South Africa
Operator: Força Popular Aérea de Moçambique (Mozambique Air Force)
Aircraft type: Tupolev Tu-134A (C9-CAA)

Mozambique's President Samora Machel was among 35 persons killed when the aircraft crashed about half-a-mile (800m) inside the South African border and 40 miles (65km) west of Maputo, Mozambique, where it was to have landed at the end of a flight from Lusaka, Zambia. Four others aboard, including the pilot, survived with various injuries. The pilot had reported being unable to locate the city's airport during the very-high-frequency omni-directional range procedure approach, conducted in darkness and during heavy rain, with thunderstorm activity in the area, just before the twin-engine jet slammed into a hill at an elevation of about 2,000ft (600m), its undercarriage down and flaps extended at the moment of impact. Despite the break-up of the aircraft, there was no fire. The Soviet flight crew assigned to C9-CAA was found to be negligent in continuing a descent without establishing their exact position and in engaging in an impertinent discussion during this time, as well as for not filing a flight plan and not taking on enough fuel to reach an alternative destination should a diversion have been necessary.

Date: 30 October 1986 (c.17:00)
Location: Near Wamblan, Jinotega, Nicaragua
Operator: Fuerza Aérea Sandinista (Nicaraguan Air Force)
Aircraft type: Mil Mi-17 (294)

The turbine-engine helicopter plummeted to earth 125 miles (200km) north of Managua as it was approaching to land, and 21 Nicaraguan servicemen aboard were killed. A soldier riding as a passenger and the aircraft's pilot, one member of its crew of three, survived. Different accounts attributed the crash to mechanical failure and to the local weather, with conditions of poor visibility, although Contra rebels claimed to have shot down the Mi-17.

Date: 2 November 1986 (c.19:25)
Location: Near Zahedan, Baluchestan va Sista, Iran
Operator: Islamic Republic of Iran Air Force
Aircraft type: Lockheed C-130

The four-engine turboprop transport struck a mountain near the Pakistani border about 10 miles (15km) east of Zahedan, where it was to have landed at the end of an internal flight from Bakhtaran. Including a crew of seven, all 103 Iranian military personnel aboard were killed in the accident, which occurred in darkness. Failing to follow the instructions of the control tower, the aircraft had not maintained the minimum altitude of 6,500ft (1,980m) during the approach, with an altimeter error or defect given as the reason for the disaster.

Date: 25 November 1986 (time unknown)
Location: Near Sarowbi, Laghman, Afghanistan
Operator: Afghan Republican Air Force
Aircraft type: Ilyushin Il-18

The four-engine turboprop transport was shot down, reportedly by Afghan rebels using an anti-aircraft missile, 50 miles (80km) east of Kabul, killing all 40 Afghan and Soviet military personnel aboard.

Date: 2 January 1987 (c.16:30)
Location: Off Bata, Equatorial Guinea
Operator: Ejército del Aire (Spanish Air Force)
Aircraft type: CASA 212-100 Aviocar (T.12B-32)

The twin-engine turboprop transport crashed in the Atlantic Ocean immediately after it had taken off from Bata Airport on a passenger service to Malabo, on the island of Bioko, after transmitting a distress message. Searchers subsequently recovered the bodies of the 22 persons killed in the accident, which included a crew of Spanish military personnel; there were no survivors. Prior to the crash, the pilot's request for permission to land had been denied because another aircraft was on the same runway. Subsequently, the Aviocar plummeted into water that ranged from 5 to 15ft (1.5–5m) deep and about 700ft (200m) off shore. According to one source, there were indications that its right power plant was stopped at the moment of impact, a further indication of a mechanical failure.

Date: 13 January 1987 (c.13:30)
Location: Near Asmara, Erythrea, Ethiopia
Operator: Ethiopian Air Force
Aircraft type: Antonov An-12

All 54 Ethiopian military personnel aboard were killed when the four-engine turboprop transport crashed a few minutes after taking off from Asmara's Johannes IV Airport, on an internal flight to Addis Ababa. The accident reportedly resulted from a 'technical malfunction', with a loss of control apparently occurring after the aircraft had turned back and was attempting an emergency landing.

Date: 9 February 1987 (c.11:30)
Location: Near Khowst (Matun), Paktia,
   Afghanistan
Operator: Afghan Republican Air Force
Aircraft type: Antonov An-26

The twin-engine turboprop transport was reportedly shot down by Afghan guerillas, who apparently used a Stinger missile, about 25 miles (40km) from the Pakistani border and shortly after it had taken off from Khowst, on an internal flight to Kabul. According to Afghan government radio, all 36 persons aboard lost their lives, including a crew of six, and that a number of the passengers were civilians.

Date: 30 March 1987 (c.11:00)
Location: Near Samkani, Paktia, Afghanistan
Operator: Afghan Republican Air Force
Aircraft type: Antonov An-26

The twin-engine turboprop transport was shot down by a Pakistani F-16 jet fighter, firing an air-to-air missile, and crashed in flames while on an internal flight from Kabul to Khowst, Paktia. All 40

persons aboard were killed; the passengers included some civilians. Pakistan identified the An-26 as a 'warplane', and claimed it had intruded into its own airspace.

Date: 11 June 1987 (c.06:30)
Location: Near Qalat, Zabol, Afghanistan
Operator: Afghan Republican Air Force
Aircraft type: Antonov An-26

During an internal flight to Kabul, the twin-engine turboprop transport was shot down by Moslem guerrillas, reportedly with a Stinger missile, some 120 miles (190km) north-east of Kandahar, from where it had taken off earlier. Among the 55 persons aboard the aircraft, including a crew of three, there were only two survivors, both of whom suffered serious injuries. According to the guerillas, the downed aircraft was a military Il-14, and that all five crew members lost their lives.

Date: 18 June 1987 (c.10:00)
Location: Near Montelillo, San Martin, Peru
Operator: Fuerza Aérea del Peru (Peruvian Air
   Force)
Aircraft type: Antonov An-26 (392)

Operating on a domestic civil passenger flight to Saposoa, with an ultimate destination of Iquitos, the twin-engine turboprop transport crashed in a gorge about 370 miles (600km) north of Lima, from where it had taken off earlier. All 46 persons aboard, including a crew of six military personnel, were killed in the accident, which occurred in adverse weather conditions. In its final radio transmission, the aircraft was reportedly about 10 minutes from its destination, but no specific details about the crash or possible cause were released.

Shown in civilian livery, this CASA 212 Aviocar is similar to the Spanish military aircraft that crashed at sea off Equatorial Guinea. (Philip Jarrett)

A Soviet-built Antonov An-26, shown in civil livery, but otherwise similar to the Afghan military transports lost to hostile action during a four-month period in 1987. (Martin Bowman)

Date: 8 December 1987 (c.22:30)
Location: Near Santa Rosa, Lima, Peru
Operator: Fuerza Aviacion Naval del Peru
(Peruvian Naval Aviation)
Aircraft type: Fokker F.27 Troopship Mark 400M
(AE-560)

The twin-engine turboprop transport, carrying as passengers members of the nation's top soccer team, crashed in the Pacific Ocean approximately 3 miles (5km) off shore and 5 miles (8km) north-west of Jorge Chavez International Airport, serving the city of Lima, where it was to have landed following an internal flight from Pucallpa. Among the 43 persons aboard, including a crew of six military personnel, only the pilot was rescued alive, having remained afloat for about 10 hours. The accident occurred in darkness and during a heavy fog after the pilot had reported an instrument indication that the undercarriage had not been properly extended, although this must have resulted from a faulty light, as the control tower reported seeing the gear down as the aircraft circled the airport. Searchers had recovered 21 bodies within 10 days of the crash, the wreckage having sunk in water that was around 120ft (35m) deep. No information as to the possible cause of the accident was released by the Peruvian military authorities.

Date: 14 December 1987 (c.21:30)
Location: Off North-eastern Brazil
Operator: Força Aérea Brasileira (Brazilian Air
Force)
Aircraft type: Lockheed C-130H (C-130.2468)

All 29 persons aboard perished when the four-engine turboprop transport crashed in the Atlantic Ocean about 10 miles (15km) off the island of Fernando de Noronha, where it was to have landed following an internal flight from Recife. The victims included the crew of six military personnel; the passengers were civilians. The crash of the aircraft occurred in darkness during its landing approach, for reasons that, if known, were not disclosed.

Date: 8 March 1988 (c.21:45)
Location: Near Clarksville, Tennessee, US

First aircraft
Operator: US Army
Type: Sikorsky UH-60A (85-24462)

Second aircraft
Operator: US Army
Type: Sikorsky UH-60A (87-24605)

The two turbine-engine helicopters collided in mid-air, then crashed and burned at the Fort Campbell military reservation, and all 17 American servicemen aboard both aircraft were killed. Involved in the accident were the leader of a flight of three rotorcraft (85-24462), which altogether had just picked up some three dozen soldiers and was itself carrying 10 passengers plus a crew of three, and the individual UH-60 (87-24605), which had been on a training flight with four crewmen aboard. The group had just taken off and was climbing when the pilots of the two other aircraft observed, in the darkness, the navigation lights of the lone helicopter at their 3 o'clock position, and successfully initiated evasive action. However, the flight leader was struck by 87-24605, the impact shearing off the aft section of the former's tail boom and two of the latter's four main rotor blades. The collision occurred at an above-ground height of approximately 150ft (50m), in visual meteorological conditions, with a ceiling of 8,000ft (2,500m) and a visibility of 7 miles (11km). In a brief statement, military authorities attributed the accident to 'pilot error, to wit, a reasonable mistake in judgement'. Considered as contributory were restrictions to vision due to door posts and structural components of the aircraft and the limited field of view of the night-vision goggles being used by both crews, which also hampered their ability to see each other.

Date: 10 April 1988 (c.15:10)
Location: Near Mazare-e Sharif, Balkh,
   Afghanistan
Operator: Afghan Republican Air Force
Aircraft type: Antonov An-26

The twin-engine turboprop transport was shot down near the Soviet border by Afghan guerillas, using an anti-aircraft missile, while on an internal flight from Maymaneh, Faryab, to Mazar Sharif, Balkh. All 29 persons aboard the aircraft (23 passengers and a crew of six) were killed.

Date: 18 June 1988 (time unknown)
Location: Central Mozambique
Operator: Força Popular Aérea de Libertacao de
   Moçambique (Mozambique Air Force)
Aircraft type: Mil Mi-8

The turbine-engine helicopter crashed in the province of Zambezia, killing 21 military personnel aboard. Four members of the aircraft's crew survived with injuries.

Date: 15 August 1988 (time unknown)
Location: Northern Afghanistan
Operator: Afghan Republican Air Force
Aircraft type: Antonov An-32

All 39 military personnel aboard lost their lives when the twin-engine turboprop transport, on an internal flight to Kunduz, was shot down by rebels, using a surface-to-air missile.

Date: 17 August 1988 (c.16:30)
Location: Near Bahawalpur, Punjab, Pakistan
Operator: Pakistan Air Force
Aircraft type: Lockheed C-130B (23494)

Pakistan's President Mohammed Zia ul-Haq was among 30 persons killed in the crash of the four-engine turboprop transport, which occurred 60 miles (100km) from the Indian border and about 10 minutes after it had taken off from Bahawalpur on an internal flight to Islamabad. It was determined that the crash probably resulted from an act of criminal sabotage, possibly with a low-intensity explosive device or even through interference or incapacitation of the four-man military crew.

Date: 28 August 1988 (c.16:00)
Location: Near Kaiserslautern, West Germany
Operator: Aeronautica Militare Italiano (Italian
   Air Force)
Aircraft types: Aermacchi MB.339PAN (x3)
   (MM54474); (MM54481) and (MM54483)

A demonstration by the 'Frecce Tricolori' (Tricolour Arrows) at an air show being held on this Sunday afternoon at Ramstein Air Base ended

A fireball marks the collision of three members of the Italian Air Force Frecce Tricolori aerobatic team during the Ramstein air show. (AP/Wide World Photos)

in the worst peacetime military aviation disaster in the history of Western Europe when three of the precision flying team's 10 jet aircraft collided during a low-altitude manoeuvre. One jet was making a loop perpendicular to the other two looping groups when it hit the leader of a five-aircraft formation at an approximate height of 200ft (60m) above the ground, who in turn hit the No. 2 aircraft. The singleton then crashed and exploded in a crowd of spectators, while the second aircraft fell at the airfield and the third into a forest area. Killed in the tragedy were all three pilots and 70 persons on the ground, the latter including the crew of a US Army UH-60 turbine-engine helicopter standing by their aircraft. More than 500 other persons suffered injuries. The collision was attributed to 'misjudgement' on the part of the solo pilot.

Date: 19 November 1988 (c.20:30)
Location: Near Miram Shah, Waziristan, Pakistan
Operator: Afghan Republican Air Force
Aircraft type: Antonov An-26

The twin-engine turboprop transport was shot down in darkness, apparently accidentally, by Pakistani anti-aircraft fire about 100 miles (150km) south-west of Peshawar, after straying out of Afghan air space. All 34 persons aboard the An-26 were killed.

Date: 10 December 1988 (c.20:00)
Location: Eastern Afghanistan
Operator: Afghan Republican Air Force
Aircraft type: Antonov An-32

All 25 persons aboard lost their lives when the twin-engine turboprop transport was shot down by a Pakistani jet fighter while on an internal flight to Kabul from Khowst, Paktia. The warplane had reportedly violated Afghan air space, downing the An-32 in darkness.

Date: 11 December 1988 (time unknown)
Location: Near Leninakan, Armenia, USSR

First aircraft
Operator: Soviet Air Force
Type: Ilyushin Il-76

Second aircraft
Operator: Soviet Air Force
Type: Mil Mi-8

The four-engine jet transport, which had been on an earthquake relief flight and was approaching to land in evening darkness, collided with the turbine-engine helicopter, and the fixed-wing aircraft then crashed and burned. Including the nine members of its crew, 77 Soviet military personnel aboard the Il-76 were killed, and the sole surviving passenger, who had been seated in a truck being

One of the MB.339PAN jets plunges into the crowd at Ramstein Air Base, in West Germany, resulting in heavy loss of life among spectators. (AP/Wide World Photos)

carried in its cargo compartment, was seriously injured. All five occupants of the rotorcraft survived.

Date: 31 January 1989 (c.12:10)
Location: Near Abilene, Texas, US
Operator: US Air Force
Aircraft type: Boeing KC-135A (63-7990)

Operated by the Strategic Air Command, the jet tanker crashed and burst into flames seconds after taking off from Runway 16 at Dyess Air Force Base. All 19 persons aboard lost their lives, including a crew of seven military personnel; among the passengers were four civilian dependents. Only seconds after becoming airborne, the KC-135 slammed to earth approximately half-a-mile (0.8km) beyond the end and 600ft (180m) to the right of the extended centreline of the runway, its

Top: *A Strategic Air Command KC-135 jet tanker lifts off from Dyess Air Force Base in a slight wing-low attitude.* **Above:** *Seconds later, its crash is marked by a cloud of dust.* (US Air Force)

undercarriage retracted and flaps set at 30 degrees at the moment of impact. The accident occurred in visual meteorological conditions, but gusty winds were blowing from a due westerly direction at the time, with a cross-wind component alone of 20 knots or greater. There was no evidence of failure in the aircraft's instruments, flight controls or power plants, despite eye-witness accounts of smoke or vapor emanating from an engine, which could indicate trouble in its water injection system. Improper piloting technique was, however, reported to have factored in the crash.

Date: 20 March 1989 (c.07:00)
Location: Near Hunghae, Kyongsang-Pukdo, South Korea
Operator: US Marine Corps
Aircraft type: Sikorsky CH-53D (157140)

The turbine-engine helicopter was participating in a troop lift mission when it crashed and burst into flames in a mountainous region along the nation's south-eastern coast about 15 miles (25km)

north-west of Pohang, and some 250 miles (400km) south-east of Seoul. Killed in the accident were 19 of the 34 American servicemen aboard, including both pilots; the other two members of its crew and the 13 surviving passengers suffered various injuries. Flying on a north-westerly heading in the second position of a two-aircraft formation, 157140 initiated a right turn at an approximate altitude of 350ft (105m) above the ground in preparation for setting down at the designated landing zone, with its undercarriage extended. During this 180-degree turn, the banking angle of the helicopter increased, as did its rate of descent, until the moment of impact, which was on an almost due southerly heading. Just before the crash, control of the aircraft was passed from the second pilot to the pilot-in-command, and the CH-53, which had initiated a flare at an unknown height, struck the ground with its tail rotor and aft pylon, coming to rest in a drainage ditch, its air speed indicator frozen on a reading of around 50mph (80kph). The crash site was in a ravine approximately half-a-mile (0.8km) wide and at an elevation of around 250ft

(75m). The weather conditions were not considered a factor, and there was no evidence of pre-impact mechanical failure. The accident apparently resulted from an error in judgement and insufficient co-ordination on the part of the flight crew, combined with an absence of 'situational awareness' during the initial turn and subsequent approach. The pilots may not have been thoroughly briefed as to the intention of the flight leader or as to the intended destination, possibly resulting in confusion. It was further noted in the investigative report that under the circumstances, a 'highly-aggressive, relatively-inexperienced' pilot could have been lulled into a sense of complacency regarding the performance characteristics of the aircraft when operating at a high gross weight, at which time it would handle differently. The low-altitude manoeuvre, called an 'overhead break', had been routinely practiced by pilots returning from a mission, when an aircraft's gross weight is much less. Furthermore, the published course procedures at the Pohang base required a higher altitude, 1,000ft (300m) above ground level and 500ft (150m) while on the downwind leg. Contributing to the number of fatalities was the fact that none of the passengers had been wearing head protection and some were not seatbelted, both of which violated existing regulations. The fact that none had been wearing helmets, which in this case was to allow for the differentiation of personnel during the force-on-force segment of the exercise, proved particularly tragic in this instance, as some of those killed may have been knocked unconscious in the crash and succumbed to the effects of the post-impact fire. Further insistence on the use of headgear was recommended in the report on this accident. Additionally, high banks by aircraft in this squadron were officially suspended.

Date: 22 June 1989 (c.17:40)
Location: Near Urcubamba, Junin, Peru
Operator: Fuerza Aérea del Peru (Peruvian Air Force)
Aircraft type: de Havilland DHC-5 Buffalo (329)

All 62 persons aboard perished, including a crew of five military personnel, when the twin-engine turboprop transport crashed and burned in the Andes Mountains about 20 miles (30km) northwest of Tarma and some 100 miles (150km) east of Lima. The aircraft slammed into a slope at an approximate elevation of 15,000ft (5,000m) around 10 minutes after it had taken off from San Ramon, which was an en-route stop during a domestic civil passenger flight originating at Pucallpa, with an ultimate destination of Lima. Although no official cause was given, one source indicated that the Buffalo had been considerably overloaded with passengers, animals and freight at the time of its departure from San Ramon, and in his last radio transmission, the pilot reported losing altitude.

Date: 23 July 1989 (time unknown)
Location: Near Jalalabad, Nangarhar, Afghanistan

First aircraft
Operator: Afghan Republican Air Force
Type: Mil Mi-8

Second aircraft
Operator: Afghan Republican Air Force
Type: Mil Mi-8

The mid-air collision between the two turbine-engine helicopters, which occurred some 60 miles (100km) east-south-east of Kabul, claimed the lives of all 30 aboard both aircraft, 15 in each.

Date: 26 July 1989 (time unknown)
Location: Near Chana, Moxico, Angola
Operator: Force Aérea Populaire de Angola (Angolan Air Force)
Aircraft type: Antonov An-26

The twin-engine turboprop transport, which had been on an internal flight from Luena to Cazombo, was shot down near the Zambian border, 25 miles (40km) from its destination, either by rebels or accidentally by government forces. Among

A de Havilland DHC-5 Buffalo turboprop transport, the type flown by the Peruvian Air Force that crashed during a commercial flight. (de Havilland/Boeing Canada)

the 48 persons personnel aboard the aircraft, including a crew of four, 42 were killed and all six survivors suffered serious injuries. After a missile had reportedly struck one power plant, the An-26 crashed while attempting a forced landing.

Date: 21 September 1989 (time unknown)
Location: Central Afghanistan
Operator: Afghan Republican Air Force
Aircraft type: Mil Mi-8

All 26 military personnel aboard were killed when the turbine-engine helicopter crashed and burned while on an internal flight to Kabul from Baghran, Helmond.

Date: 21 September 1989 (time unknown)
Location: Near Baghran, Helmond, Afghanistan
Operator: Afghan Republican Air Force
Aircraft type: Mil Mi-17

The crash of the turbine-engine helicopter, which occurred about 250 miles (400km) south-west of Kabul, claimed the lives of all 24 military personnel aboard the aircraft.

Date: 18 October 1989 (time unknown)
Location: Off Azerbaijan, USSR
Operator: Soviet Air Force
Aircraft type: Ilyushin Il-76MD (SSSR-76569)

The four-engine jet transport, carrying paratroopers and a crew of seven, crashed in the Caspian Sea while attempting an emergency landing after fire had erupted in its port outer power plant. All 57 Soviet military personnel aboard were killed.

Date: 27 October 1989 (time unknown)
Location: Near Yelizovo, Russian Soviet Federated Socialist Republic, USSR
Operator: Soviet Air Force
Aircraft type: Antonov An-26

All 36 persons aboard lost their lives when the twin-engine turboprop transport crashed into a mountain about 20 miles (30km) north of Petropavlovsk-Kamchatsky as it was attempting to land in adverse meteorological conditions. The victims of the accident included both military personnel, among them the aircraft's crew of six, and civilian dependents, who were travelling as passengers.

Date: 23 November 1989 (time unknown)
Location: Albania

First aircraft
Operator: Albanian People's Army/Air Force
Type: Mil Mi-4

Second aircraft
Operator: Albanian People's Army/Air Force
Type: Mil Mi-4

The two helicopters, which were transporting medical personnel and some of the survivors of a bus accident, collided in mid-air and crashed. Killed in the second tragedy were all 24 persons aboard both aircraft, 12 in each. No further details about the collision were available, including its exact location.

An Ilyushin Il-76 jet transport, similar to aircraft flown by the Soviet Air Force that crashed in the Caspian Sea. (Philip Jarrett)

Date: 21 December 1989 (c.14:00)
Location: Near Guayaramerin, Beni, Bolivia
Operator: Fuerza Aérea Boliviana (Bolivian Air
    Force)
Aircraft type: Lockheed C-130A (TAM-62)

The four-engine turboprop transport crashed in a jungle area 370 miles (600km) north-east of La Paz shortly after it had taken off from Guayaramerin Airport, on an internal flight to Santa Cruz, and all but four of the 28 persons aboard were killed. Among the passengers were women and children; the survivors including two of the aircraft's crew of 10 military personnel. No details were given regarding the suspected cause of the accident.

Date: 23 January 1990 (c.07:45)
Location: Near Sabaneta, Federal District,
    Venezuela
Operator: Armada Venezolana (Venezuelan Navy)
Aircraft type: CASA 212-200 Aviocar (ARV-0210)

The twin-engine turboprop transport crashed and exploded on El Junquito Hill, 15 miles (25km) west of Caracas, about 5 minutes after it had taken off from that city's Simon Bolivar International Airport, on an internal communications flight to Puerto Ayacucho, Amazonas. All 24 persons aboard lost their lives in the accident, including nine civilian passengers; the rest were military personnel, including the aircraft's crew of three. A probable primary or contributing factor were the conditions of reduced visibility, with rain and a low overcast, in which the crash occurred.

Date: 27 January 1990 (c.17:30)
Location: Near Kinkala, Pool, Congo
Operator: Force Aérienne Congolaise (Congolese
    Air Force)
Aircraft type: Nord 262C-66 (TN-230)

All 23 persons aboard were killed when the twin-engine turboprop transport, on an internal flight from Pointe-Noire to Brazzaville, crashed 50 miles (80km) south-east of its destination. The victims included some civilians; the rest of the passengers and the aircraft's crew of four were military personnel. The crash was probably related to the bad weather conditions encountered by TN-230, with rain and winds of more than 40 knots.

Date: 17 February 1990 (c.19:30)
Location: Near Ngwerere, Likouala, Zambia
Operator: Zambian Air Force
Aircraft type: Hawker Siddeley 748-2A (602)

The twin-engine turboprop transport, which was on an internal flight to Lusaka from M'bala, Likouala, crashed in darkness 5 miles (10km) north of the capital city. All 28 persons aboard perished, most of whom were military personnel, including the crew of five. Last reported descending in preparation for landing at Lusaka International Airport, the aircraft subsequently plummeted into a field.

Date: 1 March 1990 (time unknown)
Location: Near Meerut, Uttar Pradesh, India
Operator: Indian Air Force
Aircraft type: MiG-23

After its pilot had successfully ejected from the stricken aircraft, the jet fighter crashed into two tanker trucks on a road about 70 miles (110km) north-east of Delhi, killing 50 persons on the ground.

Date: 27 March 1990 (time unknown)
Location: Near Kuito, Bie, Angola
Operator: Force Aérea Populaire de Angola
    (Angolan Air Force)
Aircraft type: CASA 212-300 Aviocar (T-410)

The twin-engine turboprop transport, on an internal Angolan flight, was shot down by a rocket fired by National Union for the Total Independence of Angola (UNITA) forces about 20 miles (30km) from Kuito, killing all 25 persons aboard the aircraft, including a crew of five.

Date: 20 April 1990 (time unknown)
Location: Near Kinshasa, Zaire
Operator: Force Aérienne Zairoise (Zairean Air
    Force)
Aircraft type: Lockheed C-130H (9T-TCG)

The four-engine turboprop transport, which was on an internal flight to Gbadolite, Equateur, crashed about 3 minutes after it had taken off from N'dola Airport, serving Kinshasa. All but four of the 24 persons aboard the C-130 were killed in the accident, some of them military personnel; among the survivors was a 2-year-old girl, one of its civilian passengers. Reportedly, one blade had separated from the aircraft's No. 3 propeller and then struck the No. 4 power plant, resulting in serious damage and leading to the crash.

Date: 10 August 1990 (time unknown)
Location: Near Shindand, Farah, Afghanistan
Operator: Afghan Republican Air Force
Aircraft type: Antonov An-12

The four-engine turboprop transport crashed and exploded some 120 miles (190km) south of Herat shortly after it had taken off from the military base at Shindand, killing all 83 persons aboard (78 passengers and a crew of five). According to an unofficial report, the disaster resulted from 'mechanical failure'.

A section of the aircraft's fuselage is still recognisable following the crash of the US Air Force C-5A near Ramstein Air Base. (US Air Force)

Date: 29 August 1990 (00:34)
Location: Near Kaiserslautern, Germany
Operator: US Air Force
Aircraft type: Lockheed C-5A (68-0228)

Operated by the Military Airlift Command, the wide-bodied jet transport crashed and burned in a field immediately after taking off from Ramstein Air Base, killing 13 of the 17 American military personnel aboard. The survivors, who included one member of the aircraft's crew of eight, suffered various injuries. Bound for Rhein-Main Air Base, also in Germany, the C-5 had just lifted off from Runway 27 when it began to drift to the left, initially clipping a number of trees with its port wing. Ultimately, it struck the ground approxi-

mately 3,000ft (1,000m) from the end of the runway and 500ft (150m) south of its extended centreline. The accident occurred in darkness, and there was thunderstorm activity in the area at the time, with broken layers of cumulo-nimbus and alto-cumulus clouds at 5,000ft (1,500m) and 10,000ft (3,000m), respectively. Investigation revealed some physical evidence that a power plant thrust reverser had deployed during the take-off, but there was no absolute proof of such an occurrence nor how it could have happened. It was concluded, however, that such a deployment must have involved either its No 1 or 2 engines, and had to be uncommanded. Under the circumstances, the resulting asymmetrical thrust condition would have led to a loss of control.

1991–1998

The end of the Cold War, which could perhaps best be symbolized by the tearing down of the Berlin Wall in 1989, marked not only a shift in the world diplomatic scene but also in strategic military policy. The US and USSR began dismantling nuclear bombers and missiles once held in large numbers under what became known as the 'Balance of Terror'. Other weapons were aimed away from population centres. The worth of tactical air power was well illustrated during the Persian Gulf War in 1991, where it enabled American-led western forces to drive the occupying Iraqis from Kuwait in a matter of days, with remarkably few casualties. The war also saw the first large-scale use of such high-tech weaponry as 'smart' bombs, cruise missiles, and the revolutionary Stealth jet fighter. Technology can also receive credit for a general improvement in the military safety record, with the exception perhaps of the forces of the former Soviet Union, which were in considerable disarray following the break-up of the nation into a number of independent countries. As with commercial aviation, however, safety improvements often only come after tragedy. It took the mid-air crash between American and German military transports to bring about the installation by both countries of collision-avoidance systems, as were already in use aboard airliners. As military aviation moves into its second century of 'heavier-than-air' flight, it can look back at its past with pride and look ahead to its future, aware of its responsibilities – and its risks.

Date: 10 January 1991 (c.18:00)
Location: Near Paramo Mucuti, Merida, Venezuela
Operator: Armada Venezolana (Venezuelan Navy)
Aircraft type: CASA 212 Aviocar 200 (ARV-0209)

The twin-engine turboprop transport, which had been on an internal flight from Caracas to the city of Merida, crashed into a mountain 35 miles (55km) south of its destination. All but one of the 22 persons lost their lives, including the crew of three, and the sole survivor was seriously injured. Most of the victims were Venezuelan military personnel. Initially diverting to Santa Barbara due to adverse meteorological conditions, the aircraft had proceeded on towards Merida, but about half-an-hour later the crew reported being unable to land due to the weather and declared an emergency, with the accident occurring shortly thereafter, around dusk. Ironically, ARV-0209 had been transporting a funeral party with the body of a Navy aviator killed a few days earlier, and the passenger who survived this crash had also survived the previous one. The victims of the second accident also included family members of the pilot killed earlier.

Date: 5 February 1991 (time unknown)
Location: Near Nea Ankhialos, Magnisia, Greece
Operator: Royal Hellenic Air Force
Aircraft type: Lockheed C-130H (748)

All 63 Greek military personnel aboard were killed when the four-engine turboprop transport struck Mount Othris about 100 miles (150km) north-west of Athens and approximately 25 miles (40km) from Nea Ankhialos Air Base, where it was to have landed at the end of an internal flight from Elefsira. The crash occurred as the aircraft was letting down in instrument meteorological conditions, but no further details were made available.

Date: 14 February 1991 (time unknown)
Location: Near Taisha, Morona Santiago, Ecuador
Operator: Fuerza Aérea Ecuatoriana (Ecuadorean Air Force)
Aircraft type: de Havilland DHC-6 Series 300 (FAE-447)

Operated by Transportes Aereos Militares Ecuatorianos on a non-scheduled domestic passenger service of the military airline to Taisha from Macao on behalf of a missionary group, the twin-engine turboprop crashed and burned at an approximate elevation of 5,000ft (1,500m) on Mount Paso Macuna, only about 100ft (30m) below its summit, and 20 miles (30km) from its destination. Including a crew of three military personnel, all 22 persons aboard the aircraft were killed in the accident, which occurred in adverse weather conditions.

Date: 22 February 1991 (time unknown)
Location: Near Cazombo, Moxico, Angola
Operator: Force Aérea Populaire de Angola (Angolan Air Force)
Aircraft type: Antonov An-26

The twin-engine turboprop transport was shot down some 250 miles (400km) east of Luena by UNITA rebel forces, using a Stinger surface-to-air missile, and all 47 persons aboard lost their lives, including a crew of four military personnel. Most of the passengers were civilians.

Date: 21 March 1991 (time unknown)
Location: Near Ras-al-Mishab, Saudi Arabia
Operator: Royal Saudi Air Force
Aircraft type: Lockheed C-130H (469)

The four-engine turboprop transport, its passengers all Sengalese soldiers returning from duty in the Persian Gulf War, crashed about 15 miles (25km) south of Khafji as it was attempting to land at Ras-al-Mishab, in conditions of poor visibility due to oil fires in nearby Kuwait. Killed in the accident were 98 military personnel aboard the aircraft, including its six Saudi Air Force crewmen; three soldiers survived with serious injuries.

Date: 21 March 1991 (c.02:15)
Location: Off Southern California, US

First aircraft
Operator: US Navy
Type: Lockheed P-3C (158930)

Second aircraft
Operator: US Navy
Type: Lockheed P-3C (159325)

This disastrous mid-air crash occurred during an anti-submarine warfare training exercise. Designated as the 'on-station' aircraft, 159325 was being relieved by 158930, having provided sonobuoy contact as part of the operation. The two four-engine turboprop patrol aircraft collided at an approximate altitude of 3,000ft (1,000m) and some 60 miles (100km) south-west of San Diego, and both then plummeted into the Pacific Ocean. All 27 crewmen from both aircraft, 14 aboard 158930 and 13 aboard 159325, lost their lives. Searchers recov-

ered a small amount of debris, but none of the victims' bodies. Both aircraft had been based at the Moffett Field Naval Air Station, located near San Jose, California. The altitude separation to be used in the turn-over had been established in pre-flight briefings by their crews. Though both were operating under visual flight rules procedures, horizontal separation at the scene would have been afforded through air-to-air tactical air navigation (TACAN) facilities. In addition, the aircraft were in radio contact with each other. According to radar transcripts, 158930 had, prior to the accident, descended from its en-route altitude, and was maintaining its height, while 159325 had ascended an estimated 300 to 1,000ft (100–300m). Just before impact, the former was headed generally north, the latter generally east. The crew of a Navy helicopter observed the fireball produced by the collision. It was dark at the time, and the meteorological conditions consisted of intermittent rain, with the cloud level down to around 2,000ft (600m) and a visibility of between 5 and 10 miles (10–15km). There was also thunderstorm activity in the area. The weather was considered a possible contributing factor. Although the exact sequence of events could not be determined, the accident apparently occurred after one crew either misunderstood the other's intentions, lost situational awareness at a critical time, or violated a previous understanding or agreement made in radio communications as to how each P-3 would shift altitudes in order to effect the turn-over. Significantly, the flight of 159325 had been marked by equipment failures, an inoperative autopilot system, and extended time in turbulent weather conditions, which reportedly caused airsickness among some of its crewmen. These factors, combined with the added distractions of reported interference on its crew intercom system and fatigue associated with the length of time on station and the night-time duty, could have contributed to the accident had this crew been at fault. As previously mentioned, 159325 was the aircraft that deviated from the self-assigned swap height of 2,500ft (750m), although this could have been agreed upon between both crews by radio. Despite a recommendation for such, the investigative report noted no plans to retrofit the US Navy's P-3 fleet with crash-survivable flight data recorders.

Date: 25 March 1991 (c.08:15)
Location: Near Bangalore, Karnataka, India
Operator: Indian Air Force
Aircraft type: Hindustan Aeronautics 748 Series 2

The twin-engine turboprop transport, which was on an 'air experience' flight, its passengers comprising trainee engineers and cadets, crashed shortly after take-off from Yellahanka Air Base. All 28 Indian service personnel aboard were killed, including the crew of three. Climbing to an approximate height of 150ft (50m), the aircraft began to loose height until it slammed to earth about half-a-mile from the airfield. The fiery accident may have been related to power plant failure.

Date: 27 July 1991 (time unknown)
Location: Near Maymaneh, Faryab, Afghanistan
Operator: Afghan Republican Air Force
Aircraft type: Mil Mi-8

All 30 persons aboard lost their lives, including an estimated crew of five military personnel, when the turbine-engine helicopter was shot down by rebel forces. Most of the passengers were civilians.

Date: 5 October 1991 (c.15:00)
Location: Condet, Java, Indonesia
Operator: Tentra Nasional Indonesia-Angkatan Udara (Indonesian Air Force)
Aircraft type: Lockheed C-130H (A-1324)

A total of 148 Indonesian military personnel were killed in the flaming crash of the four-engine turboprop transport in a south-eastern suburb of Jakarta. The victims included a guard on the ground; there were no survivors among the occupants of the aircraft (135 passengers and a crew of 12). Reportedly, one power plant of the C-130 had caught fire, and the crash occurred during an attempted emergency landing at Perdonakusuma Halim Airport, from where it had taken off shortly before, on an internal flight to Bandung.

Date: 1 November 1991 (time unknown)
Location: Near Karakent, Azerbaijan, USSR
Operator: Azerbaijan Air Force
Aircraft type: Mil Mi-8

The turbine-engine helicopter was shot down by rebel forces, and all 40 persons aboard lost their lives.

Date: 20 November 1991 (time unknown)
Location: Nagoro-Karabak, Azerbaijan, USSR
Operator: Soviet Air Force
Aircraft type: Mil Mi-8

The turbine-engine helicopter slammed into a cloud-obscured hill and exploded after its pilot reported being unable to see anything. All 23 persons aboard the aircraft, including a crew of three military personnel, were killed in the crash. There was another report that the aircraft had been shot down.

Date: 28 January 1992 (c.16:20)
Location: Azerbaijan, Commonwealth of Independent States
Operator: Azerbaijan Air Force
Aircraft type: Mil Mi-8

All 47 persons aboard were killed, including a military crew, when the turbine-engine helicopter was shot down about 5 miles (10km) south of Stepanakert. The aircraft had been en route from Agdam to Shusha when it was hit by a surface-to-air missile, exploding in mid-air.

The scene of devastation where the Indonesian Air Force C-130H transport crashed on Java, with a loss of nearly 150 lives. (AP/Wide World Photos)

Date: 6 February 1992 (c.10:00)
Location: Evansville, Indiana, US
Operator: US Air Force
Aircraft type: Lockheed C-130B (58-0732)

Operated by the Kentucky National Guard, the four-engine turboprop transport struck a motel and then crashed into a restaurant and exploded. The five military crewmen (and only occupants) of the aircraft and 11 persons on the ground were killed, while nine others suffered injuries. Additionally, a police officer who assisted in the post-crash rescue effort and who was among those hospitalized, succumbed more than a week later. The impact and resulting fires also destroyed eight vehicles and damaged some 20 others. During the approach phase of a touch-and-go practice routine being conducted at Evansville Regional Airport, the aircraft was advised by the control tower to return to its home base, Standiford Field, located at Louisville, in neighbouring Kentucky. Abandoning the approach, it then climbed to an approximate height of 1,700ft (520m) above the ground before going into a rapid descent. Subsequently, the C-130 slammed to earth approximately 1 mile (1.5km) south of the departure end of Runway 22, its undercarriage retracted but flaps extended to 50 degrees. Although the cause was not officially reported, an unnamed military source attributed the crash to the failure of the pilots to maintain sufficient air speed during a simulated engine failure due to distractions with air-traffic control instructions and their check-list routine, resulting in a stall.

Date: 16 April 1992 (time unknown)
Location: Nairobi, Kenya
Operator: The 82 (Kenyan) Air Force
Aircraft type: de Havilland DHC-5 Buffalo (214)

Soon after it had taken off from Eastleigh Air Base, the twin-engine turboprop transport crashed in the Nairobi suburb of Kaloleni. Killed in the morning accident were all 46 persons aboard the aircraft, two of whom were civilian dependents but the rest Kenyan military personnel, including the crew of four, plus six others on the ground. About half-a-dozen others suffered injuries. The left power plant had failed and the corresponding propeller consequently autofeathered following the aircraft's departure from Runway 06, and the pilot initiated a left turn in an attempt to return to the airfield. But while turning on to the final leg of the circuit, 214 entered a low overcast, and the pilot apparently lost sight of the runway, causing him to overshoot the approach course. As he tried to effect realignment, the aircraft stalled and plummeted to the ground with its undercarriage down and flaps extended, then skidded into a block of apartment buildings and exploded. No determination could be made as to the reason for the engine malfunction.

Date: 5 July 1992 (c.17:00)
Location: Near Iyakochchi, Sri Lanka
Operator: Sri Lanka Air Force
Aircraft type: Shaanxi Y-8D (CR872)

All 19 military personnel aboard were killed, including a crew of six, when the four-engine

Military personnel search through the remains of the Air National Guard C-130 that crashed into a motel and restaurant in Evansville, Indiana, US. (AP/Wide World Photos)

turboprop transport, basically a Chinese-built Antonov An-12, crashed and burned approximately half-a-mile (1km) from the Elephant Pass Army Garrison. The aircraft was apparently shot down by rebel forces while approaching to land at the military installation.

Date: 14 July 1992 (time unknown)
Location: Near Nakhichevan, Azerbaijan,
  Commonwealth of Independent States
Operator: Russian Air Force
Aircraft type: Antonov An-12V (SSSR-11111)

The four-engine turboprop transport crashed and burned immediately after it had taken off from the Nakhichevan airport, bound for Rostov-na-Donu, Russian Federation, killing 29 Soviet military personnel. Five others aboard, including two members of the aircraft's crew of seven, survived with serious injuries. There was one report that the aircraft had experienced fuel exhaustion.

Date: 14 July 1992 (time unknown)
Location: Near Bir Fadl, Yemen
Operator: Unified Yemen Air Force
Aircraft type: Antonov An-12

The four-engine turboprop transport crashed and exploded about 5 miles (10km) from the Aden airport, where it was to have landed at the end of a flight from the island of Socotra. All 58 persons aboard lost their lives, including a crew of six military personnel; most of the passengers were civilians. The aircraft had been held for a time in a traffic pattern because of reduced visibility conditions associated with a sandstorm, and the accident occurred after the pilot announced he was diverting to Sana'a.

Date: 26 September 1992 (c.18:00)
Location: Near Lagos, Nigeria
Operator: Federal Nigerian Air Force
Aircraft type: Lockheed C-130H (911)

The four-engine turboprop transport crashed in a swamp, killing all 152 persons aboard. Except for four civilians, the victims were military personnel, mostly Nigerian, including three Air Force crewmen, but also from Ghana, Tanzania, Zimbabwe and Uganda. The accident occurred about three minutes after the aircraft had taken off from Murtala Muhammed Airport, serving the capital city, on an internal flight to Kaduna. Two of its power plants had malfunctioned initially, followed by a third, possibly as the pilot-in-command was attempting to ditch the C-130 in a canal, with the resulting crash occurring around dusk and in clear weather conditions. Fuel contamination was mentioned as the cause of the multiple engine failure.

Date: 5 November 1992 (time unknown)
Location: Near Anapa, Russian Federation,
  Commonwealth of Independent States
Operator: Russian Air Force
Aircraft type: Mil Mi-6

The turbine-engine helicopter crashed while transporting military personnel and their families from Rostov-na-Donu back to their home base, located near Krasnodar. All but one of the 29 persons aboard were killed in the accident, including the aircraft's crew of five; the surviving passenger was seriously injured. Although the cause was not officially reported, overloading of personal baggage may have been a factor in the crash.

Date: 11 November 1992 (time unknown)
Location: Near Tver, Russian Federation,
  Commonwealth of Independent States
Operator: Russian Air Force
Aircraft type: Antonov An-22 (SSSR-09303)

The four-engine turboprop transport crashed and burned 125 miles (200km) north-west of Moscow, shortly after taking off from Migalovo Air Base, on a chartered freight service to Yerevan, Armenia. All 23 persons aboard lost their lives, including a crew of seven military personnel; a few of the passengers were civilians. The aircraft had climbed to an approximate height of 800 (250m) before it lost height and slammed to earth beyond the end of the airport runway. Improper loading and excessive weight were believed to have factored in the accident. Not explained was the registration of the aircraft, identical to an An-22 reported missing over the North Atlantic Ocean in 1970.

Date: 11 November 1992 (time unknown)
Location: Off Bombay, India
Operator: Indian Air Force
Aircraft type: Mil Mi-8

Possibly after its rotor blades struck an oil rig, the turbine-engine helicopter crashed in the Arabian Sea, and 20 persons aboard the aircraft were killed.

Date: 30 November 1992 (c.21:20)
Location: Northern Montana, US

First aircraft
Operator: US Air Force
Type: Lockheed C-141B (65-0255)

Second aircraft
Operator: US Air Force
Type: Lockheed C-141B (66-0142)

Operated by the Military Airlift Command, the two jet transports collided in mid-air about 10 miles (15km) north of Harlem, and both then crashed

The front fuselage section of 66-0142, one of the two US Air Force C-141B jet transports involved in the mid-air collision over Montana, is pictured where it came to rest. (US Air Force)

and burned. All 13 crewmen of both aircraft, seven in 65-0255 and six in 66-0142, were killed. The collision occurred at a height of around 25,000ft (7,500m) in darkness and meteorological conditions consisting of scattered clouds at lower altitudes, a visibility of 7 miles (11km) and moderate turbulence. The two involved in the accident were among four transports engaged in a training mission, and had just completed mid-air refuelling. Proceeding on a west-south-westerly heading at the time of the collision, both aircraft then suffered catastrophic structural failure, and wreckage was scattered across the open terrain over an area of approximately 8 miles (13km) long by about three miles (5km) wide. No information pertaining to the possible or probable cause of the accident was disclosed.

Date: 14 December 1992 (time unknown)
Location: Near Lata, Georgia, Commonwealth of Independent States
Operator: Russian Air Force
Aircraft type: Mil Mi-8T

The turbine-engine helicopter was shot down by Georgian rebel forces, using a surface-to-air missile, some 25 miles (40km) east-north-east of Sukhumi, and all 61 persons aboard were killed.

Date: 10 February 1993 (time unknown)
Location: Near Daraim, Badakhshan, Afghanistan
Operator: Afghan Republican Air Force
Aircraft type: Mil Mi-8

The turbine-engine helicopter, which was reportedly overloaded and poorly maintained, crashed some 200 miles (320km) north-east of Kabul while on a flight to Daraim, located about 20 miles (30km) south of Faisabad, where it had taken off from earlier. All 30 persons aboard were killed.

Date: 27 April 1993 (time unknown)
Location: Near Kholm (Tashqurgan), Samangan, Afghanistan
Operator: Afghan Republican Air Force
Aircraft type: Antonov An-32

All 76 Afghan military personnel aboard were killed, including an estimated crew of five, when the twin-engine turboprop transport, which was on an internal flight from Kabul to Mazar-i-Sharif, crashed into a hill 40 miles (65km) east of its intended destination. The accident occurred in evening darkness, with low clouds and fog.

Date: 27 April 1993 (c.23:00)
Location: Off Libreville, Gabon
Operator: Zambian Air Force
Aircraft type: de Havilland DHC-5D Buffalo (319)

The twin-engine turboprop transport, which was carrying the Zambian national soccer team, its manager and support staff, plummeted into the Atlantic Ocean about five minutes after it had taken off from the Libreville airport, an en-route refuelling stop during a service originating at Lusaka, Zambia, with an ultimate destination of Dakar, Senegal. Including a crew of five military personnel, all 30 persons aboard were killed in the crash, which occurred in evening darkness and apparently resulted from a power plant fire leading to a loss of control.

Date: 6 July 1993 (time unknown)
Location: Near Ochamchire, Georgia, Commonwealth of Independent States
Operator: Georgian Air Force
Aircraft type: Mil Mi-8

The turbine-engine helicopter was shot down by Abkhazi forces some 30 miles (50km) south-east of Sukhumi, and all 23 persons aboard were killed.

Date: 4 October 1993 (time unknown)
Location: Near Svanetia, Georgia, Commonwealth of Independent States
Operator: Georgian Air Force
Aircraft type: Mil Mi-8

The turbine-engine helicopter crashed during an internal refugee flight to Svanetia from Abkhazia, killing all 60 persons aboard.

Date: 15 December 1993 (time unknown)
Location: Near Libmanan, Camarines Sur, Philippines
Operator: Philippine Air Force
Aircraft type: Lockheed C-130H (4761)

All 29 persons aboard perished, including a crew of six military personnel, when the four-engine turboprop transport struck a wooded mountainside and exploded about 20 miles (30km) north-west of Naga City, where it was to have landed at the end of an internal flight from Manila. The afternoon accident occurred in adverse weather conditions, with heavy rain and zero visibility, reportedly after the aircraft had descended below a safe altitude during its landing approach.

Date: 17 March 1994 (c.22:30)
Location: Near Nagornyy Stepanakert, Karabakh, Azerbaijan, Commonwealth of Independent States
Operator: Islamic Republic of Iran Air Force
Aircraft type: Lockheed C-130H (5-8521)

The four-engine turboprop transport was shot down by Armenian forces while en route to Tehran from Moscow, Russian Federation, and all 32 persons aboard were killed, including a crew of 13 Iranian military personnel. The passengers comprised of the families of the Iranian embassy staff on their way home, the aircraft was hit by a missile while flying in darkness.

Date: 23 March 1994 (c.14:30)
Location: Near Fayetteville, North Carolina, US

First aircraft
Operator: US Air Force
Type: General Dynamics F-16D (88-0171)

Second aircraft
Operator: US Air Force
Type: Lockheed C-130E (68-10942)

Third aircraft
Operator: US Air Force
Type: Lockheed C-141B (66-0173)

The jet fighter and the turboprop transport collided in mid-air as both were approaching to

The impact point of the crashing F-16 jet fighter (in the foreground) and the destroyed C-141 transport following the disaster at Pope Air Force Base. (US Air Force)

land at Pope Air Force Base, and the former then crashed and skidded across the tarmac into a staging area where some 500 army paratroopers were preparing to board parked aircraft, including the C-141. Hit by debris, the jet transport was destroyed in a fiery explosion. The disaster claimed the lives of 23 military personnel on the ground and injured 100 others. Both airmen in the F-16 ejected and parachuted to earth, while the damaged C-130 landed safely without injury to its five-member crew. An official inquiry regarded as a major factor in the collision confusing instructions given to the F-16 by a civilian tower controller at Fayetteville Regional Airport, who first issued it a traffic advisory concerning the C-130, then cleared 88-0171 for a straight-in approach to Runway 23 at the military base during a simulated engine failure. After the advisory, the fighter pilot did not ask the tower about the position of the transport, and did not break off the simulated flame-out. A trainee controller tried to alert the fighter pilot regarding the presence of 68-10942, but used the wrong call sign. The collision occurred in visual meteorological conditions at an approximate altitude of 300ft

(100m), with the F-16 striking the stabiliser of the C-130. Camouflage painted, 68-10942 had been nearly impossible to see against the forested terrain in the background.

Date: 14 April 1994 (c.09:35)
Location: Northern Iraq

First aircraft
Operator: US Army
Type: Sikorsky UH-60 (87-26000)

Second aircraft
Operator: US Army
Type: Sikorsky UH-60 (88-26060)

Following the end of the Persian Gulf war and occupation of Kuwait by Iraqi forces three years earlier, the US National Command Authority instituted Operation *Provide Comfort*. With the intention of protecting the Kurdish population in an area of Iraq designated as a security zone, American, British and other coalition military aircraft began patrolling in what was known as a Tactical Area of Responsibility (TAOR), north of the 36th Parallel. Iraqi aircraft were prohibited from entering this area, but had nevertheless tested coalition forces on numerous occasions, leading to several skirmishes. The sequence leading up to this tragedy began with the departure of the two turbine-engine helicopters from Zakhu, bound for the towns of Irbil and Salah ad Din, also in Iraq; they were carrying as passengers the Turkish and US co-commanders of the Military Co-ordination Center (MCC) and their party to a scheduled meeting with UN representatives and officials of the Kurdish Democratic Party. In accordance with prescribed procedures, the flight

contacted an Airborne Command and Control System (AWACS), actually an American Boeing E-3B jet aircraft flying above, informing the en-route controller of their intended destination. Also on patrol in the area were two US Air Force F-15C jet fighters. About two minutes after the fighters had entered northern Iraq, the lead pilot reported radar contact with a low-flying target. At the time, the helicopters had been proceeding on a course of about 100 degrees at a speed of around 150mph (250kph). The TAOR controller, also aboard the E-3, acknowledged the radio transmission, responding with a 'clean there', indicating no such contacts. Attempts by the F-15 pilots to identify the rotorcraft by electronic means were unsuccessful, so the the fighters then made one pass in an attempt to identify them visually. It was at that point that the lead pilot misidentified the UH-60s as Soviet-built, Iraqi-operated Mi-24 Hind helicopters; his wingman saw them but could not make positive identification. The F-15s then attacked the two friendly helicopters, which at the time were flying through a valley in a staggered left trail formation at a height of between 100 and 200ft (30–60m) above the ground, shooting down both. The lead fighter brought down the trailing helicopter with an AIM-120 air-to-air missile fired from behind at a range of approximately 5 miles (10km). In what may have been an escape manoeuvre, the lead UH-60 turned on to a north-easterly heading and entered a narrow, steep gorge, but seconds later it too was hit with a Sidewinder air-to-air missile fired by the second F-15, also from behind and at a distance of around 2 miles (3km). The two rotorcraft burst into flames when struck, then crashed 30 miles (50km) north-north-east of Irbil and about 10 miles (15km)

This Sikorsky HH-60 helicopter is similar to the two US Army aircraft misidentified and shot down over Iraq by two US Air Force F-15 jet fighters. (Sikorsky)

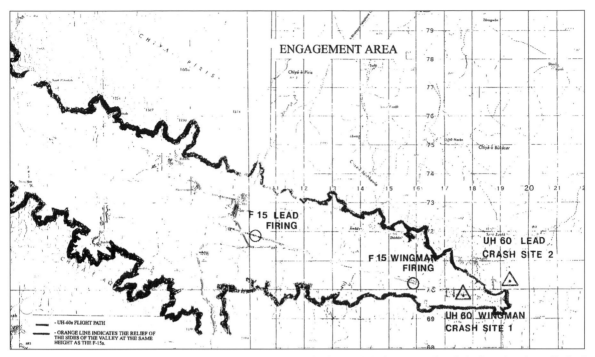

The position of the two F-15 fighters and the two UH-60 Black Hawk helicopters shortly before the 'friendly fire' disaster. (US Air Force)

from the Turkish border. Including eight US military crewmen divided evenly between them, all 26 persons aboard both helicopters lost their lives, 13 in each one. This tragedy was attributed to a chain of events that began with the break-down of clear guidance from the Combined Task Force, which oversaw the entire operation, to its component organisations. The result was a lack of co-ordination between helicopter flights and other air operations within the TAOR. Additionally, personnel were found to have been lacking in consistent, comprehensive training, and in some cases possessed an over-simplified understanding of the proper Rules of Engagement. Still another factor was the high degree of independence given MCC personnel in helicopter operations, without sufficient consideration being given to the potential threat of engagement with coalition combat aircraft operating in the area. Information about these flights were not adequately communicated to the task force staff. The AWACS surveillance section had assigned the helicopter flight a 'friendly general' track symbology and an 'H' character programmed to appear at its location whenever an identification friend or foe (IFF) Mode 1 'squawk', or reply, was detected. (This code is designed to confirm the friendly status of an aircraft and in this case would be used outside of the TAOR.) There was no evidence that the en-route controller performed a Mode IV IFF check on the helicopters, which, though not directed, is an implied duty. (This

code is used to differentiate between friend and foe, and its use would be important within the TAOR.) The helicopter crews were apparently not aware that a different Mode 1 code was to be used when flying within the no-fly zone. Neither the en-route controller nor the senior director had instructed the helicopter crews to switch to the TAOR clear frequency, nor had advised them that they were still emitting the incorrect Mode 1 Code. Both IFF and radar contact with the helicopters were lost when they entered a mountainous region at a low altitude. As a result, the AWACS computer continued to move the 'H' symbol based on the last available heading and air speed information from the helicopters. However, the en-route controller failed to note this information, and never transferred control of the flight to the individual monitoring the TAOR. Although the air surveillance officer had marked the helicopters' last known position with a computer-generated 'attention arrow', the blinking alert light was automatically dropped after 60 seconds. Minutes later, the en-route controller dropped the symbology representing the helicopters from the radar scopes, the only visual reminder of their presence in the area. It could not be ascertained why the F-15 pilots were unsuccessful in identifying the UH-60s through their IFF Mode IV interrogation system (despite an initial, momentary, friendly response). This probably resulted from one or a combination of factors, namely, both fighter pilots selecting the wrong interrogation code; the incorrect processing of the transponder signals from the helicopters by the fighters' air-to-air interrogators; improper loading of both UH-60 IFF codes; possible garbling of the helicopters' friendly IFF responses caused by the use of the same code by both Army crews in close proximity to each other, or an intermittent loss of the 'line-of-sight' radar contact between the fighters and the helicopter flight due to the mountainous terrain and the latter's low altitude, which could have precluded a successful Mode IV interrogation. Significantly, the American Secretary of Defence regarded the IFF system as a back-up rather than a primary means of identifying aircraft. The F-15 pilots themselves were found to have had only limited recognition training during the previous four months, and neither had ever seen a UH-60 Black Hawk in the configurations of these two, ie, with sponsons and external fuel tanks. Their identification pass was made at a speed of around 520mph (840kph), and at an altitude and distance from which it would have been unlikely for them to detect the markings on the helicopters, despite the daylight and good weather conditions in the area, with unlimited visibility. Investigation also revealed that the en-route controller on duty at the time of the tragedy had previously received three 'unsatisfactory' ratings in simulated flights in the areas of safety, airspace co-ordination and aircraft positioning. However, he had performed well in two recent training exercises. He would later be acquitted by a military court of charges stemming from his actions on the day of the shoot-down. The 'friendly fire' incident spurred a sweeping review of command and control procedures in joint US military air operations, and of Air Force AWACS crews in the areas of operational readiness and training.

Date: 2 June 1994 (c.18:00)
Location: Near Campbeltown, Strathclyde, Scotland
Operator: Royal Air Force
Aircraft type: Boeing/Vertol Chinook HC. Mark 2 (ZD576)

The worst helicopter disaster in the history of the RAF occurred during a flight that had originated at Aldergrove Air Base, near Belfast, Northern Ireland. The passengers included a number of anti-terrorist specialists from the Royal Ulster Constbulary, who were on their way to a security conference at Fort George, located near Inverness, Scotland. Observed at a height of under 500ft (150m) over the North Channel, the turbine-engine rotor-craft was seen to change its direction, towards Corran, then began to ascend and finally disappeared into a low cloud base. Subsequently, it slammed into Beinn Na Lice ('The Mountain of the Stone Slab') only about half-a-mile (800m) from the lighthouse on the Island of Kintyre, at an approximate elevation of 800ft (250m), bursting into flames on impact. All 29 persons aboard were killed, including a four-man military crew. An investigative report attributed the accident to what it described as 'gross negligence' on the part of the flight crew for proceeding towards the high ground in a heavy fog below a safe altitude. The pilots then selected an inappropriate rate-of-climb in order to clear the rising terrain. Significantly, the helicopter's newly-installed power plant control system may have been susceptible to icing, which in this case could have necessitated flight below the clouds, rather than in them, in order to avoid such conditions. Subsequent to the crash of ZD576, the RAF announced plans to install its rotor-craft with flight data recorders and cockpit voice recorders to aid in accident investigations.

The unrecognisable remains of the Chinook helicopter that crashed in Scotland, resulting in the worst rotary-wing disaster in the history of the RAF. (PA News)

Date: 29 June 1994 (time unknown)
Location: Near Logar, Afghanistan
Operator: Dostum-Galboddin Militia
Aircraft type: Antonov An-32

The twin-engine turboprop transport was shot down by Afghan ground troops, and 50 of the 70 persons aboard the aircraft were killed.

Date: 5 August 1994 (c.08:50)
Location: Near Boda, Russian Federation, Commonwealth of Independent States
Operator: Russian Air Force
Aircraft type: Antonov An-12

All 47 persons aboard were killed when the four-engine turboprop transport crashed and burned on a hillside in Eastern Siberia while attempting to land. Most of the victims were military personnel, including the crew of six. The accident occurred in conditions of poor visibility due to heavy rain and fog 3 miles (5km) from the aircraft's destination, near the end of an internal flight from Dzhida, and was reportedly precipitated by a power plant fire.

Date: 14 October 1994 (c.22:00)
Location: Near Formoso do Araguala, Tocantins, Brazil
Operator: Força Aérea Brasileira (Brazilian Air Force)
Aircraft type: Lockheed C-130E (C-130.2460)

The four-engine turboprop transport, on an internal flight from Rio de Janeiro to Belem, Para, crashed in darkness 250 miles (400km) north-north-west of Brasilia, and all 21 military personnel aboard were killed. It was considered possible that the load of munitions being carried by the aircraft had exploded in the air.

Date: 26 October 1994 (time unknown)
Location: Near Cuito Cuanavale, Cuando Cubango, Angola
Operator: Force Aérea Populaire de Angola (Angolan Air Force)
Aircraft type: Mil Mi-8MTV (H-534)

The turbine-engine helicopter was shot down by rebel forces, 250 miles (400km) south-south-west of Luena, killing all 22 military personnel aboard the aircraft.

Date: 25 November 1994 (time unknown)
Location: Near Cuito Cuanavale, Cuando Cubango, Angola
Operator: Force Aérea Populaire de Angola (Angolan Air Force)
Aircraft type: Mil Mi-17 (H-584)

During a medical evacuation flight, the turbine-engine helicopter was shot down by UNITA rebel forces, and 22 military personnel aboard were killed. The aircraft's four crewmen survived.

Date: 17 June 1995 (time unknown)
Location: Near Cuvela, Benguel, Angola
Operator: Force Aérea Populaire de Angola (Angolan Air Force)
Aircraft type: CASA 212 Aviocar 200 (T-401)

The twin-engine turboprop transport, which was on an internal flight from Ondjiva to Catumbela, and carrying as passengers members of a local soccer club, crashed 10 miles (15km) east of its destination, while approaching to land. Including its three military crew members, 48 persons aboard the aircraft were killed; the five survivors suffered various injuries. The primary factor in the crash was believed to have been adverse weather conditions, though in addition to that the transport had been reported been overloaded.

Date: 18 July 1995 (time unknown)
Location: Near Antananivo (Tananarive), Madagascar
Operator: L'Armée de l'Air Malgache (Malagascar Air Force)
Aircraft type: Douglas C-47A

Having been chartered to carry a French medical team back from Maintirano, the vintage twin-engine transport crashed while preparing to land at Ivato Airport, serving Antananivo. The accident claimed the lives of 34 persons aboard the aircraft, including the five members of its military crew. Six passengers survived with serious injuries. It was unofficially reported that both engines of the C-47 had malfunctioned during the landing approach, with the resulting crash occurring some 1,500ft (500m) from the end of the runway.

Date: 9 September 1995 (c.07:15)
Location: Near La Macarena, Meta, Colombia
Operator: Fuerza Aérea Colombiana (Colombian Air Force)
Aircraft type: CASA 212 Aviocar 200 (FAC.1152)

Operated by the military airline Servicio Aeronavegación a Territorios Nacionales (SATENA) and on a scheduled domestic flight from Villavicencio to the resort town of La Macarena, the twin-engine turboprop crashed and burst into flames in a tropical forest region near its destination and 70 miles (110km) south-east of Bogotá. All 21 persons aboard the aircraft were killed, including its crew of four military personnel; one passenger was found alive but later succumbed to injuries. The Aviocar slammed into a hillside during a rain and fog 5 miles (10km) from the local airport as it was trying to land after initiating a missed approach procedure, the second of two unsuccessful landing attempts.

Date: 13 September 1995 (c.07:20)
Location: Gulf of Mannar
Operator: Sri Lanka Air Force
Aircraft type: Antonov An-32 (CR-861)

All 81 persons aboard perished, including five military crewmen, when the twin-engine turbo-prop transport crashed 25 miles (40km) north-west of Colombo, Sri Lanka. Bound for Palay, in the Tamil region of the nation, the aircraft had taken off from Ratmalana Airport, located near the capital city, before it plunged into the sea from an approximate height of 8,000ft (2,500m). The pilot had radioed that he had an instrument problem and that he was returning to his departure point, and may have lost control during the 180-degree turn. At the time of the accident, the meteorological conditions in the area were adverse, with thunderstorm activity and a heavy overcast.

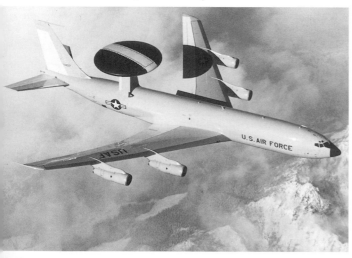

BIRD STRIKE

Date: 22 September 1995 (c.07:45)
Location: Near Anchorage, Alaska, US
Operator: US Air Force
Aircraft type: Boeing E-3B (77-0354)

The modified Boeing 707-320B jet, used as an Airborne Warning and Control System (AWACS) aircraft, crashed and exploded shortly after taking off from Elmendorf Air Force Base, on a routine training mission. All 24 crewmen aboard perished. Investigation revealed that a flock of 100 or more Canada geese, which had been roosting on the grass adjacent to the runway, rose into the air and were ingested into the two port engines of the E-3 five seconds after the commander was heard to call 'rotate' on the cockpit voice recorder tape. This resulted in the immediate, uncontained and catastrophic failure of the No. 2 power plant and severe compressor stalls in the No. 1, leading to an asymmetrical thrust condition. The aircraft began a slow left-hand climbing turn before it initially struck the ground with its port wing tip and then slammed into the hilly, wooded terrain approximately 1 mile (1.5km) north-north-east of the departure end of Runway 05, which it had used, its undercarriage still down and flaps partially extended at the moment of impact. The local weather at the time consisted of scattered clouds down to about 1,500ft (500m) and layers at higher altitudes, a visibility of 7 miles (11km) and light to moderate turbulence. Only two minutes

Left *A US Air Force Boeing E-3B AWACS aircraft, identical to the one that crashed after taking off from Elmendorf Air Force Base in Alaska.* (Boeing)

Below *A swath cut in the forest marks the site of the E-3B crash, which was attributed to a bird strike.* (US Air Force)

before the crash, a C-130 transport had disturbed the birds that would bring down 77-0354, but while this had been observed by the tower controller, he did not inform either the AWACS crew or Airfield Management. Also cited were the procedures employed to reduce the bird hazard at the base, which were described as 'inadequate'. Four officers assigned there in fact received 'administrative discipline' for their failure to provide leadership in this area.

Date: 8 November 1995 (c.21:00)
Location: Near Luyaba, Cordoba, Argentina
Operator: Fuerza Aérea Argentina (Argentine Air Force)
Aircraft type: Fokker F.27 Friendship Mark 500 (TC-72)

Operated by the Argentine military airline Lineas Aéreas del Estado (LADE) on a domestic flight from Comodoro Rivadavia, Chubat, to the city of Cordoba, the twin-engine turboprop transport crashed at an approximate elevation of 8,000ft (2,500m) in the Sierra Grande range of mountains, 10 miles (15km) from Villa Dolores. All 53 persons persons aboard, including a crew of five, were killed. The passengers on the flight consisted of military personnel and their dependents, including about 20 children, who were on their way to the 25th anniversary of a flight academy graduation. At the time of the crash, which occurred in darkness and adverse weather conditions consisting of thunderstorm activity, accompanied by heavy rain, strong winds and turbulence, TC-72 had been on the direct course between Villa Reynolds and Cordoba. However, it was also observed to be very

low before it slammed into the mountain about 1,000ft (300m) below the summit, and exploded.

Date: 22 November 1995 (c.19:00)
Location: Off Jaffna Peninsula, Sri Lanka
Operator: Sri Lanka Air Force
Aircraft type: Antonov An-32 (CR-862)

The twin-engine turboprop transport, which was on an internal flight from Colombo, its passengers mostly soldiers, crashed in the Indian Ocean while attempting to land at Palay Air Force Base. Including a crew of six, all 63 persons aboard the aircraft were killed. The last contact with the An-32 was when the pilot asked for the approach lights to be switched on; the subsequent accident occurred in darkness.

Date: 22 January 1996 (c.12:00)
Location: Off Point Pedro, Sri Lanka
Operator: Sri Lanka Air Force
Aircraft type: Mil Mi-17

All 39 military personnel aboard lost their lives when the turbine-engine helicopter was shot down by Tamil rebels, plummeting into the Indian Ocean.

Date: 11 February 1996 (time unknown)
Location: Near Kandahar, Afghanistan
Operator: Taliban Militia
Aircraft type: 'Helicopter'

The crash of the rotorcraft claimed the lives of all 20 persons aboard.

A Soviet-built Antonov An-32 turboprop transport, the type flown by the Sri Lanka Air Force and involved in two major crashes in the latter half of 1995. (Philip Jarrett)

Date: 26 February 1996 (c.19:00)
Location: Near Jabal Awliya, Khartoum, Sudan
Operator: Silakh al Jawwiya as Sudaniya (Sudanese
    Air Force)
Aircraft type: Lockheed C-130H

The four-engine turboprop transport, which had
been on an internal flight from Al-Ubayyid,
crashed and burned 25 miles (40km) south-west of
the city of Khartoum while attempting an
emergency landing due to an in-flight fire. All 91
military personnel aboard (85 passengers and a
crew of six) were killed in the accident, which
occurred in darkness and good weather conditions.

Date: 9 March 1996 (time unknown)
Location: Near Mesones Muro, Amazonas, Peru
Operator: Aviación del Ejército Peruana (Peruvian
    Army Aviation)
Aircraft type: Mil Mi-17 (EP-561)

The turbine-engine helicopter, which was on an
internal flight from Condorcanqui to Bagua,
crashed into a mountain ridge and exploded north
of its destination, killing all 23 persons aboard.
Nearly half of the victims were civilian passengers,
the rest Peruvian military personnel, the latter
including the aircraft's crew of four. The heavy fog
in which it occurred was probably a significant
factor in the accident.

Date: 3 April 1996 (c.16:00)
Location: Near Dubrovnik, Croatia
Operator: US Air Force
Aircraft type: Boeing CT-43A (73-1149)

This mission of economic revitalization of a war-
torn nation would end in tragedy on a rocky
mountainside due to a series of errors by an experienced flight crew and flaws reaching into the upper
levels of the Air Force command structure. The
aircraft involved had been converted from a navigational trainer so as to have passenger-carrying
capability. Having taken off earlier from Tuzla, on
the next to last segment of a five-leg flight to
various locations within Bosnia-Herzegovina and
Croatia, the twin-engine jet was to have landed at
Cilipi Airport, serving Dubrovnik, but it crashed
and burned during the final phase of a non-directional beacon (NDB) instrument procedure
approach to Runway 12. Including a crew of six
military personnel, all 35 persons aboard were
killed; the other occupants consisted of a contingent
of American business officials, headed by US
Secretary of Commerce Ron Brown. Searchers
found in the wreckage one passenger showing signs
of life, but she was pronounced dead after being
taken to a hospital. With its undercarriage extended
and flaps set at 30 degrees, the CT-43 had slammed
into St John Hill at an approximate elevation of
2,200ft (670m), or only about 100ft (30m) below its
summit, 2 miles (3km) to the left of the runway
threshold. Impact speed was calculated to have
been approximately 170mph (270kph). At the time,
the meteorological conditions in the area consisted
of a low overcast, with broken clouds at 400ft
(120m) and solid coverage at 2,000ft (600m), and a
visibility of about 5 miles (10km) in light rain. The
wind at ground level was from a direction of 120
degrees at 12 knots. The investigation of the crash
was conducted without the use of either a flight
data recorder or a cockpit voice recorder, which
normally would have been installed on an equiva-
lent civil jet transport, relying instead on examination of the wreckage and reconstruction of the
aircraft's flight path. Although the flight of 73-1149

A US Air Force Boeing T-43A – similar to the Boeing 737 derivative that crashed in Croatia. (Boeing)

from Tuzla was actually slightly ahead of schedule, this was somewhat disrupted when the crew attempted to take a course through restricted air space, which resulted from improper planning on their part. This mistake was corrected by an air-traffic controller in an E-3 Airborne Warning and Control System (AWACS) aircraft, but the re-routeing of the flight added some 15 minutes to the trip. During its descent in preparation for landing, the aircraft's air speed was too high for the application of the correct flap setting, as required by Air Force directives, but instead of entering a holding pattern in order to effect such stabilisation, the pilots began their approach to the runway without clearance from the controlling air-traffic facility, also in violation of prescribed procedures. Clearance was obtained following passage of the final approach fix (FAF), but the speed at the time remained around 90 to 115mph (145–185kph) above the norm. From the FAF to the point of impact, 73-1149 maintained a heading of 110 degrees, a deviation from the correct course of 119 degrees. When considering the 25-knot wind blowing from a south-easterly direction at the flight altitude, a course correction of 6 degrees would have been required, with the crew using the aircraft's radio magnetic indicator and setting the heading 'bug' on its horizontal situation indicator to 125 degrees. The 'bug' was in fact set at 116 degrees, and the pilot's course select window also indicated the wrong bearing. Whereas the NBD procedure at Dubrovnik required two automatic direction finder (ADF) receivers, examination revealed the single unit with which the CT-43 was equipped to be tuned to the FAF beacon, designated 'KLP'. The crew could not have identified the missed approach point without a second ADF, and the tuning of the same receiver to different beacons during a final approach would not have been allowed under Air Force regulations. Examination of the ground-proximity warning system (GPWS) installed on 73-1149 indicated that it did not activate at any time prior to impact, this because it was not designed to respond to this combination of terrain profile, aircraft configuration and flight path. The system would in fact have been desensitised when the aircraft's undercarriage and flaps were extended, so as to avoid false alerts. (It was noted in the accident report that a newer, enhanced GPWS would have provided nearly 40 seconds of early warning to the crew of the CT-43.) The fact that both engines were at higher-than-normal power settings at the time of the crash indicated that the crew may have been initiating a missed approach procedure or pulling up after making visual contact with the ground. That the aircraft had even attempted to land at Dubrovnik Airport represented a failing by the Air Force Command to comply with governing directives from higher

The charred rear fuselage section of the aircraft on which US Secretary of Commerce Ron Brown and 34 others were killed. (AP/Wide World Photos)

headquarters, as the non-precision approach procedure being used there had not been authorised.
These directives required a review of all instrument
approach procedures not approved by the US
Department of Defense to consider the overall
safety of the procedure, including the accuracy of
navigational facilities and obstacle clearance. A
waiver had been requested, but was denied by
higher authorities. The approach at Dubrovnik was
found to be improperly designed with regard to
obstacle clearance and featured an excessively low
minimum descent altitude. Nor was radar monitoring available there. In an effort to reduce
controlled-flight-into-terrain type accidents, the US
Air Force distributed 100 video tapes on the subject
to various flying wings, and also announced the
development of a greatly-improved terrain avoid-
ance system for use in some of its aircraft.

Date: 12 June 1996 (c.19:00)
Location: Near Rollingstone, Queensland,
    Australia

First aircraft
Operator: Australian Army Aviation
Type: Sikorsky S-70 (A25-113)

Second aircraft
Operator: Australian Army Aviation
Type: Sikorsky S-70 (A25-209)

The two turbine-engine helicopters collided in
mid-air and crashed 35 miles (55km) west of
Townsville, killing 18 Australian servicemen.
Among the 10 injured survivors of the accident

were nine of the 15 aboard one aircraft; only one of
the 13 aboard the other escaped with his life. Six
helicopters were engaged in a night counter-terrorist
exercise, flying in an abreast formation, and
approaching their drop zone, when the lead aircraft
banked to the right. The others failed to follow,
however, and when the former's pilot, perhaps
fearing a collision, tried to turn back, the main rotor
of his aircraft struck the No. 2 helicopter. Following
the collision, the No. 1 exploded and slammed to
earth in an inverted attitude, while No. 2 crashed
and burned during an autorotative landing.
According to the investigative report on the
accident, the pilots involved may have been
stressed, fatigued and inadequately prepared, and
just prior to the accident were flying some 700ft
(200m) lower than required in order to see the
designated target. Other factors may have been
confusion as to the location of the drop zone, a
possible course deviation by the group and limitations in the night-vision goggles being used, including a lack of peripheral vision, acute fluctuations in
light gain and limited depth perception.

Date: 15 July 1996 (c.18:00)
Location: Near Eindhoven, Noord-Brabant, The
    Netherlands
Operator: Force Aérienne Belge (Belgian Air
    Force)
Aircraft type: Lockheed C-130H (CH-06)

The four-engine turboprop transport crashed
and burned while landing at Eindhoven Air
Base, located about 50 miles (80km) south-east of

*The burned-out hulk of the Belgian Air Force C-130H transport that crashed at an air base near Eindhoven,
Holland.* (Associated Press)

Rotterdam. Including the four Belgian Air Force crew members assigned to the aircraft, 34 military personnel aboard lost their lives; the passengers consisted of a Dutch Army band returning from Villafranca, Italy, seven of whom survived with serious injuries. Numerous bird carcasses were found at the accident site, indicating that during the visual approach to Runway 05, the C-130 had collided with large flocks of lapwings and starlings, which caused, in sequence, the failure of its Nos 3, 1 and 2 power plants. The resulting loss of power and asymmetric thrust condition led to a loss of directional control, making it veer to the left during its landing flare. The port wing then hit the ground, and the transport finally came to rest adjacent to the runway. The accident occurred in fair weather conditions, with scattered clouds at around 5,000ft (1,500m) and good visibility. The wind was from a direction of 10 degrees at 10 knots. Contributing to the heavy death toll was the failure of the base air-traffic control officer to inform rescue workers of the passengers on CH-06. As a result, the fire-fighters concentrated on extinguishing the blaze, assuming the crew was already dead and that there were no other occupants. They did not gain entry to the cabin for more than half-an-hour after the crash, even though most or all of those aboard had probably survived the impact. Subsequent to the accident, the Belgian and Dutch governments asked the International Civil Aviation Organisation (ICAO) to modify its flight plan procedures to ensure that destination airports are aware of the number of passengers aboard an arriving aircraft.

Date: 27 November 1996 (c.23:50)
Location: Near Mokhovo, Russian Federation, Commonwealth of Independent States
Operator: Russian Air Force
Aircraft type: Ilyushin Il-76T (RA-76804)

Operating on an internal cargo flight to Petropavlovsk-Kamchatsky, the jet transport crashed into a mountain and exploded about 10 miles (15km) from Abakan, itself located in Siberia 2,500 miles (4,000km) east of Moscow, from where it had taken off shortly before. All 23 persons aboard (13 passengers and a crew of 10) perished. Overloading was believed to have been a factor in the accident, which occurred in darkness.

Date: 24 December 1996 (c.15:00)
Location: Near Nellore, Andhra Pradesh, India
Operator: Indian Air Force
Aircraft type: Hindustan Aeronautics 748 Series 2 (H1032)

All 22 persons Indian military personnel aboard (17 passengers and a crew of five) were killed when the twin-engine turboprop transport crashed

in a field about 100 miles (150km) north of Madras, Tamil Nadu. The aircraft had been on an internal flight from Tanbaram Air Force Base, located near Madras, to Hyderabad, Andhra Pradesh, and the accident occurred after the pilot reported the failure of a power plant. Cracks were reportedly found in the same engine, which had not been detected during maintenance.

Date: 2 February 1997 (c.17:30)
Location: Near Quibaxe, Cuanza Norte, Angola
Operator: Force Aérea Populaire de Angola (Angolan Air Force)
Aircraft type: CASA 212-200 Aviocar (T-400)

All 37 military personnel aboard were killed, including a crew of three, in the crash of the twin-engine turboprop transport. The aircraft had been on an internal flight from Luanda to Cafunfo, but prior to the accident was seen heading in the opposite direction, ie towards the south, and appeared to be in difficulty.

Date: 4 February 1997 (c.19:00)
Location: Northern Israel

First aircraft
Operator: Israel Defence Force Air Force
Type: Sikorsky CH-53D (357)

Second aircraft
Operator: Israel Defence Force Air Force
Type: Sikorsky CH-53D (903)

In the worst military disaster in the history of Israel, the two turbine-engine rotorcraft collided, crashed and exploded near She'ar Yeshuv in the Galilee panhandle. All 73 servicemen aboard were killed, including two four-member crews assigned to each aircraft. The two helicopters had taken off shortly before from a landing strip in Israel and were ferrying ground troops into southern Lebanon. The subsequent collision occurred in darkness but otherwise good meteorological conditions at an approximate altitude of 300ft (100m) above the ground and about 5 miles (8km) from the border of the two countries, after which one CH-53 fell atop some unoccupied houses and the other into a cemetery. Although the cause of the disaster could not be determined, possible contributing factors were a lack of knowledge by both aircraft commanders as to who was to be the flight leader and inexperience by both as lead pilots. Also, there were no clear instructions when pilots were to turn off their lights, for security reasons, when crossing into Lebanon. Among the recommendations of the investigative commission was to allow helicopters entering Lebanese airspace to fly separately in most cases, and that a flight leader must be designated in operations involving more than one aircraft.

Date: 13 March 1997 (c.18:00)
Location: Near Mirabad, Khorasan, Iran
Operator: Islamic Republic of Iran Air Force
Aircraft type: Lockheed C-130HF

The four-engine turboprop transport, carrying as passengers servicemen and their dependents, crashed in mountainous terrain 25 miles (40km) west of Mashhad, where it was to have landed during an internal flight from Dezful, Khuzestan. Including a military crew, all 88 persons aboard were killed in the accident, which occurred around dusk and was reportedly related to power plant failure.

Date: 23 April 1997 (time unknown)
Location: Near Konduz, Afghanistan
Operator: Afghan Republican Air Force
Aircraft type: 'Transport'

The aircraft, which may have been a twin-engine turboprop Antonov An-26, crashed into a mountain, killing all 36 persons aboard.

Date: 6 July 1997 (time unknown)
Location: Near Saravena, Meta, Colombia
Operator: Ejército Colombiano (Colombian Army)
Aircraft type: Mil Mi-17

Chartered from the civilian company Helicol Colombia and carrying as passengers Colombian soldiers who were to protect workers at the scene of a sabotaged oil pipeline, the turbine-engine helicopter was shot down by rebels some 220 miles (350km) east of Bogotá. Among the 25 persons killed were the four members of the aircraft's civilian crew; four soldiers survived. The Mi-17 was reportedly hit at an approximate height of 300 to 600ft (100–180m) above the ground, then crashed and exploded.

Date: 13 September 1997 (c.18:00)
Location: South Atlantic Ocean

First aircraft
Operator: Luftwaffe (German Air Force)
Type: Tupolev Tu-154M (11+02)

Second aircraft
Operator: US Air Force
Type: Lockheed C-141B (65-9405)

The two jet transports collided in mid-air and crashed about 75 miles (120km) off the coast of Namibia. Of the 33 persons aboard the aircraft, the body of only one victim – a flight attendent from the German aircraft – was recovered; there were no survivors. Pieces of wreckage were also found in the water, which was some 3,000ft (1,000m) deep in the area. Both aircraft had been flying at an approximate height of 35,000ft (10,500m), their crews apparently unaware of each other's presence, at the time of the collision. The Tu-154, carrying 12 German Marines and two civilian passengers plus a crew of 10, had been en route from Cologne, Germany, to Cape Town, South Africa, with a planned refuelling stop at Windhoek, Namibia, from where the C-141 had taken off, bound for the US via Ascension Island, with nine crewmen aboard. According to a US Air Force investigative report, the German transport had not been flying at the altitude requested in its flight plan, 39,000ft (12,000m). In fact, neither its requested nor its actual height conformed with guidelines for an aircraft flying on this particular south-easterly heading. German authorities issued a statement acknowledging the error of its crew. The American transport had been at its assigned cruising altitude when the collision occurred. Faulty procedures by the Angolan air-traffic control service responsible for the two flights was considered a contributing factor. Neither transport had been equipped with a

The Luftwaffe Tu-154M jet transport (11+02), the aircraft lost in mid-air collision with a US Air Force C-141B over the South Atlantic Ocean. (AP/Wide World Photos)

collision-avoidance system, which would have prevented the accident. Subsequently, both the US Air Force and the Luftwaffe announced plans to install the safety systems on some of their large aircraft.

Date: 6 December 1997 (c.09:45)
Location: Irkutsk, Russian Federation,
    Commonwealth of Independent States
Operator: Russian Air Force
Aircraft type: Antonov An-124-100 (UR-82005/08)

The four-engine wide-bodied jet transport, on an internal flight to Vladivostok and carrying two Sukhoi Su-27 jet fighters, crashed into a block of apartment buildings and burned only about 20 seconds after it had taken off from the Irkutsk aircraft factory. Killed in the disaster were all 23 military personnel aboard the transport (17 crew members and six passengers), and 44 other persons on the ground. About a dozen others suffered injuries. All four of the aircraft's power plants had failed in rapid succession, probably due to the uncoordinated operation of their high-pressure compressors, coupled with defective design. The An-124 fleet would be grounded for six months.

Date: 13 January 1998 (c.22:30)
Location: Near Chaman, Quetta-Pishin, Pakistan
Operator: Afghan Taliban Militia
Aircraft type: Antonov An-12

The four-engine turboprop transport crashed and burned near the Khojak Pass, 75 miles (120km) north of Quetta and about 10 miles (15km) from the Afghan border. All 51 persons aboard (45 passengers and a crew of six) were killed. Unable to land in the darkness and adverse weather conditions, the aircraft may have run out of fuel after receiving initial clearance to land at Quetta.

Date: 3 February 1998 (c.15:15)
Location: Near Cavalese, Trento, Italy
Operator: US Marine Corps
Aircraft type: Grumman EA-6B (163045)

This tragedy, which would create some diplomatic rancour between two NATO allies, began as a low-level training flight out of the Aviano Air Base, also in Italy, located near Vittorio. On at least two of the six legs of the mission, the maximum speed and minimum altitude restrictions were exceeded, culminating in the twin-jet electronic counter-measures aircraft striking and severing two cables, one about 370ft (110m) above the ground and the other 6ft (2m) lower, that were suspending an aerial tram at the Cermis ski resort, located 30 miles (50km) north-east of the city of Trento. The gondola then plummeted about 300ft (100m) to earth, and all 20 occupants were killed. The aircraft sustained substantial damage, but nevertheless returned safely to the base, its four-man crew escaping injury. The accident was attributed to error by the crew of 163045, who, according to the Marine Corps investigative report, 'aggressively' manoeuvred their aircraft, flying above the speed limit of approximately 520mph (840kph) and well below the prescribed minimum height in the area of the accident of 2,000ft (600m), and even below the altitude at which the flight had been planned, and the crew briefed, of 1,000ft (300m). Though not considered directly contributory to the tragedy, this discrepancy between the briefed and actual minimum altitudes was attributed to a squadron supervisory error, specifically, the failure to ensure a 'read-and-initial' program of providing vital information to flight crews. Significantly, it was learned that while several documents distributed to the squadron stipulated the fact, all but three of the 18 crew members assigned to the squadron were unaware of the 2,000ft minimum in the area of the

An Antonov An-124 heavy-lift jet transport, shown in the colour scheme of the Russian airline Aeroflot but otherwise similar to the military aircraft that crashed at Irkutsk. (Douglas Green)

Shown in US Navy markings, this Grumman EA-6B is otherwise the same as the Marine Corps aircraft involved in an accident at an Italian ski resort. (Northrop Grumman)

accident, which had been imposed as a noise-abatement measure. The No. 1 electronic counter-measures officer of 163045, who would also have been responsible for navigation and was positioned in the front right seat beside the pilot, later stated that the crew was neither aware of the minimum height nor the ski resort itself. Nevertheless, three separate copies of a knee board card containing that information were found in the accident aircraft. The meteorological conditions in the area at the time consisted of a few clouds at around 20,000ft (6,000m) and a visibility of 7 miles (11km).

The wind was from almost due south at 4 knots. The pilot of the EA-6B, who had not flown a low-level mission in six months and may have experienced an optical illusion with regard to his height, saw the cables at the last moment, and tried to dive below them. Rolled approximately 45 degrees to the left and in a nose-down longitudinal attitude, the aircraft struck the 2¼ inch (57mm) load-bearing cable, which supported the gondola, and the ⅞ inch (20mm) drive cable beneath it with its starboard wing, vertical stabiliser and station 5 jamming pod. Naval Air Training and Operating Procedures state

The flattened gondola car in which 20 persons lost their lives when the American military jet cut its support and drive cables while flying at extremely low altitude. (AP/Wide World Photos)

that pilots shall utilise their radar altimeter at low altitudes to maximize safety. The system on 163045 was found to have been functioning properly, though the aural height alert was not reported by the crew. No other technical failures were found that could have been a factor in the accident. The investigative board found no pattern of 'unprofessional or reckless' attitudes within the squadron that could have contributed to the accident. And although the US Marine Corps chain of command was found to be 'cumbersome and complicated', neither could they be considered a factor. It was noted in the accident report that during the 18 months before the tragedy, minimum training altitudes were in a constant state of flux, resulting in some confusion, but had been fixed at 1,000ft about six months before it actually occurred. In the light of this tragedy, the squadron commander to which the aircraft belonged was relieved of his duty and re-assigned, and the pilot and ECO-1 faced court-martial proceedings on 20 counts of negligent homicide.

Date: 12 February 1998 (c.08:30)
Location: Near Nasir, Sobat, Sudan
Operator: Silakh al Jawwiya as Sudaniya (Sudanese Air Force)
Aircraft type: Antonov An-32

Sudan's First Vice President, Lt Gen Al-Zubeir Mohammad Saleh, was among 27 persons killed when the twin-engine turboprop transport overshot the runway while landing in a heavy fog at a small airfield and ploughed into the River Sobat. Most of the 30 survivors were reported injured.

Date: 29 March 1998 (c.09:30)
Location: Primavera, Piura, Peru
Operator: Fuerza Aérea Peruana (Peruvian Air Force)
Aircraft type: Antonov An-32 (FAP-388)

The twin-engine turboprop transport, which was evacuating civilians from areas of flooding, crash-landed in a canal about a mile from Piura/Captain Guillermo Airport, from where it had taken off earlier and was attempting to return due to a malfunction in one power plant. Among the 61 persons aboard the aircraft, 27 were killed, as was one person on the ground.

Date: 20 April 1998 (c.16:50)
Location: Near Bogotá, Colombia
Operator: Fuerza Aérea Ecuatoriana (Ecuadorean Air Force)
Aircraft type: Boeing Advanced 727-230 (FAE-560)

Operated by the military airline Transportes Aereos Militares Ecuatorianos as Flight 422, a scheduled passenger service being conducted on behalf of the civilian carrier Air France, and bound for Quito, Ecuador, the jet transport slammed into a mountain about four minutes after taking off from El Dorado Airport, serving Bogotá. All 53 persons aboard (43 passengers and a crew of 10) perished. Following its departure from Runway 13, the aircraft failed to make a required 90-degree procedural turn and took no action despite a ground controller's warning that it was off course. Subsequently, the aircraft struck a mountain at an approximate elevation of 10,000ft (3,000m), only about 150ft (50m) below its summit, and while on a south-easterly heading, exploding on impact. At the time of the accident, the weather conditions in the area consisted of rain and a low, broken overcast.

Date: 5 May 1998 (c.21:30)
Location: Near Tintiyacu, Loreto, Peru
Operator: Fuerza Aérea Peruana (Peruvian Air Force)
Aircraft type: Boeing Advanced 737-282 (FAP-351)

Chartered by the American firm Occidental Peruana to carry oil workers to a company camp, the jet transport crashed and burned in a swamp about 3 miles (5km) north of Andoas Airport, where it was to have landed, and 700 miles (1,100km) north of Lima. Killed in the accident were 74 of the 87 persons aboard; two members of the aircraft's crew of seven and 11 passengers survived with injuries. Following an internal flight from Iquitos, the 737 slammed into a swamp during the final phase of an NDB procedure approach to Runway 12 in darkness and during light rain.

Date: 12 May 1998 (c.19:30)
Location: Near Nema, Mauritania
Operator: Force Aérienne Islamique de Mauritanie (Mauritanian Air Force)
Aircraft type: Xian Y-7-100C

The twin-engine turboprop transport crashed during a sandstorm shortly after it had taken off, killing 39 persons aboard. There were three survivors. Except for seven civilians, the fatalities were military personnel.

Date: 25 May 1998 (c.10:20)
Location: Near Longtiang, Laos
Operator: Lao People's Liberation Army Air Force
Aircraft type: Yakovlev Yak-40 (ZPX 01)

All 26 persons aboard were killed when the jet transport, which was carrying a Vietnamese delegation on an internal Laotian flight from Vientiane to Xiang Khoang, crashed in a jungle region during a heavy rainstorm. The aircraft struck a jungled mountainside at an approximate elevation of 6,000ft (1,800m) and exploded, possibly after a premature descent as it was preparing to land.

Index